SOCIOLOGY
AND THE
STUDY
OF RELIGION

SOCIOLOGY AND THE STUDY OF RELIGION

Theory, Research, Interpretation

THOMAS F. O'DEA

BASIC BOOKS, INC., PUBLISHERS

NEW YORK / LONDON

FOR JANET AND MICHAEL

PREFACE

This book presents several studies which have appeared roughly over a decade in a number of journals and which together make up a consistent and coherent body of research, interpretation, and theoretical discussion in the sociology of religion, and indeed in the scholarly study of religion generally. In bringing them out in this form it is hoped that they may become the object of critical evaluation and appraisal by those seriously engaged in intellectual enterprise in this field and that they may enter according to their intrinsic worth into the general background of religious study. This book is presented to its readers with the hope that it may be of interest as a contribution to sociology and to the substantive study of the religious groups and situations with which it is concerned. Were these studies all to be rewritten today they might well be written somewhat differently. This is especially the case with some of them as is stated in the introduction. Yet unless the scholarly mind atrophies, the scholar always moves somewhat beyond each of his formulated positions and as a consequence could condemn himself to continual rewriting. As they stand it is felt that these chapters possess the intrinsic sociological merits and the substantive interest to make their present publication a genuine contribution to the study of religion in our day. Like all such studies they represent an impressive slice of one man's intellectual capital.

The author wishes to express his gratitude to a great number of people most of whom could not possibly be named here. When one thinks one is most original one is often shocked and surprised and curiously enough gratified to recall or to discover that he but presents in new light the accomplishment, achievement, or insight of his teacher. The present writer wishes to thank all those who aided directly and indirectly in the research and intellectual effort after comprehension which these chapters

represent. They include teachers, colleagues and students, graduate and undergraduate. To them he is most indebted and most
grateful. There must be mentioned by name in this preface
which has little space for names, Renato Poblete, S.J., and Evon
Z. Vogt, friends and colleagues, for their original working with
him in the research and writing of chapters ten and five respec-
tively of this volume and for their gracious permission to include
them in a collection of his own studies. He also is grateful to
Mrs. Hinda Elmore of the Institute of Religious Studies at the
University of California at Santa Barbara for her most valuable
help. He also wishes to express his thanks to the staff of Basic
Books, Inc., for their efficient and understanding cooperation in
the always difficult but little appreciated task of converting a
collection of "writings" into a "book." Thanks are also deserved
by and freely granted to my wife who as a student in this field
first suggested the merit of collecting these studies together in
one place and who aided in the final stages of preparing this
publication under conditions which were not the most propitious
to intellectual endeavor. Finally gratitude is expressed to the
various journals who have so graciously granted permission to
reprint these articles in this form. Proper acknowledgment to
them is made in the appropriate places in this volume.

December 1969   THOMAS F. O'DEA
                                             Institute of Religious Studies
                                             University of California,
                                             Santa Barbara

CONTENTS

SECTION III

IDENTITY AND COMMUNITY

SECTION IV

SOCIOLOGY OF RELIGION: SOCIOLOGICAL THEORY

SOCIOLOGY AND THE STUDY OF RELIGION

INTRODUCTION

The sociological study of religion has become increasingly popular in this country, whether judged by activity or production, the sale or the writing of books, or the offering of and enrollment in courses in colleges and universities. This growth seems to reflect two notable tendencies in our contemporary intellectual life. The first is the continuing popularity of the social sciences; the second, the increasing concern with religious studies which is also to be seen in an increase in academic departments, course offerings, and enrollments of graduates and undergraduates.

These phenomena allow for various interpretations and are no doubt related to and reflective of basic changes taking place in American society. One interpretation which seems eminently plausible to the author may be suggested here. The distinctive social experience of our time is one of crisis, conflict, turmoil, and widespread malaise in political, intellectual, and religious life. Such a situation suggests to many of our contemporaries that social science may have something important to contribute to understanding our predicaments and clarifying our experience. The social sciences represent the endeavor to adapt, extend, and apply systematically the attitudes (intellectual and emotional disciplines) and the methodology (perspectives, methods, and techniques) of the natural sciences to the study of human problems. In this way it is hoped to go beyond a commonsense understanding of our experience and to achieve insights not available on that level. Although this demands fragmentation of perspective and specialization of method, it makes possible a more controlled and more concentrated attention to the aspects chosen for investigation. Moreover, it is hoped that later discussion and synthesis will put the pieces together in a larger whole, deeper and better grounded than the products of commonsense thought, which will provide valid and relevant information and insight. It is felt that not from any one social science, but from all of them together, will such a deepening take place. This interdisciplinary aspect of the social sciences has found less institutionalized support in university structure and practice than the specialized social sciences themselves; yet it remains an important part of social science research and teaching.

Moreover, it is widely recognized that our present historical situation is one which calls in question and renders problematic the chief answers to the questions of man's being and becoming which were formulated in the past. This critical process is not new. For many decades now we have been living through what St. Simon called a "critical" period. The long-term revolutions in which we have been involved since the last decades of the eighteenth century—the Industrial Revolution and the democratic revolution—bring us to a new kind of confrontation with the human condition. The accomplishments of science, the rapidity of communications, and the vast increase in higher education all combine to accelerate the dynamic characteristics of our time. It appears to multitudes in one form or another that the culture of the past is not alone adequate to provide the guidelines in this rapidly and often chaotically changing world in the forms in which it has been formulated and come down to us. Nevertheless, many recognize that these traditions contain the insights of untold generations, and to lose contact with them would be to empty out the substance of our heritage at a time when we need it most.

In such a situation many sense an imperative to return to a reconsideration of the roots of our culture and, most important, to those religious roots which provided such guidelines for life in the past. It is hoped that some understanding of religious experience, and of the formulations of the meaning and implications of that experience in religious institutions and traditions, will be fruitful in enabling us to confront our present predicaments with greater depth and sharper insight. Furthermore, in a period of culture contact between Europeans and Americans on one side and the people of Asia and Africa on the other, an idea that had earlier been grasped and formulated by scholars takes on a larger appeal: we can learn much from non-Western religious traditions.

However, it is widely recognized that regardless of what may be the character of the personal commitment of faith and fellowship of those involved, this re-examination of the Western religious tradition and confrontation of the religious traditions of the non-Western world must be objective and conducted with the intellectual tools of advanced scholarship. One consequence of this has been the vast expansion of religious studies in our colleges and universities and their greatly increased popularity with students.

As a social science and an academic discipline, sociology stands in a somewhat fortunate position with regard to these developments. Sociologists are able to become important contributors in the many-sided interdisciplinary study of religious phenomena; they stand also in a position to enrich sociology itself by bringing back into the field the fruits of their study of religion as part of that interdisciplinary experience. Such developments, indeed, are still in their preliminary stages. They can be counted on to meet with both encouragement and resistance. Whether their apparent promise will be vindicated by the experience of the next two generations, no man at this time can tell. Whether forces in the political world and the international arena will so radically alter the situation that the whole venture loses meaning, we do not know.

The articles brought together in this volume reflect both of the tendencies described above. They stand in their own right as contributions to sociology: to research, to interpretation, and to theory. They also command some attention as explorations of the complex and many-sided religious life of America. The first section includes four chapters dealing with the American Catholic experience. Indeed, they represent an early use of that term as a sociologically derived concept to be utilized in sociological analysis. In these, research, contemporary and historical, together with its interpretation, presents important aspects of that experience revealed through the sensitizing virtues and analytical powers of a properly applied sociological theory. With respect to their substantive content, it is interesting to note that all these chapters were published as articles originally before the Second Vatican Council. That Council marks a great watershed in Catholic life generally and in the relationship of Catholic to non-Catholic groups and institutions in America.[1] The chapters themselves reflect and analyze the preconciliar condition. Indeed, the study of St. Benedict Center was done in 1949, although for a number of reasons it was not published until 1961. The actual pressures on Catholic intellectual life before the new day of postconciliar Catholicism is thus reflected and interpreted with some sophistication and in some depth. The fourth chapter, an essay in interpretation, was written in 1958 and reflects the prethaw situation in Catholic-Protestant relations in this country. From the theoretical point of view, these chapters say some things about the development of religious institutions and about intergroup relations which the character of the situation at that time made highly evident to observation and analysis. However, we shall discuss the theoretical significance of the chapters in a moment.

Section II presents four studies in the Sociology of Mormonism, one of them done in collaboration with the well-known anthropologist E. Z. Vogt. They were all done as part of or in connection with the Comparative Study of Values Project of the Harvard Laboratory of Social Relations. Again, sociology is seen to enhance our grasp of an important subgroup and an important religious tradition in American life. Here the paradigm of comparative analysis which in many ways represents the sociological equivalent of (or at least substitute for) experiment in large-scale field studies is made use of to compare a Mormon and a non-Mormon group and several Mormon groups. The analysis of the Mormon conception of time indicates the close relationship between the Mormon experience and the general American experience itself.[2]

Section III presents a rather sophisticated frame of reference for the study of intergroup relations and specifically of anti-Semitism. There has been a tendency in studying such relationships, especially when they are asymmetrical in some important respect (such as minority-majority group relations), to concentrate on one of the groups involved. In some cases it is the minority group that is the focus of investigation. In others, as in the postwar study of anti-Semitism, it was the majority. Many years ago Everett C. Hughes, in a study of French Canada, sharply called our attention to the fact that the study of any minority required seeing the whole setting—the minority group-majority group setting—in its wholeness and complexity.[3] In an essay in the *Cahiers Internationaux de Sociologie* in 1951, Georges Belandier showed how the study of colonialism required that the investigator take the entire "colonial situation" as his context and see the reciprocal relationships of colony and mother country. He declared that "every present-day problem of the sociology of colonized peoples had to be considered in terms of this totality."[4] Yet for many years after the publication of these two works the study of anti-Semitism remained oddly one-sided. One even got the impression that it was considered rather bad form to call attention to the importance of such contextual research and interpretation. The first chapter in the third section, "The Changing Image of the Jew and the Contemporary Religious Situation: An Exploration in Ambiguities," was originally presented to a conference on poll data and anti-Semitism sponsored by the American Jewish Committee and was published in *Jews in the Mind of America.*[5] It not only makes use of total context as its basic frame of reference but analyzes the significance of reciprocal negative influence in such a setting in the development of mutual hostile imagery.

In the second chapter in this section, the problems of Puerto Rican immigrants in metropolitan New York are seen in relation to a specifically religious response. This chapter is also a product of collaboration. The field work was done by Renato Poblete, S.J., now a sociologist of religion in Chile, and the chapter was written by both him and the present writer.

The fourth section consists of five theoretical chapters. Before discussing that section, however, it may be well to note that beyond the substantive significance of the first three sections, they too are of considerable theoretical interest. The concept of "Sect" introduced by Ernst Troeltsch and developed and criticized by many others finds here two interesting treatments. The first chapter in Section I, the one on St. Benedict Center, presents us with an example of sectarian development within preconciliar American Catholicism. The study was done before the excommunication of the Center, which its original draft predicted, and which happened much sooner than was expected. Here we see a sect forming not primarily in protest against the church, but as a defensive reaction in the face of situational strain. However, the typical dynamics of sectarian development made the Center a protest group and led to its excommunication. In the second chapter in Section III, the one written in collaboration with Poblete, we see the sect arising again not primarily as a protest group; indeed, in any manifest sense not as a protest group at all. Rather in the immigrant situation it represents a response to anomie and the outcome of a quest for genuine community.

In the chapters in Section I we see the kind of disarticulated relationship that can come to prevail between a minority group and the culture of the larger society—a disarticulation that exhibits both a cognitive and an affective dimension. We have called this disarticulated relationship "askewness." In the St. Benedict Center case we see it as a source of severe strain. In understanding this strain, the historical dimension shows itself of strategic importance. The situation in which the Center group found itself was the product of a long historical preparation. The importance of knowing the history of the group for the understanding of the social and cultural structure of the situation becomes quite apparent in this case. In the analysis of Catholic attitudes toward foreign policy we see such askewness as a cognitive-emotional residue of determining significance present on the latent level of preconciliar Catholic consciousness in this country. The relationship of such a concept to Mannheim's idea of "perspective" as a factor in the sociological determination of knowledge is obvious.[6] It is seen here, however, as a cognitive-affective complex, the precipitate in implicit awareness of a long historical experience. In the third chapter on the Catholic immigrant, such an askewness is further explored in terms of some of the cognitive disarticulations involved and their sociological significance. In both the chapter on anti-Semitism and the chapter "The Ideologists and the Missing Dialogue," the reciprocal effects of having two groups in confrontation in certain kinds of situation are explored. The concept of "ideology" as used is an interesting one. The term here refers not to the usual "isms," but rather to comparable historically conditioned definitions of the situation which are highly abstract and verbal, greatly economized and oversimplified, and quite rigid. Such mental precipitates of group experience have the function of facilitating the relating to the situation of those who hold them and of enabling them to take a defensive-aggressive posture in the encounter. But they facilitate what is basically a dysfunctional relationship, and the accompanying posture is self-defeating. Such dysfunctionality seems the inevitable result of an oversimplification whose economy, abstractness, and rigidity distort reality and thereby ensure unrealistic response.

These chapters are concerned with the group experience and its relation to developing group identity. Such group evolution of self-definition becomes an important dimension in the development of individual identity. One aspect of the crisis of our time is often described as an identity crisis. Assimilation and mobility, psychic, social, and geographical, so characteristic of American society, the loss of consensus on values and traditions, and widespread affluence combine with the religious crisis to compound it and to bring about severe problems of identity for many. In the treatment here of the Catholic and Mormon experiences we see some important elements involved in identity as these develop in the historical experience of subgroups and subtraditions of our society. In the chapter on anti-Semitism the interesting phenomenon of "counteridentity" is to be seen. Identity is reinforced and can come to consist in part in not being like the others. What is suggested here is the significance of the historical aspect of self-definition or identity.

But perhaps most interesting is the way in which a number of these chapters put sociology and history together. There has long been interest in this most vital and significant endeavor, although it appears still confined to a minority.[7] Several of these chapters may be described as examples of historically oriented sociology. They attempt to bring about what Cahnman and Boskoff called a "rapprochement and reunion" between the two disciplines and urge the significance of that rapprochement for a profounder sociology. That history has to gain as well is quite true, but we are now discussing sociology. This combination of sociological and historical approach brings us to the business of interpretation. All sociologists, of course, make interpretations. Even the most rigorously constructed experimental study needs to be interpreted; that is to say that it needs to be understood in terms of a body of theory and thereby related to other phenomena to which it would not appear so related without such a use of theory. But interpretation can and, indeed, should be more than that. Interpretation should be the application of sociological theory in the attempt to explore and understand historical or contemporary events and situations. The works of important sociological figures in the past fall in whole or in part into this category. Yet there is some tendency today to avoid it or to consider it less than hardheaded. Such a tendency probably conceals the underlying fear that interpretation is extremely difficult in itself and that it is not easy to judge and control in the training of graduate students. These considerations should not be lightly dismissed. Nevertheless, the graduate student should be taught to interpret as well as to construct models, conduct interviews, make observations, and where possible do experiments. He should be taught that interpretation makes stringent demands—demands that the material be known, demands that theory be genuinely comprehended and applied with sensitivity and a sense of nuance, demands that comparative checks be made wherever possible, whether as part of the study or as an outside control.

The importance of *understanding (Verstehen)* in sociology is now generally conceded, although opinions concerning the requisite degree and depth of such understanding of the people and cultures being studied differ and still remain matters of conflict.[8] However, since the appearance of the works of Dilthey, Weber, and Freud and the development of phenomenology, it is no longer possible to embrace a naïve behaviorism. What Aron says of the historian and the past is true for the sociologist and the present as well: "Between observation of facts, explanation by causes on one hand, and aesthetic appreciation on the other, comes the understanding which should logically be independent of both and precede both. Lacking this, the historian mutilates or is ignorant of the spiritual reality of the past."[9] Parsons has emphasized the necessity of the sociologist's taking both the "point of view of the actor" and also the "point of view of the observer."[10] That is to say, the sociological investigator looks at the object situation both from the point of view of the participants, their definitions of it and relations and responses to it, and from the point of view of sociological theory which categorizes significant elements of the situation in terms of a structured social system and its typical relationships to culture and personality functioning. Such an approach makes possible both a deeper *understanding* of what the people observed are living through and an *explanation* why certain things happen out of their control and against their intentions. *Interpretation is the process and product of such understanding and explanation.* The observer looking at the situation from the viewpoint of theory is in a position to see that actions initiated by the participants with a certain meaning for them and aimed at certain results take on a changed significance for others involved differently in the complex situation with them and, because of certain inherent tendencies in interaction or certain peculiar characteristics of this particular society, are bound to have unforeseen and unintended consequences. The observer is in the position to see both the *meaningful* and the *functional* integration of the situation and their consequences. Interpretation is then a basic element in "doing sociology," and the bias against it is really against developing interpretation as a self-conscious kind of sociological practice removed from immediate observational studies. From such a point of view the interpretation in the first chapter in

Section I is justified; that in the second is not. The distinction appears quite groundless. If the writer controls the strategic facts of Catholic immigration and assimilation in the United States and if he is able to see these from the point of view of the participants on the one hand, and if he knows the history of the United States in the century between 1846 and 1946 and has a good grasp—a genuine comprehension—of sociological theory on the other, he is in a position to offer an interpretation which will have considerable worth. Whether or not this has been done in the second the reader must judge for himself.

The question arises that a particular interpretation is not the only one possible. That is, indeed, the case. Theoretically a plurality of interpretations is possible. History is rewritten, if not in each generation, at least from time to time and written differently as new groups of men under new conditions ask new questions of the past. With interpretation which is central to both history and sociology, much depends on the kind of question asked of the situation studied. Max Weber has pointed out that the selection of problems for research is highly influenced by values. In this way values play a strategic part in affecting the direction of science. But directions of research can also be influenced by purely theoretical problems; that is, by questions which arise in the clarification of the propositions of the body of theory itself and their relations to each other. However, once problems are selected, objectivity means that they be studied by canons of procedure which are as free as possible of distortions by the value preferences or desires of the individual researcher, his group, his country, or even his civilization. Yet it must be remembered that the sociologist and the historian are part of a present historical situation: they, like all men, are historical beings, conditioned by and part of the very situations they study. Theory, together with understanding of their situations, gives them a partial and relative transcendence over the here and now, providing them with some leverage in making interpretations and predicting possible outcomes. But this transcendence is only relative and is basically rooted in the perspective of a time, a culture, a discipline, and an individual. All interpretations are perspectival and therefore partial. More than one is possible in viewing any situation. Yet what theory would suggest is that in a number of different interpretations done in answer to quite different questions, certain common elements would appear.

Max Weber has said:

> The cultural problems which move men form themselves ever anew and in different colors, and the boundaries of that area in the infinite stream of concrete events which acquires meaning and significance for us, i.e., which becomes an "historical individual" are constantly subject to change. The intellectual context from which it is viewed and scientifically analyzed shift. The points of departure of the cultural sciences remain changeable throughout the limitless future as long as a Chinese ossification of intellectual life does not render mankind incapable of setting new questions to the externally inexhaustible flow of life. A systematic science of culture, even only in the sense of a definitive, objectively valid, systematic fixation of the problems which it should treat, would be senseless in itself.[11]

Interpretation enables us to utilize universal concepts and particular items of understanding to clarify a particular unique situation. It brings together the analytic use of general categories—strain, askewness, social class, conflict, defensiveness, and so on—with an understanding of particular specific elements to deepen our knowledge of such individual complexes. Weber was quite aware of the uniqueness of specific historical configurations, "the historical individual," and the importance of such unique structures in influencing the future.[12] But he thought that the unique historical configuration could also be analyzed in terms of generalized categories and that as a consequence an understanding of its unique elements together with a potentially general explanation (one admitting of comparative treatment with other configurations) of its strategic structural elements would be possible.

In addition to its having made a prediction that subsequently was verified, the St. Benedict Center chapter is interesting to us here. There we see the selection and identification of what Weber called "an historical individual," a significant configuration, in this case the situation of a small Catholic group in the context of Harvard University. Situation here refers to a complex of ideas, values, and social relationship, especially power and prestige relationships. In the study, this situation is looked at from the point of view of the participants and also from the overall point of view of the observer whose observation is guided by theoretical considerations. What is seen is that the Center comes to embody and express a kind of meaningful response to Harvard which with time becomes increasingly extreme. How are we to understand that complex response? Here the history of the strands or elements making up the situation becomes strategic. Catholicism and secularism, Catholicism and Protestantism, Ireland and England, Irish immigration and assimilation in America, social status differences—each of these complexes contributes important constituents to the situation, and the situation could be understood only by understanding the history of each of these elements and its relationship to the present situation. Here we go to history because the precipitates of the past are real, present, and effective in some form in the present. We have no way of achieving understanding of those present-past elements except through an understanding of their history. They are present as precipitates of history and are rendered understandable by knowledge of that history. In this sense the investigator does not simply take the point of view of the participants. He seeks to know the effective thrust of the participants' point of view through a knowledge of how it came to be. It is interesting to note that one level of investigation was entirely excluded from the study by circumstances. There is no account going beyond and behind the *motifs* of observed response to the psychological level of motivation. The motifs of response are understood in relation to their "appropriateness" to the situation as the participants in the Center experienced it and defined it for themselves. Obviously, such social behavior canalized and directed a variety of individual motivational systems into common or reciprocal behavior. It was practically impossible to investigate individual attitudes and motivation under the circumstances in which the study was originally made. Yet for an understanding of the Center and a prediction of its likely fate in the future in relation to the church, the study as it stands proved to be completely adequate. Here the historical grasp of specific content and the sociological insight into the unfolding of process go together as the warp and woof of insightful interpretation.

A French sociologist has noted the importance to the social sciences of the "way in which anyone perceives and divines what is going on in another consciousness." He says:

> In his sociology, Simmel puts the question in Kantian terms: "On what condition is society possible?" And he answers by indicating, among other conditions, the knowledge that individuals at all times have of each other. But this communication between personalities is a condition of historical knowledge as well as of social life.[13]

What this suggests is that *understanding* has deep roots in forms of knowledge by no means conscious or explicit. While the sociologist tries to make as many as possible of his assumptions and premises conscious, he will do well to remember that even his most explicit communication is rooted in a more holistic communication experience. The sociologist is part of what he studies in this fundamental way. There is, beneath all the individual differences, all the historically effected differences among groups, all the wide differences of various cultures, a certain psychic unity immanent in men which, though little understood in itself, is the basis of all communication and all understanding of self and others. We do not deny the importance of attempting the clarification of this source of knowledge and of developing checks upon it less obscure than it is itself at its deepest roots. The object side of such knowledge may be seen in the analogousness of all human situations despite their tremendous empirical variability. We are all part of the "group-situation" context and hence all participants in a substrate which undergirds our communication. In this sense the sociologist is part of what he studies.

Second, man is not an ahistorical essence, but rather, as we have said, a being who comes to be in a specific social and historical setting which forms him to his depths in certain respects. The sociologist approaches his object of study as part of his times in this deep way. These things too he must strive to understand; but his belongingness is no less real, and the transcendence he gains from self-understanding is, as we have already seen, quite relative. This means that the point of view of the observer and the point of view of the actor interpenetrate each other. When one takes the point of view of the actor, he is himself the observer taking it vicariously and partially, from his own perspective and for his own reasons. When he takes the point of view of the observer, he does so as one who is himself an actor and knows what the social entities designated by his categories of analysis "feel" like in life. Hence his grasp of what he studies is at once both "internal" and "external."

An eminent English historian writing in 1934 suggested that "history and sociology are, in fact, indispensable to one another. History without sociology is 'literary' and unscientific, while sociology without history is apt to become mere abstract theorizing." He spoke of the "mutual distrust between history and sociology and the attempt of each to assert its own independence and self-sufficiency." He continued: "In reality sociology and history are two complementary parts of a single science—the science of social life. They differ, not in their subject matter, but in their method, one attempting a general systematic analysis of the social process, while the other gives a genetic description of the same process in detail."[14]

In fact, of course, sociologists and historians do both. Gibbon generalized when he characterized the establishment of Christianity in the Roman Empire in the fourth century and the rise of Islam in the Middle East in the seventh both as "revolution." Edward Hallett Carr has noted that the "historian is not really interested in the unique, but what is general in the unique."[15] Perhaps it would be more accurate to say that the historian is interested both in the unique and in what is general in the unique, while the sociologist is interested in the general and its effect on the unique. Dawson's term, a genetic description of process, seems best. It does justice to both the unique and the general aspects of the reality studied by the historian. He is also right about the aims of sociology: the systematic analysis of social process. And again:

> History by itself is not enough, for it is impossible to understand a society or a culture in purely historical terms. Underlying the historical process and the higher activities of civilized life there are the primary relations of a society to its natural environment and its functional adaptation to economic ends. The sociologist has to study not only the inter-social relations of man with man, but also that primary relation of human life to its natural environment which is the root and beginning of all culture. Here sociology approaches the standpoint of the natural sciences and comes closer to the biologist than to the historian, for the study of a society in its mutual relation with its geographical environment and its economic activity has a real analogy with the biologist's study of an organism in relation to its environment and its function.[16]

Sociology approaches the natural sciences not only in its grounding in ecology as noted by Dawson but also in its use of abstract and general categories to study interaction and interindividual relationships, social structure, and social process—what Dawson has designated as "the inter-social relations of man with man." But sociology also approaches history and the humanities in its concern with understanding as well as explanation and as basic to and interpenetrating with its explanation. In this position sociology might become especially well equipped to play the role of mediator between the scientific point of view and that of the humanities, both of which it shares—to play the role of culture broker between what C. P. Snow called the two cultures. It has not, of course, so far risen to that challenge. Aristotle commented that history is more philosophical than poetry and more poetic than philosophy. We must recall that for Aristotle philosophy represented abstract knowledge analogous to that of natural science in our day, and poetry stood for the concrete experiential knowledge we associate with literature. For Aristotle, history was the equivalent or analogue of our history and social science. What he is saying is that history united what the French distinguish as *savoir* (knowing abstractly) and *connaître* (knowing through experience). This is what sociology could and should do in our own day. At any rate, the sociologist must also be something of a historian, the historian something of a sociologist. As Hallett Carr has put it, "I would say that the more sociological history becomes and the more historical sociology becomes, the better for both. Let the frontier between them be kept wide open for two way traffic.[17]

The chapter in Section II on Mormonism and the avoidance of sectarianism examines simultaneously an important empirical question—how did Mormonism avoid becoming a sect?—and a significant theoretical consideration—the valences to be attributed to structural and meaningful elements as against historical elements in influencing the actual outcome. It shows also the importance of maintaining the concrete cultural context even in the examination of a theoretical problem.

In the final part of this volume, Section IV, five chapters in various senses theoretical are presented. The first two attempt to state in different ways, for different purposes, and a dozen years apart, a significant discussion of the sociology of religion. The second of the two appeared originally in the *American Catholic Sociological Review,* together with a rather comprehensive bibliography. Because of Catholic sponsorship of that journal, the article was interpreted by some, especially those who had not read it, as a "confessional" or apologetic document.[18]

That "conclusion" becomes difficult to maintain if one is acquainted with the chapter itself. It is not only denied explicitly, which is never, of course, definitive, but the implications of the presentation are difficult to interpret as favoring or promoting any sectarian interest. It was criticized from other quarters as being too "polemical." Perhaps it is too bad that "institutionalized sociology" in America is so conflict-shy; but, good or bad, that quality is one, I believe, which we all share to one extent or another. Were I writing that second chapter again I believe I would eschew the polemical tone it shows in places, which seemed justified at the time and in the circumstances of the original writing. However, I do believe that the significant theoretical points made in that chapter are still quite valid, though some fourteen years later I would no doubt present them somewhat differently.[19]

The third chapter in this section appeared originally in the *Journal for the Scientific Study of Religion* and represents an example of theory building through empirical induction. It is, I believe, an important contribution to the sociology of religion and to sociological theory generally. The fourth chapter explores the possibility of an applied sociology of religion and suggests some interesting ideas concerning how little we really know and the relation of theory and practice.

The final chapter stands somewhat apart. It is an essay in applying the insights of sociological theory to analysis and interpretation. It was originally given as a paper at the Colloquium on Value Motivation sponsored by the Religion in Education Foundation at Carmel, California, in December, 1967, and it appeared first in the Report of that meeting. It represents an example of the use of a historically oriented sociology to analyze the present condition of Western man. It is the most ambitious piece of interpretation in the whole book. For this reason, for its theoretical sophistication, and for the importance of the conclusions it suggests, it makes a fitting final contribution to the volume.

This chapter suggests that sociology can, indeed, be relevant on the deepest levels of contemporary concern. It suggests that sociological analysis and interpretation can pose real problems and contribute to the clarification of contemporary experience. Troeltsch no doubt was right when he spoke of history as "an immeasurable, incomparable profusion of always-new, unique, and hence individual tendencies, welling up from undiscovered depths." He was quite accurate in speaking of its phenomena as "always-new and always-peculiar individualizations."[20] The activities of men spring from and express what Weber called "the eternally inexhaustible flow of life." In them men act out ever new, yet in some respects ever-recurring, dramas of meaning, relation, and achievement. That is why the idea of a "closed system of concepts, in which reality is synthesized in some sort of *permanently* and *universally* valid classification and from which it can again be deduced" is, in Weber's words, to be characterized as "meaninglessness."[21] Yet as men we can understand what other men have thought and done, and as men we can appreciate the predicaments other men have faced. As intelligent beings we can discover some at least of the consequences of past actions, some at least of the antecedents of present conditions. Sociology has its perspective, its mode of study and analysis, to offer in this venture. Yet while a total closed system is impossible, a vocabulary and syntax of analysis are not only possible but available.

Sociological theory presents us with such conceptual and analytic tools today. Closed or relatively closed models are, of course, possible for particular, well-delineated problems, but such models derive from and hark back to the larger, less systematic body of many-sided sociological theory. That theory can be helpful to men today in enabling them to achieve a better understanding of their predicaments and of the factors which have shaped and formed them. Thus, inherent in sociological analysis and interpretation is an increased clarification of experience which enhances understanding of our situation and, by enabling us to see how we have been conditioned by circumstances and events, enhances our freedom as well.

In this last chapter it is said: "Man is emerging into the historical epoch in which the long implicit question 'what is man doing in this earth?' becomes a matter of conscious thought and genuine decision, a matter of practical policy—indeed perhaps a prerequisite for survival." The sociology of religion is the sociological study of man's deepest relation to being and his most fundamental sense of direction. As such it confronts significant responsibilities in our day. Its challenge is to be both scholarly and relevant, for relevant scholarship has an important role in the clarification of experience in our present time of crisis. Today one hears much discussion about whether or not the university and the college are "relevant." At times it is suggested that less emphasis should be put on learning and scholarship and more energy be devoted to action. It seems to the present writer that it is precisely in the sphere of scholarship and teaching that the institutions of learning are prepared to make their most significantly relevant contributions. It also seems that one of our most important needs today is for a kind of clarification of our situation which becomes impossible without both critical thinking and the continued availability of the values and insight of our accumulated traditions. We suggested at the beginning that the sociology of religion had profited by the coincidence of continuing interest in the social science and a new increase in the desire to study the religious traditions of both West and East. Upon this favorable conjunction of circumstances there devolve responsibilities as well. In deepening the character of thinking and research in their own field, the sociologists of religion will perhaps make their best contribution to meeting the crisis of our time.

NOTES

1. For an analysis of the significance of the Council, see Thomas F. O'Dea, *The Catholic Crisis* (Boston: 1968).

2. This theme is further explored in Chapter 6 and in Thomas F. O'Dea, *The Mormons* (Chicago: 1957).

3. Everett Cherrington Hughes, *French Canada in Transition* (Chicago: 1943).

4. Georges Balandier, "The Fact of Colonialism: A Theoretical Approach," Joseph E. Cunneen, tr., *Cross Currents*, II, No. 4, 29 (Summer, 1952), reprinted from *Cahiers Internationaux de Sociologie*, Vol. XI (1951).

5. Charles Herbert Stember, *et al., Jews in the Mind of America* (New York and London: 1966).

6. See Karl Mannheim, *Ideology and Utopia* (New York and London: 1949).

7. For example, see Werner J. Cahnman and Alvin Boskoff, eds., *Sociology and History: Theory and Research* (New York: 1964), and Edward N. Saveth, ed., *American History and the Social Sciences* (New York: 1965).

8. See Aaron Cicourel, *Method and Measurement in Sociology* (New York: 1964).

9. Raymond Aron, *Introduction to the Philosophy of History*, George J. Irwin, tr. (Boston: 1961).

10. Talcott Parsons, *The Structure of Social Action* (Glencoe: 1949).

11. Max Weber, *The Methodology of the Social Sciences*, Edward A. Shils and Henry A. Finch, eds. and trs. (Glencoe: 1949).

12. See especially the treatment of the development of theodicy in Max Weber, *Ancient Judaism*, Hans H. Gerth and Don Martindale, trs. (Glencoe: 1952).

13. Aron, *op. cit.*, p. 60.

14. Christopher Dawson, "Sociology as a Science," in Sir J. Arthur Thomson and J. G. Crowther eds., *Science for a New World* (London: 1934), quoted from the reprinting in *Cross Currents*, IV, No. 2 (Winter, 1954), 129.

15. Edward Hallett Carr, *What Is History?* (New York: 1965), p. 80.

16. Dawson, *op. cit.*, p. 130.

17. Carr, *op. cit.*

18. See, for example, the footnote in Kingsley Davis, "The Myth of Functional Analysis as a Special Method in Sociology and Anthropology," *American Sociological Review*, XXIV (December, 1959), 766.

19. I did this, for example, in Thomas F. O'Dea, *The Sociology of Religion* (Englewood Cliffs, N.J.: 1966).

20. Ernst Troeltsch, *Christian Thought: Its Theory and Application* (New York: 1957), p. 44.

21. Max Weber, *op. cit.*, p. 84.

THE AMERICAN CATHOLIC EXPERIENCE: A SOCIOLOGICAL PERSPECTIVE

O N E : Catholic Sectarianism: A Sociological Analysis of the So-Called Boston Heresy Case

This chapter is based on a study, made in 1949 and first published in 1961, of the so-called Boston Heresy Case. The incident was unusual inasmuch as an important case of heresy in the American Catholic Church had not occurred for a very long time. The substance of the study was completed before the group found itself in conflict with ecclesiastical authority and at a time when the members themselves and the non-Catholics who knew them considered their position orthodox and even "official." The study predicted the likelihood of excommunication, though at the time it appeared that ecclesiastical authority was largely, if not completely, unaware of the true significance of this interesting religious development in one of the most Catholic regions of America.

Strains Inherent in the Contemporary Position of the Catholic Church

Social institutions embody a fundamental dilemma, providing, as they do, both the established context requisite for human behavior and at the same time imposing restrictions on the thinking and action of individuals. The former aspect is required for and is the basis of stable and continuing human activity, but

From *Review of Religious Research*, Vol. III, No. 2 (Fall, 1961).

the latter can prove itself an inhibiting force with respect to creativity and spontaneity and can in some situations contribute a certain rigidity and defensiveness in the face of the challenge which new developments in the ongoing life of the society present to individuals and groups.

Nowhere is this dilemma so apparent as in organized religion. The reasons for this derive from two sources. First, the religious experience is the experience of ultimacy and the sacred, both of which transcend established social forms and place individuals at the limit or boundary situation in terms of cognition of and the affective response to the human situation apperceived in that modality. Second, the religious institutions are, in our civilization, old institutions displaying that autonomy of individual wishes and motivation characteristic of established social forms in a particularly severe form.

Moreover, the religions of the Judeo-Christian tradition, emphasizing, as they do, the importance of man's relation to the transcendent, are placed in the position where they cannot readily (or over any long period of time, successfully) simply adapt to society. They must always embody an element of "relative disarticulation" with other social institutions and with the general run of consensual values in the society of which they are a part. In fact, when they are most true to their own visions, they will be least at home in the "world," understood as the general context of secular values and conduct characteristic of their social settings. And contrariwise, when they fit best into that world, their position is always one in which they stand in danger of slighting or even partially betraying their insights into what is required for an appropriate response to their vision of the transcendent God.[1]

It was this basic dilemma of Christianity which Troeltsch so remarkably spelled out in his great work *The Social Teachings of the Christian Churches,* but it is a Christian dilemma which but continues in new forms the older paradox to be seen in the conflict among the biblical Hebrews of the royal and priestly versus the prophetic understanding of the special relation to transcendence which Israel conceived as its peculiar covenant. With the institutionalization of religion—whether in the national entity of biblical Israel or the Christian community of the church—this basic disarticulation undergoes a number of remarkable transformations. Social institutionalization represents the objectification and establishment of a certain relative autonomy for culture patterns which were originally the significant content of the minds and attitudes of remarkable men who underwent original religious experiences. Then the problems of adjusting values whose relation is characterized by a relative contrariety undergo a metamorphosis into conflicts between social institutions, and all the secondary motivations of vested interests become built into them. For example, the disarticulation between the response to ultimacy embodied in Christianity and secular values of an essentially penultimate nature (and which make up the greater part of the value systems of all cultures) is transformed into a conflict between the church, as the institutional embodiment of the former, and the secular community, as the manifestation of the latter.

Modern Western civilization is the product of the Judeo-Christian religion on the one hand and the secularization process, which was to a considerable degree a revolt against it, on the other. There is a great historic irony in this, since the Christian ages with their creationist theology prepared the way for an acceptance of secular values, once the economic and social situation had brought into being the requisite classes for the assertion of their autonomy. Yet despite the undoubted truth of Tillich's statement that the Catholic Church was the schoolmistress of Europe until the fourteenth century, it is equally true that medieval Christianity slighted the legitimacy of secular values in practice, attempted to make a pseudomonastic ideal the model for the Christian lay life, and asserted an imperialist supremacy of the church in relation to other institutions of society. When it is recalled that this all took place within an institutionally hardening ecclesiastical structure and an explicit intellectualized world view which tended toward a certain rigidity of closure (despite the internal disarticulations it contained), it is not surprising that the modern world from the fourteenth century on found it necessary to revolt against the older Catholic structures and to proclaim secular values: science, nature, and politics. While this was characteristic of the Mediterranean world, the revolt in the north took another direction: the attempt to assert a partially deinstitutionalized Christianity against the rigidity of Catholic structures in the realms of thought, worship, and ecclesiastical polity.

The Catholicism of the fourteenth century represented a compromise between (1) the inner content of the Christian experience and the processes of institutionalization and their

product, and (2) between an Augustinian view of secular values
and the new assertion of the legitimacy of the secular developing
in Italy and elsewhere. Reinhold Niebuhr is quite right when he
states that Catholicism was too humanistic for the north, too
Christian for the south. It was, moreover, institutionally rigid and
caught in the net of vested interests. Despite its impressive self-
reform (which, however, came too late to prevent schism and
revolt), it remained in the anomalous position of half-progenitor
and half-alien in the modern world.

As a result of these developments, the relative disarticulation
between Christianity and the world, which is the permanent
condition and crisis of religions of transcendence, expresses itself
in our day in a complete alienation of the modern temper from
the Christian spirit. Catholics tend to see the former as characterized by the failure to center life on God. This condition of
Western thought and values is the result of a complex historical
development which includes the rise of cities, trade, nations,
worldly learning, and modern science. One specific aspect of the
process has found particular expression in America: the utopian
aspirations of a democratic and scientistic chiliasm. Catholics are
often protected by the structure of Catholic thought and institutional forms from feeling the full impact of this cultural context,
and as a result Catholic life in America is often characterized by
a number of strains the sources of which often remain obscure.

Although in the United States the secession of humanism and
its bearers from the older orthodoxy was largely against a
dominant Protestantism, the resulting antagonism and disarticulation were often directed against the Roman Catholic Church as
the survival of medievalism, ecclesiasticism, superstition, and
tyranny. This situation of disarticulation and defensiveness was
made more difficult for American Catholicism by the fact that its
members were largely immigrants who were being incorporated
into American society at the lowest social level. A lower-class and
largely immigrant Catholicism grew up segregated into something like a ghetto in the midst of a prospering and expanding
society based on secularism—more precisely on scientism and
capitalism. If, from one point of view, America was, indeed, a
welcome haven to the immigrants, it also exacted a heavy price
"down to the third and fourth generation" of those that loved
her. The record of American Catholicism and of American
Catholics as a group is one of assimilation with its conflicts and

compromises, its successes and failures, its humor and pathos, and perhaps, above all, its ambiguities.[2]

The fact is that the American Catholic is generally of humble lineage, of a background often relatively segregated from the main currents of American culture, and, as a result, is often uneasy about his relation to important aspects of American culture when he is not downright defensive. His somewhat greater vulnerability to the appeals of a radicalism of the right must be seen in this light, for it is of central importance to understanding its structure and content.

Recent years have seen a considerable change in this condition with the remarkable social mobility of Catholics in politics and business, and even—though with significant lag—in intellectual life. Yet for American Catholics the general problems of social mobility have been complicated by the fact that non-Catholic intellectual circles which ultimately set the tone of the culture, establishing the cultivated and civilized climates of opinion, were first Protestant and later secularist.[3] Hence the American Catholic must often confront circles to which he is not simply socially inferior but also, in terms of the self-definitions of such groups, intellectually and culturally inferior as well. As a student in a secular college he is immersed in an intellectual atmosphere which combines indifference and antagonism to his fundamental faith position. As an intellectual he must face the difficult task of reuniting the separation between his religion and secular learning and values which the centuries have produced—and often be misunderstood by his coreligionists who either do not see the vastness of the problem or react against the whole disturbing spectacle with a semisectarian defensiveness. It is small wonder that a few years ago, with the tendency for anti-Catholicism to become the anti-Semitism of the liberals, some Catholics embraced anti-intellectualism as the antisecularism of those unable to meet the stringent demands of the modern encounter which assimilation and social mobility had thrust upon them. Since Communism is the most identifiable and most aggressive expression of secularist thought in our day, it is to be expected that there developed among Catholics a broad and uncritical anti-Communism, which attacked all forms of secular liberalism.

The position of contemporary Catholicism, then, is characterized by two sets of strains. One arises from the defensive position of Christianity as a whole in the face of the modern civilization which developed in a condition of semisecession from its ranks. The second derives from the rigidity of overinstitutionalization which characterized and still characterizes Catholic thought and organization. Yet in terms of sociological analysis it cannot be denied that these two conditions have played a positive role in preserving the integrity of Catholic thought and institutions.

It would be a complete misreading of the record to conclude that modern Catholicism had failed to perceive its problems and to face the challenge to its present position. The present century has seen a veritable "Catholic renaissance" in thinking and in the renewal of the forms of worship. It remains true, however, that the repercussions of positive adaptive developments have been restrained within the context of institutional and intellectual rigidities.

Catholic thinking has, indeed, been unaware of the strains outlined above. The pressures of its present position push its members toward extreme responses the more they become aware of the true sociological and intellectual dimensions of their present position in modern society and culture. The late Emmanuel Cardinal Suhard has analyzed the two phenomena known as integralism and modernism in Catholic circles as two errors evoked by the strains of secularization, and he charted for the French Church, which had been plagued by both, a middle way. These are, in fact, but less extreme expressions of reactions which in heightened form reveal themselves as sectarianism in one case and apostasy in the other.

This chapter presents an abbreviated report of research in which both of these extreme responses had originally been studied. It confines itself, however, to sectarianism. It is the great irony of the American Catholic experience that the immigration of a lower-class church, defensive in the face of its partial alienation from the contemporary culture, rendered an entire ecclesiastical structure somewhat sectarian in its response to its cultural milieu, dominantly Protestant in its content. An extreme phenomenon, implicitly tantamount in Catholic terms to heresy and in this case actually ending as heretical, outright sectarianism, reveals in exaggerated form aspects of response to strain often present in a less palpable way among the great majority who occupy more modal positions.

The St. Benedict Center

In 1940 in Cambridge, Massachusetts, a Catholic student group was formed which became known as St. Benedict Center. Located in the shadow of Harvard University houses and but a short walk from the Harvard Yard, the Center attracted Harvard students as well as others from the colleges and universities in Greater Boston. Its evening lectures often drew as many as 250 to 300 students. In 1946, in addition to student activities and lectures, the Center became a school, receiving students under the G.I. Bill and offering classes in Scripture, philosophy, church history, classical languages, and other subjects. In the same year, it began to publish a quarterly entitled *From the Housetops*. Its spiritual director was a Jesuit priest—a talented writer and able lecturer—who had been regarded in Catholic circles as a genial commentator.

During its development the Center came to identify its chief aim with opposition to secular education, which by the fall of 1946 could be said to have constituted its *raison d'etre*. Its members, some of whom were Catholic students away from home, some commuters, some converts, were told by their leaders (some of whom were faculty members of Boston College) that the modern world was a place of great peril to their faith; they were counseled to meet it with a policy combining withdrawal and militant opposition. Lectures and articles in the quarterly put this policy into effect. Many non-Catholics came to the Center to see "what the noise was all about." Many at Harvard considered the position of the Center to be the "official" position of the Catholic Church, and it became somewhat of a scandal.

Opposition to secular education was at first understood largely as opposition to secularism in education at secular colleges and universities. This was soon expanded to Catholic withdrawal from such institutions and to criticism, often of a distorted kind, of secularism in Catholic institutions and in the policies of Catholic educators. Opposition to Catholic students' attending secular colleges grew into opposition to Catholic graduate students' attending secular universities and to the superiors of religious orders for sending their members to do graduate work at secular universities. Ironically enough, the priests and nuns who came to Harvard for graduate work were often older than many of the self-appointed counselors at the Center.

The Center came to oppose any Catholic participation in interfaith co-operation and even to oppose friendly relations with Protestants. One began to detect a desire to draw as sharp a line of demarcation as possible between Catholic and non-Catholic. These tendencies and policies were finally summed up in an insistence on a narrow and unequivocal interpretation of the dictum *extra ecclesiam nulla salus*.

These tendencies and policies revealed themselves as three themes, which sum up the basic attitudes of the Center group. These are documented from the contents of the ten issues from September, 1946, to the spring of 1949 of *From the Housetops*.

1. OPPOSITION TO SECULAR EDUCATION
AND TO CATHOLIC STUDENTS' ATTENDING SECULAR
COLLEGES AND UNIVERSITIES

Secularism in colleges is so complex a phenomenon that its nature and its modes of opposition to Catholic faith are hard to define. Catholics must nevertheless recognize it as their main enemy. . . . Any Catholic student choosing a secular college exposes himself to these dangers [Vol. I, No. 1].

What they [Catholic students who enter secular colleges] desire is a liberal education; what they receive is instruction inevitably detrimental to their faith [Vol. I, No. 2].

Never have so many Catholics gone to secular colleges . . . . In one more generation, will there be any Catholic loyalty left? [Vol. III, No. 1].

2. OPPOSITION TO SECULAR EMPHASIS IN
CATHOLIC EDUCATION

A Plea for No Appeasement

1. To reestablish uncompromising orthodoxy. . . .

2. We must know that not only is it against the Church for Catholic students to go to secular colleges, but it is a scandal for Catholic clergy to go there also.

3. We must break with State Boards of Education made up of heretical and atheistic men whose concept of man's nature is limited and whose view of men's destiny is utilitarian and humanistic, who

rule that our college curricula resemble in content the courses taught in secular colleges.

4. We must not place on the faculty of Catholic Colleges secular college men except on recommendation of priests who will take responsibility for their orthodoxy. We should not place on the faculty of Catholic Colleges priests who have received the greater part of their training in secular colleges.

5. We must remove the prestige which has been given to schools of Social Work, Experimental Psychology, and Psychiatry based on the teaching of Sigmund Freud and his successors [Vol. I, No. 3].

The large enrollment of religious at every secular university in this country is a scandal both to Catholics and non-Catholics [Vol. I, No. 3].

3. THE ATTEMPT TO DRAW A SHARP LINE BETWEEN
CATHOLICS AND NON-CATHOLICS

. . . [Interfaith co-operation means to] make terms with Christ's enemies [Vol. I, No. 3].

If we are to preserve our faith today we must know our enemies. The greatest enemy of the Catholic Church today is not Communism, as many suppose. It is heresy—Protestantism. . . . It requires courage to attack the real enemy, Protestantism. Still it must be done if we are to save our own souls and the souls of those Protestants of good will who would come into the Church if a sufficiently strong challenge were presented and a sharp line drawn between the Church and its enemies.

And let us not be afraid of calling Protestants names. Nothing is so useful in removing surface cordiality. In this day of weakened faith name-calling is considered impolite. Very well, let it be so. Politeness is not one of the cardinal virtues [Vol. II, No. 4].

The file of *From the Housetops* contains ten issues, comprising 193 titles which fill 638 pages. Of these, 125 are prose titles; 68 are poetry. Of the former, 32 are more or less direct (most of them very direct) expressions of the three themes presented above. Thirteen more may be called philosophical articles; in some of these the three themes may be found, but they are not the dominant content. The 32 articles which are more or less direct expressions of the dominant themes fill 149 pages out of a total of 638. Thus about one quarter of the publication is devoted to these themes directly, while other features often indirectly reflect them.

On the other hand, there is striking unawareness of, or unconcern with, the general problems of the day. The magazine began publication one year after the end of World War II, yet the war is hardly ever mentioned except in poetry. There is no discussion of the moral problems raised by the atom bomb. Current problems in politics and economics are ignored. The magazine is directed to students, yet there are no articles discussing problems in the humanities or sciences. While teaching in secular institutions or in Catholic colleges is attacked, there is no real attempt to discuss intellectual problems from the point of view of the Christian faith or to take up the concrete problems of Christian education. No Catholic work in any academic field is discussed. There is one book review in the whole two and a half years: Arnold Toynbee is called a trickster and a magician for his *Study of History*. Only among the philosophical articles is there any recognition of modern problems as posing something other than targets for polemics.

Significant also is the general tone of the magazine, imbued as it is with three striking characteristics: (1) a note of urgency, (2) distortion of the present situation of the church in America, and (3) opposition to the policies of the church in America.

Incipient Sectarianism and Legitimate Authority

The reaction of St. Benedict Center to secularism at a distinguished institution of learning was characterized by separatism and by both defiance of and withdrawal from the demands of the secular sphere. The demands of the secular sphere in this instance included at minimum some serious attempt to confront secular learning and modern science in the spirit of the original patristic confrontation of classical learning: "For 'thy foot shall not stumble' if thou attribute to Providence all good, whether it belong to the Greeks or to us" (St. Clement of Alexandria, *Stromateis,* I, v. 28), or of the medieval confrontation of Greek and Arabic science: *Non respecias a quo sed quod sane dicatur memoriae recommenda* (St. Thomas Aquinas, *De modo studendi*). This task—not an easy one under the circumstances—would have required an equanimity which was rendered more difficult of achievement by the insecurity of a minority group in a climate of opinion varying from alien through uncongenial to hostile, the group itself occupying a position of social and intellectual inferiority. It is this condition which parallels the marginality characteristic of the circumstances in which so many Protestant sects have arisen. In some two and a half years of publication of *From the Housetops,* a period in which the Center was at its height as a Catholic student group, the quarterly shows no serious endeavor to meet this task. Polemical opposition is preferred, and Catholic intellectual and even social ghettoism is advocated. It is this reaction which parallels the reaction of separatism and exclusiveness that characterizes Protestant sectarianism. As in the Protestant examples, isolation was preferred not only to compromise but to entrance into the world, even for the latter's sanctification.

All these sectarian tendencies were summed up in a narrow, literalist, and unequivocal interpretation of *extra ecclesiam nulla salus,* an interpretation which held "that the baptism of desire is a device of 'liberal' Catholics to christianize heretics" and displayed a spirit that "not only alienates Protestants of good faith but also is a positive scandal to Catholics."[4] The taking of an exclusivist stand on this interpretation is somewhat analogous in Catholic circumstances to characteristics of Protestant sects: the emphases on conversion and voluntary election. This becomes all the more obvious when the Center's sectarian interpretations become the basis of the presumption to "correct" those of duly constituted ecclesiastical authority.

The Center displayed the sectarian *notae* of austerity and the conviction of persecution. While it did not advocate a Protestant interpretation of "the priesthood of believers" or of "private interpretation," its leaders—laymen and in one prominent case a laywoman—spoke in a manner of persons "having authority" and highly suggestive of attempted usurpation of ecclesiastical authority. The Center, like most sects, spoke "with authority" and certainly met Wach's criterion of claiming to be "renewing the original spirit" of the church.

By March, 1949, St. Benedict Center had become an incipient sect within the body of the Catholic Church. It was inevitable that as such it would sooner or later become involved in serious conflict with ecclesiastical authority. When the time would arrive a decision would have to be taken—a decision to remain within the church and modify itself or to become a fully developed sect outside of and in opposition to the church. (This was as far as the original study went. The events of the next several days are analyzed on the basis of material in the Boston *Herald, Post,*

Globe, and *Traveler.* The events more than amply confirmed the writer's conclusion.)

The Time of Decision

On Thursday, April 14, 1949, the Boston papers announced in banner headlines that four Boston College teachers had been dismissed. Said the morning *Post:*

> Three members of the Boston College faculty and a teacher at Boston College High School were discharged today.

The evening *Globe* of the same day declared, "B.C. Replies to Ousted Teachers," and quoted the college president as saying:

> These gentlemen in question were under contract at Boston College to teach philosophy and physics. They had been cautioned by me and others in authority here to stay within their own fields and leave theology to those who were adequately and competently prepared.
>
> They continued to speak in class and out of class on matters contrary to the traditional teaching of the Catholic Church, ideas leading to bigotry and intolerance.
>
> Their doctrine is erroneous and as such could not be tolerated at Boston College. They were informed that they must cease such teaching or leave the faculty.

The four teachers, two of whom were converts, accused Boston College of teaching heresy. As reported in the Boston *Globe,* April 14, 1949, they declared such heretical instruction consisted in teaching

> both explicitly and implicitly that (1) there may be salvation outside the Catholic Church, (2) a man may be saved without admitting that the Roman Catholic Church is supreme among the churches, (3) a man may be saved without submission to the Pope.

At four o'clock in the afternoon of the next day, which was Good Friday, worshipers at six Catholic churches in Boston, including the Cathedral, were surprised to see before the church two and in some cases three men carrying placards which read "No Salvation Outside the Church" and offering for sale a publication entitled *From the Housetops.* About an hour before the picketing began, the newspapers had received an anonymous phone call from a person who said he represented St. Benedict Center, informing them that there would be "something doing at four o'clock" outside a number of churches which he specified. The following day, April 16, the Associated Press reported "Vatican sources" as saying that the "Boston College controversy" was in the jurisdiction of the Boston Archbishop.

In the meantime the connection between the discharged teachers and the Center had become more generally known. On the evening of the next day, April 17, the spiritual director of the Center issued a prepared statement in their defense, while the discharged four themselves announced that they were appealing "directly to His Holiness the Pope" since they felt that the Boston College president could not have acted "without consulting His Excellency the Archbishop." The St. Benedict Center group were openly revolting and in usual revolutionary fashion by-passing conventional channels of authority. They had decided to make, or at least under the pressure of the events they found themselves making, an intransigent stand on their narrow sectarianism which had now been focused on and symbolized by an unequivocal and literalist understanding of *extra ecclesiam nulla salus*. Incipient sectarianism had led to open "protest"—in defiance of ecclesiastical authority.

The response was not long in coming. On Monday, April 18, the Archbishop declared that the spiritual director of the Center "because of grave offense to the laws of the Catholic Church has lost the right to perform any priestly function, including preaching and teaching religion." His Excellency further revealed that the Center's chaplain had been "defying the orders of legitimate superiors for more than seven months" and since the first of January of that year had "not possessed the faculties of this Archdiocese." He further decreed that the Center was forbidden to Catholics and that those who took part in its activities would "forfeit the right to receive the Sacrament of Penance and Holy Eucharist" (Boston *Globe,* April 19, 1949).

The next day the "silenced" priest declared the Archbishop's action to be "invalid," and the board of directors of the Center stated that the Center was "not founded by a decree of the Archbishop and would not be dissolved by such" (Boston *Globe,* April 20, 1949). The Center was now in fact a dissenting sect.

At this time the Center group formed itself into an organization called the "Slaves of the Immaculate Heart of Mary" while continuing their rebellion against ecclesiastical authority, thus displaying a sectarian combination of dramatized humility and arrogant revolt. The record of sectarianism and revolt continued despite expulsion of the spiritual director from the Society of Jesus, rulings of the Supreme Sacred Congregation of the Holy Office at Rome, and excommunication. The Center group members adopted a peculiar habit in dress. They had about forty members, some of whom withdrew from Catholic colleges in the area. The group continued its conflict against church authority, which was sometimes dramatized in publicity-seeking ways, such as bursting into the office of the late Cardinal Archbishop of Chicago. Sometime afterward they became openly anti-Semitic and advocated such views in their public meetings.

Conclusion

It has been pointed out that Catholicism, as a result of its place in the structure of Western society and its past history, is subject to two major strains. The first arises from its defensiveness in the face of modern secular culture and modern thought. The second derives from the rigidities of its institutionalized structures both in thought and organization. Moreover, American Catholicism, beginning as a lower-class social phenomenon whose members have experienced considerable recent social mobility, finds these two strains especially magnified. In the St. Benedict Center case, an originally Catholic group embodying the Catholic point of view and Catholic values found itself confronted by that vast and impressive manifestation of modern secular culture which is Harvard University. In this encounter the bearers of the minority culture and values were thrown on the defensive. To the elements of value uncertainty must be added the complications introduced by social mobility.

Moreover, a university, which is an institutionalized context of intellectual encounter, contains an important element of anomie in its very structure and content. In its libraries and lecture halls, viewpoints brought by the students from home, where they were often semiconsciously internalized, meet the challenge of the explicit examination and criticism of ideas. Students in college and university are exposed to the "dangers" involved in the "examined life." Thus the academic atmosphere is one which in any case would produce some degree of student anxiety and defensiveness. The element of criticism and appraisal and consequent anxiety was made more serious for Catholics by the askewness we have discussed in the relation between Catholicism and the dominant viewpoints of secular culture. Moreover, the Center attracted converts to Catholicism whose reaction against their own backgrounds increased the tendency to aggression and defense.

Thus in this case the element of defensiveness which is inherent in the contemporary position of Christianity was rendered more aggravated by the concrete encounter with Harvard. The general status of Catholics in the social structure of the United States further aggravated this strain by adding the uncertainties of social mobility and the strains of minority social status.

The second source of strain, the rigidities of Catholic thought and organization, was important in this case since there was not in the Harvard area at the same time the kind of intellectual movements in Catholicism that would have represented a creative response to the problems involved in meeting the encounter with secularism. This lack was the result of both the class and ethnic background of Boston Catholics and the inhibition of creative movements by the rigidities of overinstitutionalization. Had such a movement existed, it would have provided a creative outlet for Catholics in such circumstances and also the intellectual and emotional support that could have eased the effects of strain. Such support and such a creative possibility could have prevented individuals from being driven into a radically defensive position.

As a consequence, a number of Catholic students led by a Jesuit priest and several adult Catholic lay people made the sectarian response. They attempted to escape from the field by a wholesale abandonment of modern culture and transmuted their extreme defensiveness into aggression by the assumption of a militant sectarian attitude. The extreme quality of the response testifies to the severity of the strain. Catholic action being impossible, Catholic reaction set in. This situation of the impossibility of creative action leading to reaction is one to be seen in the responses of many "right-wing" groups, both religious and secular. It is not surprising that the group in question here eventually embraced anti-Semitism since this has been fairly typical of extreme reactionary movements in Western culture.

Most Catholic students at Harvard and at other secular colleges avoid the radical effects of the strain involved in the encounter with secularism. It is to be suspected that they do it by various forms of compartmentalization. But the strains which found expression in the case at hand appear to be present for those who occupy more moderate and modal positions.

NOTES

1. A further development of this problem is contained in "Five Dilemmas in the Institutionalization of Religion," Chapter 13 of the present volume.

2. A good recent work dealing with one aspect of this development is Robert D. Cross, *The Emergence of Liberal Catholicism in America* (Cambridge: 1958).

3. A similar situation of Christians in Europe is discussed by Karl Heim in his *Christian Faith and Natural Science* (New York: 1953), pp. 16 ff.

4. Philip J. Donnelly, S.J., "Some Observations on the Question of Salvation Outside the Church," Department of Theology, Boston College (1949), privately distributed.

T W O : American Catholics
and International Life

The size of the Catholic community[1] in America (39,509,508 in 1959), the social mobility of Catholics into upper-middle class status, and the urgency of the foreign policy issues facing the nation lend a new importance to a consideration of Catholic attitudes on foreign affairs. Involved in this question is that of Catholic participation in the kinds of organization that provide the context of opinion formation concerning international relations. The present chapter is a tentative attempt to examine the strategic historical and sociological factors affecting these important problems. Its tentativeness should be stressed, for a more certain statement would require long and costly research.

We begin with two questions: one concerning Catholic participation in organizations concerned with foreign affairs discussion and education, of which the Foreign Policy Association is preeminent, and the other respecting Catholic attitudes toward foreign policy itself. The first should be approached as part of the larger problem of Catholic participation in the organizations of American society generally. The second should be discussed in terms of the main factors that have affected the development of attitudes among Catholics concerning issues involved in or related to foreign policy.

The term "Catholic," however, raises difficulty to begin with. It is not a concise category permitting hard and fast generalizations. There are various sorts and conditions of Catholics in this country, and general statements about them must be hedged with appropriate qualifications. Yet we persist in using the

From *Social Order,* X (June, 1960), 243-265.

general term with some degree of accurate designation. Is its use justifiable in a broad analysis of this kind?

Such justification can be found if Catholics by and large have shared, in addition to their religious commitment, a similar challenge in America. Are there characteristic elements or dimensions in the diverse experiences of heterogeneous Catholics in this country which, despite their varied circumstances of life, may be subsumed under the same categories of analysis without serious distortion of their different histories? Is there, in fact, a recognizable historical and sociological entity which might fairly be called the "American Catholic experience"?

We shall assume here that there is—an assumption we shall not digress to demonstrate, though we believe it quite demonstrable—and we shall assert that it has had quite recognizable results. These have affected the mentality of Catholic Americans in ways which we shall analyze. Such a conception is, of course, a very approximate delineation of a complex and variegated historical reality, and conclusions based on it will necessarily be very approximate ones.

The American Catholic Experience

The great background fact descriptive of the American Catholic experience is the fact of mass immigration. From 1820 to 1930, 37,762,012 immigrants came to the United States, 32,276,346 of them coming from Europe. From the foundation of the republic to 1820, about 250,000 newcomers came, at a rate of five to six thousand a year. In the 1820's the numbers began to increase; in the late 1840's mass immigration really commenced, with the arrival of the Irish and the Germans in large numbers. In the 124 years from 1820 to 1943, some 6 million Germans and 4,600,000 Irish came, the latter making up 70 per cent of the immigration from the British Isles in the years from 1821 to 1860. The arrival of these two nationalities brought an increasing proportion of Catholics to America, since about 40 per cent of the Germans were Catholic, and of the Irish about 4 million were Catholic, the large Scotch-Irish immigration having by and large occurred earlier.

The so-called "New Immigration" from southern and eastern

Europe, which began in the 1880's, brought new and diverse peoples to these shores, constituting in the decade of 1901–1910 72 per cent of all immigration. It consisted of Poles, Magyars, Italians, and others, some 2 million Italians arriving in the decade 1901–1910 alone. Of these "new immigrants," many were Catholic; as a result the Catholic Church in America grew from 7 million to 16 million from 1890 to 1916. In terms of Catholic assimilation, however, these new groups were generally fitted into a mode of adaptation and a church structure that was the product of earlier Irish and German experience. With the great migrations of the Irish and Germans which began in the late 1840's, mass Catholicism in America commences, and with it the American Catholic experience enters a new and decisive phase.[2]

The culture and society into which these new arrivals came was dominantly Protestant. This was true numerically, culturally, and with respect to dominance in social, political, economic, and intellectual life. The social system of nineteenth-century America rested on the twin pillars of Protestant religion and Anglo-Saxon law. It was dominated by descendants of earlier arrivals who were chiefly Protestants of English ancestry, or similar groups assimilated to them. Throughout the century, America was, to use a waggish term, a WASP enterprise—white, Anglo-Saxon, Protestant.

A WASP Enterprise

Although the second half of the nineteenth century witnessed a marked secularization of life and thought, this process proceeded on the established Protestant foundation and showed many cultural marks derived therefrom. Moreover, Protestantism remained strong; on the eve of the Great War there were some 26 million Protestant church members in this country to about 16 million Roman Catholics. The victory of the Eighteenth Amendment a few years later demonstrated that Protestant influence could still be decisive. Just one generation ago, in 1930, André Siegfried could still characterize Protestantism as the "national religion" of the United States.

The arrival of Catholics in large numbers evoked a negative response that at times flared up in unconcealed hostility. Nativism in the form of Know-Nothingism gave vent to violent local reactions in what has been called a "Protestant Crusade"; it appeared again in the second half of the century in the American Protective Association.[3] More restrained misgivings about the newcomers characterized less overt reactions. Fitting a large body of foreign Catholics into a Protestant country would not be easy.

The coming of large numbers of Catholics into a Protestant society and culture raised problems on two levels. First, there was the problem for the church qua church: how shall the Catholic Church adapt itself to its new situation? And, second, there was raised the question: how shall Catholic individuals and Catholic groups become assimilated to this new society in which from now on their destiny would lie?

America, especially in the post-Civil War period, did not permit as a long-run solution that kind of pluralism which is characterized by the coexistence of separate groups, each with its own language, culture, and social forms, maintaining its peculiar identity in a loosely confederated society. America would permit ethnic ghettos and even make them necessary, but their long-run significance was to serve as spatial and temporal zones of transition to full assimilation. At an earlier time there had been such cultural isolation for small sectarian groups, but its effect on American society was not long-lasting, and the pressures were always against anything like realization of what might be called the "Swiss model."[4] Such groups as survive today—Amish, Hutterites, and others—appear to be only bizarre exceptions proving the rule. Even as early as the 1830's de Tocqueville testified to the strong pressures for uniformity in the young republic. The most dramatic example of religiously based semiseparatism in our history, that of the Mormons, issued eventually in accommodation and assimilation to the general culture in most essential respects.

Problem for the Church

How, in these circumstances, should the church qua church meet the challenge of living in America? This question soon arose in diverse forms and for many decades became the focus of controversy—often enough intemperate—within American Catholic life, as adaptationists and the apostles of aloofness contested with each other on issue after issue. How should the church regard Protestantism? What should its attitude be toward the non-Catholic American state? Should immigrant Catholics and their offspring become culturally like their non-Catholic fellow citizens? How should the education of Catholics be conducted? What about the relation between energetic, activistic American values and Catholic values which gave primacy to contemplation? These were some of the issues confronting the immigrant church as it began its career of relating itself to the realities and possibilities of America. In short, should the Catholic Church become Americanized?

To oversimplify a complex development, it may be said that the struggle tended to divide on ethnic lines. The Irish generally said "yes"; the Germans generally said "no." To the former, with a background of oppression in Europe, American utopianism always made a telling appeal. For the latter, the preservation of German cultural identity, including the German language, seemed the most desirable, and indeed the only, context for protecting the faith of German immigrants. Out of this encounter of Catholicism and America and this conflict among Catholics, what emerged was an Americanized Catholicism and an American Catholic Church.[5] The victory was not by any means a demolishing of opposite views or a disestablishing of nationality-based Catholic organizations. The Americanization process, moreover, left a heritage of difficulties. Yet the genuineness of the accomplishment is beyond doubt. Indeed, the Catholic Church became an effective Americanizing force, offering to the descendants of immigrants a reference group rooted in the past, but not simply of ethnic significance. The Catholic Church in America has itself been a "melting pot." Moreover, it has culturally become quite American. If "Americanism" is, indeed, a "phantom heresy,"[6] there is nothing ethereal about such Catholic adaptations to business life as the Serra Clubs.[7] Further, the adaptation of Catholics to political life has been one of phenomenal success. Despite a real lag in the intellectual sphere, here, too, genuine contributions are being made. To give but one example, there is no doubt that the writings of John Courtney Murray, S.J., on the theology of church and state, based on the lessons of the American Catholic experience, are a significant contribution to Catholic thought generally.

The substantial victory of the "Americanizers" is attributable to three factors. The pressures of American life demanded it; the appeal of America to the Irish, who were strategic in church councils, favored it; and the desire for social mobility by the immigrants, or at least their descendants, made it inevitable. Yet the experience had effects other than simply Americanizing the church and aiding the assimilation of its members, although those two are of central significance. It left a mark on Catholic attitudes and thinking which involved some disarticulation between Catholicism and the general culture of America. It precipitated psychological residues, often of an implicit and subtle kind, that would make difficult direct and unburdened rapprochement between Catholicism and many aspects of American life.

The Americanization of the Catholic Church, a historical phenomenon of great significance, should be viewed in the context of two other accomplishments: the remarkable growth of the Catholic population throughout the nineteenth and twentieth centuries and the brute fact of sheer survival. From 1790 to 1959, the population of the United States increased from a little under 4 million to 176 million, or about 45 times. In the same years the membership of the Catholic Church grew from 35,000 to almost 40 million, or about 1,142 times. Immigration was decisive in both cases, but its relatively greater importance in the Catholic case is obvious. The church faced massive assimilation problems, and it is not surprising that considerable losses were incurred. A Catholic sociologist has recently suggested that without these losses the present church membership in America would be from 50 million to 55 million.[8] Yet the same writer states that it is astonishing that the actual losses were not greater. Survival, phenomenal growth, and substantial Americanization are the accomplishments of American Catholicism in the past 170 years, a remarkable record. The figures suggest the scope of the problems that had to be faced.

Irony in Accomplishments

These accomplishments of Catholicism in America were not without a certain irony. This irony can best be stated in terms of two sociological categories derived from the work of Ernst

Troeltsch. The fundamental problem for Christianity, Troeltsch stated, is that involved in relating activity in the world to the transcendent call of the New Testament. As a consequence, there arise two social forms of Christian community. In this sense the "church" represents the effort at adaptation, the creative search for which is characteristic of every epoch. The "sect" embodies the attitude of rejection of "compromise" and a policy of withdrawal from, or militant opposition to, the world.[9]

The influential forms of Protestantism in early America often inclined in a sectarian direction in terms of both social organization and theology. For the Puritans of Salem and Boston and the Separatists of Plymouth, migration itself was a secession from Babylon. Yet the culture that issued from Protestant settlement became a Protestant culture, embodying Protestant values as the core consensus on which American society came to rest. This fact remains true despite the secularization of the colonial period and of the decades after the Civil War. Consequently, Protestantism was able to make the kind of adaptation to secular life in America which bears important marks of what in Troeltsch's terms may be called a "church response." Despite the original sectarian elements in belief and polity, Protestantism became in fact the unofficially "established church" of the American Republic.

The Classic Example

Catholicism, on the other hand, has always offered the classical example of what Troeltsch meant by a church. Despite the defensive posture which, since 1517, history had forced upon it, the Catholic Church came to America with quite ecclesiastical orientations reflected in both its theology and its organizational forms, although its relative alienation from many aspects of modern life certainly inhibited the realization of some of their implications. It is true to say that post-Tridentine Catholicism displayed many defensive characteristics in historical situations requiring defense. Coming to America as an immigrant church entering a Protestant culture, it was forced to make its adaptation in ways that often required a defensive posture. Consequently, it was forced to behave in ways resembling a sectarian response.

Resulting Separatism

As a result, Catholics set up in many spheres separate organizations as a context for Catholic life. These range today from the Catholic Boy Scout Troop to the Catholic Association for International Peace, from Catholic grammar schools to Catholic universities. Such a response was the result of a truly ecclesiastic effort to reconcile Christ and culture.[10] But because of the defensive elements made necessary by the dominant Protestant milieu, it was an ecclesiastical response based on ecclesiastical theological positions in which lurked inescapable sectarian consequences. It involved at least a relative withdrawal from Protestant and secular society and culture; at times it involved an element of militant opposition.

The great irony of American religious history is certainly that a relatively sectarian Protestantism developed in America an ecclesiastical adaptation to society and culture, while an ecclesiastical Catholicism was forced to display elements of sectarianism in its quite ecclesiastical efforts. The result of this unintended sectarianism has been a certain askewness in the relation of Catholicism to dominant American ideas and values and a certain relative aloofness with respect to Catholic participation in the general organizations of American life.

The elements of aloofness and askewness that came to characterize the relation of Catholicism to American culture and society were increased by the secularization of culture in the second half of the nineteenth century. Earlier in Europe, because of the concrete concatenation of historical factors that prevailed, Catholicism had made an unfortunate adaptation to the rise of modern science.[11] Consequently, in the post-Civil War period, when science was making a tremendous impact on America, this inherited disability reinforced locally generated tendencies toward askewness. Secularists of Protestant background often saw in Catholicism a mighty fortress of what they deemed Christian recalcitrance to scientific progress.[12] Although a secularized culture offered in some respects more tolerance to Catholicism, it could not but make difficult a creative dialogue on fundamental intellectual issues. The generally lower-class composition of the immigrant church (a theme we shall examine later), by keeping Catholics out of intellectual pursuits, would reinforce this element of disarticulation. As naturalism came to have a strategic influence on American thought in the last third of the nineteenth century, Catholic ideas and Catholic values could not but come to appear to many as "obsolete" or "reactionary."[13]

Source of Beneficent Clericalism

A third element contributing to askewness in the relation of Catholicism to American culture was the class composition of the American Catholic population. We shall return to this in more detail in the next section, but suffice it to say here that it was such as to make clerical leadership more exclusive than would have had to be the case if upper and upper-middle class groups had been more heavily represented. Evelyn Waugh suggested several years ago that the trouble with American Catholicism was that it had no aristocracy to serve as a counterbalance to the clergy. The truth so well concealed behind this curious Anglicism is that the social structure of American Catholicism has militated against the rise of a lay intelligentsia sufficiently important to play the role of genuine lay leadership. Moreover, the attitudes of the clergy and the concrete expressions of lay initiative did not issue in happy results. Trusteeism was undoubtedly a genuine American lay Catholic response and showed the general American characteristics of a lack of restraint and a boisterousness suggesting irresponsibility. Yet had it been incorporated into the church rather than having been crushed, it might well have provided one basis for responsible lay leadership in later decades. While the result preserved Catholic communal integrity, other consequences less fortunate were part of the price. A beneficent clericalism came to characterize American Catholic life resulting chiefly from the lower-class and ethnic composition of the laity and the issue of the Trusteeship struggles. These elements could not fail to strengthen the other pressures making for aloofness and askewness, since American Catholicism was thereby deprived of an experienced lay leadership capable of tackling the cultural and social problems in a creative fashion.

The question of how the church qua church would meet the challenge of American life was answered historically by a reaction that both Americanized Catholicism and, at the same

time, produced a certain askewness in the relation between
Catholicism and American culture and an aloofness with respect
to Catholic participation in the general organizations of American life. What of the second problem: how shall individual
Catholics and Catholic groups become assimilated to America?

It is important that the question be asked in this form, and not
in terms of differences between clerical and lay assimilation.
Both priests and laymen are members of the church, and both
share in the problem of the church qua church, although the
priest is more directly involved in a structural sense. Second,
both priests and laymen share in civic responsibilities and in
ethnic loyalties, political identities and regional allegiances,
although the position of the priest in the ecclesiastical structure
and his relative isolation from areas of lay life modify the effects
of these memberships in his case. There is an old Irish rhyme
that catches the essential sociological point here:

> Is it leave gaiety
> All to the laity
> Or cannot the clergy be
> Irishmen too?

The priest shared in the Americanizing experience both as
member of the ecclesiastical organization and as a Catholic
individual in a non-Catholic society, and most times as a
member of an ethnic group.

Insofar as the individual Catholic is a Catholic, the three
dimensions of the problem for the church qua church become a
part of his individual problem. Insofar as Catholicism constitutes
for him an important reference group, an identification basic to
his own self-definition, the cultural and institutional problems
facing the church qua church as matters of objective encounter
become for the individual Catholic matters of interior personal
confrontation, of internal conflict or subjective ambivalence.
Although they impinge upon him in most varied manner, these
structured dimensions of the problem for the church become
elements of the individual's situation.

The second dimension of the individual's problem concerns
social status. Catholics came to this country quite generally at the
bottom of the socioeconomic scale and had to begin the slow
process of social mobility, one often requiring more than a single
generation. As late as 1948, a century after the Irish Famine and

the beginning of Catholic mass immigration, the Catholic Church in America still counted a greater proportion of its members in lower-class status than did either Protestantism or Judaism. In that year, 13.8 per cent of the Protestants, 21.8 per cent of the Jews, and 8.7 per cent of the Catholics belonged to the upper class; 32.6 per cent of the Protestants, 32 per cent of the Jews, and 24.7 per cent of the Catholics were reported as middle-class; and 53 per cent of the Protestants, 46 per cent of the Jews, and 66.6 per cent of the Catholics occupied lower-class status.[14] Figures on educational attainment tell the same story.[15]

Obviously, lower-class groups will have less influence in shaping the cultural ethos and in affecting national policy, at least in any direct sense, than groups more intellectually pre- pared and more strategically placed. Hence, class composition alone, because of the comparably larger lower-class percentage, will in the Catholic case make Catholic influence incommensu- rate with Catholic numbers. Hence, class status is a factor strengthening the tendencies toward askewness and aloofness deriving from the other sources we have considered.

Class composition tended to keep Catholics out of organiza- tions which were decisive in policy formation and influence. The one important exception is labor. The labor movement has been the chief source of lower-class influence on public policy, al- though it has not been the only one. Catholics have long been important in labor, to the point that self-confessed experts who claim to know the Washington scene tell us that the position of Secretary of Labor is today a "Catholic job." It is significant for our subject that the position of Secretary of State definitely is not. The class structure of American Catholics is such as to keep them underrepresented in strategic policy-influencing organiza- tions, with the important exception of the trade-unions. It is important to recall here that labor was not fully legitimated in American life until the New Deal, if, indeed, the backlog of middle-class opinion which ranges from suspicion to antagonism toward unions permits one to call its present position one of complete acceptance by the general community.

If lower-class status made the problem for the individual Catholic one of rising socially and economically, his European background soon placed him in a position that involved some break with ethnic identifications. Communities and organizations based on nationality also tended to keep Catholics aloof from the main streams of American life. Nationality groups usually did not affect the development of foreign policy, except as pressure groups concentrating on issues immediately affecting the homeland.

Americanizing Catholicism

Let us recapitulate here. The adaptation of the Catholic Church to the dominantly Protestant situation in America was an empirical, adaptive accommodation that left the fundamental relation between Catholicism and American culture characterized by a certain askewness. Adaptation produced a genuinely American Catholicism, but one that was still quite Catholic, while the general American culture remained derived from Protestant roots, often Protestant in fact, and often secularized in a direction indifferent or even hostile to religious values. Such a setting was not one admitting a comfortable congruence with Catholic ideas and value conceptions. Moreover, separate Catholic cultural institutions and social organizations, the social composition of the Catholic population, and its ethnic backgrounds and loyalties increased the askewness with respect to values and the aloofness with respect to participation. While the Americanization process was impressively successful, the structural basis of disarticulation and even conflict remained.

How has the American Catholic experience affected Catholic attitudes on issues involved in or related to foreign policy? It must be recalled that the encounter of an immigrant Catholicism and a native Protestant society and culture was also a process in which Irish and German newcomers confronted established Anglo-Saxon communities. Moreover, the Catholicism that came to this country had been affected by the experience of struggling for survival with actively hostile forces in Europe for almost three centuries; it was a Catholicism which reached the farthest point of its alienation from the modern world just about the time that mass Catholic immigration began in America. Further, the strategic bearers of its adaptationist response were Irish; they came with fresh memories of the disabilities affecting Catholics in an oppressed Catholic enclave in a Protestant kingdom.

The Age of Isms

Since the Act of Supremacy of 1534 declared that the Bishop of Rome had no more jurisdiction in the realm of England *quam alius externus Episcopus*,[16] England and Catholicism have faced each other as antagonists save for the few years of brief Marian interlude. Moreover, the eighteenth century was a time of rapid secularization of strategically important strata in English society, and the nineteenth century saw the rise of Liberalism, hostile to many basic Catholic positions. From 1848 on, socialism became a force in Europe actively inimical to traditional Christianity. In the Latin countries, its advent was preceded by laicizing tendencies, which in the French Revolution took on extreme expression. With these developments Catholicism tended to become identified with conservative forces and ideas. This was in many ways an unfortunate alignment for the church in the modern period, but one that proved unavoidable under the circumstances.

During the nineteenth century, England, once the protagonist of the Reformation, now increasingly secularized, showed considerable sympathy for liberal and revolutionary movements on the Continent. Consequently, in the nineteenth century, a period dominated by England, Liberalism, and Science (with a capital S), the church was far from at home in the world.

Important sections of American opinion were quite obviously affected by these current trends. While Americans tended to become sympathetic to European revolutionary movements, Catholic thought, traumatically affected by 1789 and 1848, tended to align itself with conservatism. The American public looked with sympathy on the Greek revolt against Turkey, the Hungarian uprising against the Hapsburgs, and the seizure of Rome by the Italian Army. When Kossuth visited Washington in the early 1850's, he was welcomed by Daniel Webster, then Secretary of State, by the President, and by both Houses of Congress. The American populace generally received him with applause. "To leading Catholics like Bishop Hughes, Orestes A. Brownson, and the editor of the *Freeman's Journal,* he was a fraud, a demagogue, and a foe of Christianity."[17] When Napoleon III was overthrown, the United States recognized the Third Republic before forty-eight hours had lapsed; three years later official American opinion was friendly to the short-lived attempt to end the Spanish monarchy. Two American historians commented many years ago, "All this was true to form. Catholic influence in Washington had as yet reached no substantial proportions and in none of the revolutions was the principle of private property impugned."[18]

Conservative Voice Dominant

There were, to be sure, Catholic voices raised in the liberal direction—John Boyle O'Reilly was one—but the general Catholic tendency was toward conservatism. This frame of mind placed influential Catholics in a position of defense of—or to use a modern term, softness toward—slavery at a time when northern opinion was shaping up in the opposite direction.

In the decades after 1861 the country was dominated by the Republican party, then the American counterpart of European Liberalism, while the march of industrialism under the hegemony of the business class caused a widespread movement for reform in both rural and urban areas. American Catholicism rejected the currently popular identification of wealth and virtue;[19] names like Terence Powderly and Ignatius Donnelly were not uncommon in movements for reform. While Catholics generally lined up with the Democrats and often enough with reform, Catholicism could not feel completely at home in association with either Liberalism with a capital L or liberalism with a lower case l. This fact remained true despite the numerous apparent exceptions, from Cardinal Gibbons' success in keeping Henry George off the *Index Librorum* to Archbishop Ireland's ardent Republicanism.

The Bishops' statement on social legislation in 1919 showed that Catholics recognized the need for reform measures. Within the church, Father John A. Ryan "fought conservatives in and outside the church, insisting that the responsibilities of Catholicism evolved with changing economic circumstances."[20] His effect was telling, indeed, as the Bishops' statement showed. Yet on the whole American Catholic thought remained derivatively conservative, and its reform impulses were based in most cases perhaps on a conservative interest in social stability founded on social justice. Obviously, the Catholic alignment on many important questions kept Catholics apart from current American liberal sympathies. Nowhere was this more the case than on those issues likely to be related to foreign events and developments.

Anti-British Heritage

In the nineteenth century America prospered in safe isolation in an economic world system organized and dominated by London and behind the protective shield of British naval supremacy. These facts were, however, far from salient in the minds of German and Irish Americans. The Irish made a strong identification with America, but they were often attracted to quite other aspects of the new land than those which elicited the loyalties of Anglo-Americans. The latter, especially perhaps in the urban East, and there among upper-class groups, tended to see as salient those aspects of American and English culture which bore a strong family resemblance. Protestant culture, parliamentary institutions, common law, and the bond of language and consanguinity stood out. The Irish were likely to give salience to those aspects of America which stood in sharp contrast to Irish experience with English rule and English institutions: republicanism as against monarchy, separation of church and state as against the Anglican Establishment, social mobility and egalitarianism as against a traditional status system and titles of nobility, and especially the anti-British heritage of 1776 and 1812.

> "I've heard whispers of a country
> that lies far beyond the say
> Where rich and poor stand equal
> in the light of freedom's day."

Washington had fought the English and was, moreover, an honorary member of the Friendly Sons of St. Patrick. Jefferson had indicted what both he and his Irish admirers considered the enormity of British misrule. Jackson had beaten the English at New Orleans and was an Irishman to boot, a Scotch-Irishman of Ulster lineage, to be sure, but an Irishman for all that. Barry had founded the Navy. Such Irish American sentiments easily coalesced with strong sentimental identifications with the "ould sod." The Irish could not but join native Anglophobes in a little twisting of the lion's tail.

The German Catholics were, as we have seen, concerned with preserving German culture and tended to cling to German social forms. This tendency to remain German was not likely to make them share the attitudes and opinions of the old stock Anglo-Americans. Moreover, the Irish and Germans tended to resent Anglo-American attitudes in the local community. The feeling of the older groups that they were the "real Americans" appeared as arrogance, and this could not but help keep alive immigrant attitudes brought over from Europe.

The end of the nineteenth century saw England and America draw together in foreign policies. This was to be seen in the Orient and in the British response to the Spanish-American War. While the Kaiser saw the monarchical principle endangered in the first diplomatic difficulties between the United States and Spain in 1897, Britain's archimperialist Joseph Chamberlain looked forward to seeing "the Stars and Stripes and the Union Jack" waving together over an "Anglo-Saxon alliance." Henry Adams thought that "the sudden appearance of Germany as the grizzly terror" had "frightened England into America's arms," but, whatever the cause, the United States was unmistakably lining up with Great Britain against the new, aggressively rising Germany. This was not a development likely to appeal to the Irish and German Americans, who were the dominant groups in the American Catholic Church. Mr. Dooley's comment apropos of "Hands across the Sea" that hot summer afternoon as he wiped off the top of his bar in his Archey Road establishment was to the point: "There are two kinds of hands, Hinessy, pothry hands and rolling mill hands, and only one kind has anny votes." The rolling mill hands tended to turn hands down on hands across the sea.

In short, the conservatism of Catholic thought and the ethnic loyalties of the Irish and Germans, reinforced by their status in local American communities, tended to align Catholic sentiment against the basic line that was developing in American foreign relations. The American Catholic experience did not prepare American Catholics on the whole to look with favor on a foreign policy friendly to Liberalism and revolution, Anglophile and, at the same time, antagonistic toward Germany. A tendency for

Catholics to align themselves with isolationism was quite understandable under the circumstances. Such an alignment often
increased the other pressures toward askewness which we have
discussed.

The Role of Religion

The role of religion in society, seen from the point of view of
functional sociological theory, is to sanctify the values and norms
strategic to the continuation of the social order and to provide
the ultimate grounding for a definition of man and his situation
that renders human life meaningful and human effort worth-
while. Students of religion and culture such as Christopher
Dawson and T. S. Eliot have emphasized this basic and central
function of religion. While this is perfectly true, it is only half of
the picture. With transcendent religions, at least, there is, as
Troeltsch has made clear in the case of Christianity, a permanent
tension between the demands of the transcendent call and the
requirements of everyday life in the institutional forms of society.
This is an abiding tension that cannot be exorcised without so
seriously truncating religion as to amount to its actual corruption.
This tension has often taken the concrete institutional expression
of a conflict between church and state. Such cases, however,
represent the effects of specific historical and sociological conditions which alter the fundamental disarticulation and involve
many accidental elements, such as the inevitable collision of two
authority structures in one society, power drives, vested interests,
political alignments, and so on. They should never be taken as
models for our thinking, since by doing so we may absolutize the
accidental features found in the historically specific case. The
basic tension is, however, inherent in the relation between a
religion of transcendence and any society whatsoever. In so-
called Catholic countries, the tension remains, often disguised in
a confusing manner by the nominally Catholic aspect of social
forms and institutions only questionably Catholic in content.

This inherent tension also has a definite function both for
religion itself and for societies committed to certain kinds of
values. It serves to keep up a degree of "healthy unadjustment"
between religion and secular values and activities and, hence, to
preserve the supramundane aspirations of religion itself. When

this is missing, as in some historic Catholic situations, or in the *Kulturprotestantismus* of the last century, religion becomes merely an expression of the highest mundane values or a concealment for less admirable orientations and strivings.

Moreover, to a society and culture which place emphasis on the dignity of the human person, this disarticulation, by underlining the centrality of the personal relation between God and the individual person, gives human worth an extrasocietal foundation. It sets up a structured barrier against tendencies which define man as basically merely a segment of society and the group and, therefore, to be dominated by societal requirements in all fields of thought and action. Maritain has given us an excellent formulation of this aspect of the question in terms of a Catholic philosophy of man and society.

The Catholic Church which came to America as the church of immigrants was a church whose relation to this basic tension had been greatly exacerbated by the events of the preceding period. The hostility of modern developments to Christianity and the alignment of Catholic thought with conservative forces, together with the concrete historically conditioned formulation of many Catholic values, had converted the basic strain into a real askewness, one that involved other elements than the disarticulation between the call of Christianity and secular concerns. The problems of adaptation to America, despite their generally successful solution, further exaggerated this strain and bent the askewness toward alienation. There is no doubt that the elements of askewness we have seen characteristic of the relation of Catholicism to America derive from this basic built-in tension. It is also true, and most important to note, that the precise forms in which we have found them are largely the product of historically specific experiences; in their concrete forms they are in no way essentially involved in the Christian commitment.

Experience as a Frame of Reference

There is, however, more than this to be considered. Experience shapes the attitudes of those who undergo it; the ideas and values, and the attitudes that embody them, once precipitated out of concrete historical situations, take on a certain relative autonomy. They are then transmitted to oncoming generations to become the frame of reference for the experience and interpretations of experience of these latter. What is involved here can best be seen, perhaps, by an analogy with social processes studied in the sociology of knowledge and the sociology of work. For example, officials whose life experience is concerned with rational and established procedural methods of problem solving often come to lose sight of the nonrational and chaotic elements characteristic of so much of human life. The training of perception and conceptualization in one direction leads to atrophy and dullness in others. As a result, we have the specialist, who is less capable of meeting problems outside his own sphere of competence than the ordinary intelligent layman. This common phenomenon was called "trained incapacity" by Veblen, "occupational psychosis" by Dewey, and "professional deformation" by Warnotte.[21] Toynbee has shown that what is involved here is not simply limited to the individual sphere. Strategic elites, he argues, as a result of successful performance in meeting a challenge, not only change their objective situations but also transform themselves in the process. As a result they are often rendered incapable of meeting a new challenge of a quite different character.[22]

The aspect of this general problem most significant for us in the present context may be stated by saying that experience shapes individuals and groups, but may shape them in ways which incapacitate them for meeting new life conditions. Moreover, this is complicated by an important psychological fact. Unsolved problems, unsolved wholly or in part, and elements of unresolved conflicts remain as residues which affect apperception and associated tendencies toward action. This is true for individuals, as clinical records abundantly testify. But groups also have an analogue of "memory" in the implicit and explicit mechanisms for the transmission of culture from one generation to the next. Hence the residues of aloofness and askewness left by the Americanization of the church still exist in the shape of the "apperceptive mass"; it is in this context that Catholics see certain current problems and events and see them as structurally analogous to their original prototypes. All learning is, of course, a "recognition" of the new in terms of the old; but when the differences in the new situation are such that the old frame of reference inherited from the past distorts one's ability to grasp the new and thereby distorts understanding and miscues response, inadequacy and even complete inappropriateness of action ensue.

Church versus Isms

The experience of value conflict with modern trends of thought and with non-Catholic culture elements has produced some residues of this character in many American Catholics. Especially is this likely to be the case with respect to the conflict between Catholicism on the one side and such phenomena as Liberalism, secularism, and the various types of leftism on the other. Second, the experience of minority status which most Catholic groups have suffered has also left residues. These all make for tender spots in Catholic sensitivities and defensiveness with respect to certain kinds of differences with other groups. Hence some issues have a symbolic significance in terms of prototypic experiences which trigger off these residues and make for responses ranging from not wholly adequate to quite inadequate in terms of the realities of current situations. "The fathers have eaten sour grapes, and the teeth of the children are set on edge" (Ezek. 18:2).

The point to be stressed is that we are not arguing a specious historicism, but rather presenting an analysis of the past factors that live on in some psychological form in the present. Their form of survival is quite understandable in terms of well-recognized psychological and sociological processes. Catholic reactions on many questions in intellectual fields, in public policy, and in problems involving values and ethics often enough show these effects to one degree or another. This in no way implies that persons exhibiting such behavior have any explicit knowledge of the prototypic situations from which such responses ultimately derive.

The analysis we have presented so far must be complicated by consideration of another important factor, one whose strategic significance for our subject in the recent period can hardly be exaggerated. The victory of the October Revolution opened a new epoch in Western and world history. Tendencies in Western thought and social and intellectual movements that had developed throughout the previous centuries—secularism, scientism, and socialism—coalesced to become the ideology of a new power structure, one bent on aggressive efforts after world domination. Consequently, a new antagonist to the chief institutions of the West and one militantly anti-Christian in character emerged on the stage of history.

A New Catalyst: Communism

At the very point when this event occurred, the Catholic Church had just emerged out of the condition of extreme alienation from Western society and culture which had characterized its position in the mid-nineteenth century. It had entered into a period of improved rapprochement with the secular world and at the same time showed signs of a new cultural vitality and creativity. The new challenge affected both its new-found external stability and its direction of development in relation to world issues.

Communism was, indeed, the incarnation of a specter that had been haunting Europe and threatening Catholicism since 1848. It was, moreover, reincarnation in altered form of trends in Western thought which had been in conflict with Catholicism for centuries. However, as the menace of Communism became increasingly dangerous to the secular civilization of the West, a new sense of common origins, common values, and common destiny came to affect the attitudes of both Catholics and secularists. There developed a tendency to stand together against the common enemy. As an expression of old threats in new form, Communism could not fail to increase the defensiveness and hence the askewness characterizing Catholic attitudes. Yet as the West more and more recognized the danger of Communism, a new solidarity became possible with non-Catholics, thus offering some alleviation of older elements of alienation.

The reflection of this change was soon visible in America. With the United States and the Soviet Union as the two opposing superpowers, anti-Communism tended to become an integral part of American patriotism. Thus the American Catholic found himself in a position where both his faith and his country faced the same threat. This offered him two kinds of "opportunity." By opposing Communism vociferously, the American Catholic could find a socially acceptable outlet for aggression generated by older conflicts, the disarticulation between

Catholicism and the temper of modernity. After all, Communism was a symbol and summation of such older elements in new aggressive form. By the same militant anti-Communism, he could by the same token urgently identify himself with America and thereby seem to solve many of the unsolved problems of askewness and aloofness whose residues were still very much a part of his consciousness. Anti-Communism thus became an occasion for a catharsis and an opportunity for identification with America.

In considering how Catholics in fact responded to this new opportunity, an important distinction should be borne in mind. Communism represents a real political and social phenomenon which constitutes a genuine threat to Christianity and to America and all free nations. As such, it should be realistically recognized and its dangers foreseen. Communism also serves as a highly visible foreign symbol of other aspects of the modern situation, many of them of native genesis—aspects that can and often do exist in quite non-Communist or anti-Communist form. Secularism and modern atheism, scientific Prometheanism and its antireligious implications, and social ideas and values which call in question the moral legitimacy and social efficacy of capitalism—all these exist and have long existed, separately and together, in the form of ideologies and movements in no sense Communist. Yet the fact is that Communism does represent one historical development of such tendencies. In this sense, Communism is the product of the Enlightenment and post-Enlightenment reform and revolutionary movements. Moreover, despite all the differences, one has often enough observed elective affinities between such tendencies and Communism itself. It is this fact that was spotted and exploited to the hilt and beyond by the charges against certain liberals of being "soft on Communism." Even where no real affinity or softness existed, the structural analogies permit a degree of symbolic identification to be made. Thus Communism is capable of appearing as the surrogate for older ideas and movements and of triggering off reactions which express residues derived from older experiences with them. As a real national enemy, Communism permits expression of aggression generated by these older frustrations against itself when the respectability and even the lack of visibility of the movements and ideas for which it serves as symbolic surrogate would make aggression difficult or embarrassing. Hence, Communism is both a real enemy and a symbolic scapegoat.

In examining opposition to Communism, it is necessary to distinguish between the reality content—Communism as a real and dangerous political and military threat—and the symbolic content: Communism as the symbol capable of reactivating older residues derived from older unresolved conflicts with ideologies and movements for which Communism now stands as surrogate, and one that it is socially permissible to attack in the present circumstances.[23] And let us add, the symbol, aggression against which can be seen as a patriotic duty and an expression of one's identification with America.

Spanish Civil War

This new symbol and new fact became an integral part of the American scene in the 1930's, a decade marked by social reform and a leftward movement of thought in many circles. Unquestionably, the catalytic event was the Spanish Civil War. The attitudes of liberals generally was to offer apparent confirmation to the symbolic affinities which Catholics were prone to see as significant in the situation. Moreover, the old association of Spain with Catholic causes increased the symbolic appropriateness. This issue became the focus for the crystallization of attitudes; once again Catholics were ranged on the opposite side from the rest of the American public generally.

On December 16, 1938, the Gallup Poll asked the question: Which side do you sympathize with in the Spanish Civil War, the Loyalists or Franco? Of those in the national sample who had opinions, 76 per cent favored the Loyalists, while 24 per cent favored Franco. When we break down this figure in terms of religious affiliation, the picture was this: Protestants, pro-Loyalist 83 per cent; pro-Franco 17 per cent; Catholics, pro-Loyalist 42 per cent; pro-Franco 58 per cent.[24] While a majority of the sample did not favor lifting the embargo imposed under the Neutrality Act to send arms to the Loyalists and were thus in agreement with dominant Catholic opinion on this point, yet the fundamental sympathies evoked by the war in Spain revealed startling differences between the state of opinion among Catholics and that of the nation generally. It is a striking expression of the kind of askewness we have been analyzing.

These figures are interesting for several reasons. They show the real askewness we have been concerned with. Second, they point up the reason why earlier we separated problems facing the church qua church from those facing the Catholic as an individual. Most "official" (with all the ambiguity of that term!) Catholic organs of opinion were solidly pro-Franco; yet 42 per cent of the Catholics in the sample, a sizable minority, indeed, took an opposite position. On this issue at least Catholics showed a much greater tendency toward nonuniformity than did their Protestant brethren. This is only what one should expect, since the tensions of the American Catholic experience and the askewness we have found characteristic of the relationship between Catholicism and dominant elements in American culture could not fail to expose many Catholics to the cross pressures of marginality on such an issue. That such would be the case is a quite likely sociological hypothesis. Yet it is the kind of fact that surprises many—so strong, indeed, is the myth of Catholic homogeneity, itself a residue in non-Catholic thinking of past experiences, even in the minds of otherwise sophisticated observers.

It was Communism as the symbol of militant secularism, rather than Communism as the symbol of social reform, that attracted Catholic aggression. Yet with the success of upward social mobility, the second element also became important. Often enough the very Catholics who enjoyed so much quoting the papal encyclical on *Atheistic Communism* were the ones who played down the papal teachings on social reform and labor or maintained a dignified silence concerning them. As a result of social mobility, in recent years Catholics have tended to abandon their old allegiance to the Democratic party in favor of a new suburban Republicanism. However, the association of leftist ideas with the New Deal is also partly responsible, for it caused somewhat of a symbolic reaction toward conservatism. In this situation of real and symbolic conservatism, there appeared the tendency to use the Communist charge against reform to assuage Catholic consciences at a time when the church was stressing papal social teachings.

Continuing Alignments

The alignments that began to form in the 1930's continued into the forties and fifties. The confusion of symbolic and reality responses at the beginning of the last decade was enough to confound even the elect. Some people opposed the administration for not preventing the Korean war and simultaneously for fighting it when it was not prevented and, at the same time, while opposing the stopping of Communism at the 38th parallel, denounced the government as being in the hands of Communist dupes or, even worse, agents. Our statesmen were denounced for losing China singlehandedly, while those who raged often showed no interest in stopping Communism in the rest of Asia. Especially were Communists to be looked for everywhere at home. Moreover, this display of symbolic reactions, carried to the point of mass neurosis which made political life a Donnybrook, gave the descendants of immigrants an additional avenue for expressing a strident identification with America and of showing their brand of Americanism superior to the questionable loyalties of the corrupt offspring of the older stock. If Al Smith's 1936 "walk" was the symbol of Catholic conservatism derived from social mobility, the figure of Alger Hiss in the 1950's was the symbolic target of the new catharsis. Catholics were not alone in this reaction, since Communism had analogous symbolic resonance for non-Catholic conservatives, frustrated by twenty years of reform administrations, for which the word "treason" became such a subjectively satisfying synonym. The hysterical anti-Communism of the early 1950's was a national aberration, and Catholics were in a minority. Yet there is unhappily a somewhat wry appropriateness in the fact that a Catholic surname, and one with the most honorable Celtic antecedents, became its generally accepted designation.

The trouble with such symbolic reactions, however, is that while they permit a discharge of pent-up frustration, their very divergence from reality usually prevents them from altering the situation that makes catharsis necessary. Too often they lead us, Pied Piper fashion, down the road to the unreal. By alienating those who heed their siren call even farther from reality, they only increase the askewness which rendered one vulnerable to their original appeal. The symbolic aspects of the anti-Communist reaction could not fail to increase the askewness between Catholicism and fundamental aspects of American culture. While it made possible some degree of rapprochement with secularist forces of a more conservative kind, even there it offered at best only a symbolic, not a real, answer to the problems involved. Perhaps, however, catharsis did dispel enough emotion to produce a degree of psychological calm. At any rate, new developments were at the very time preparing the way for dissipation of extreme behavior.

The residues of unsolved problems remain, and we must expect them to influence Catholic reactions in the future. At the present moment, however, we are in the midst of a great change. The present transformations in our society will affect the heritage of the past in many ways and alter the expression of older attitudes. The competition between the United States and the Soviet Union has changed American attitudes toward revolution in the direction of caution and has thus brought large sections of opinion closer to traditional Catholic positions. It is, in fact, the very survival of our values and our way of life, and not the "emancipation" of oppressed mankind from the shackles of tradition in moments of revolutionary ardor and fulfillment, that concerns us at present. As part of this problem, nuclear war presents itself to us as a grim prospect. The result is that foreign policy has become freighted with reality implications of a truly terrifying nature, a future whose outcome we do not see.

When real situations become extremely threatening, two reactions are possible. One is to give up symbolic responses, however satisfying for subjective reasons, and face squarely the problem of survival. The other is to take refuge from the dangers of reality in a completely symbolic sphere and to confirm the ancient adage that whom the gods destroy they first make mad. Americans in the latter half of the 1950's appear to have chosen the former, aided by the relief and fatigue derived from their symbolic saturnalia of a few years before. We Americans have discovered the inefficaciousness of the Black Mass. This is true for both Catholics and non-Catholics, although it should not be assumed that unreal symbolic reactions are completely a thing of the past. Yet the new sense of reality has brought a new confrontation of responsibility. The relative absence of inappropriate symbolic response in the Catholic reaction to the current opportunity and necessity to negotiate with the Russians, a situation involving serious dangers as well as some promise, is a good example of the new frame of mind.

Second, the new situation is characterized by our transformation into an affluent society, dedicated to consumption, affording social mobility in the presiding bureaucratic structures by way of educational attainment. The replacement of capital resources by college training as the chief avenue of social mobility has obvious advantages for the newer groups in the population. Closely related to this is a third dimension: the current breakdown of ethnicity. There is certainly a great deal to be said for the Herberg thesis that ethnic identification is being replaced by membership in the three major religious groupings.[25] Protestantism, Catholicism, and Judaism are, in Herberg's terms, becoming recognized and accepted as the basic reference groups for membership in American society. They are the "three great religions of democracy." Advancement in a bureaucratic society by educational attainment based on mass education and the end of ethnic cultural and spiritual ghettos explains largely the present increasing Catholic mobility into the upper-middle class. A new kind of Catholic outlook will necessarily evolve from such a development.

A fourth change, not unrelated to the three above, is the rise in the postwar period of a significant Catholic lay intelligentsia, self-conscious, self-critical, and Catholic, a category in which many clerics must also be included. The publication of highly intelligent, quite objective, and acutely critical evaluations of American Catholic life by American Catholics in recent years is one of the most significant cultural developments of the time, a fact recognized by the more shrewd non-Catholic observers. It is a sign of the vitality and fast approaching maturity of an Americanized Catholicism.

The Challenge

These developments are part of the new America that is emerging in our day. America has become the inheritor of the older British role of organizing and maintaining a world in which a society such as ours can survive. As such, it is faced with the responsibility of defending the entire Western heritage, a challenge which we struggle, often inadequately, to meet. It is at the same time an America which has largely solved the problems of production and faces the newer, often obscure, problems of humanizing and ethicizing a consumption society based on plenty.[26] As such, its strategic elite is no longer basically the older entrepreneural class, but rather one composed of governmental, business, and educational bureaucrats. In such a society, there necessarily develops a large middle and upper-middle class based on technical know-how and administrative skill. Mass immigration, however, ended a generation ago, and the assimilation cycle has almost run out. The Americanization of groups near to immigration and the bureaucratization of public life coincide to affect social mobility.

What will the America of thirty years hence look like? In what ways will it be continuous and in what ways discontinuous with the America out of which it has emerged? Who, indeed, can answer these questions? Too few of us really think very much about them. One thing at least is sure. The participation of Catholics in the general life of America will become of greater volume and significance. The new Catholic upper-middle class will make a large difference in terms of Catholic participation in the organizations which influence policy making. Even in Catholic organizations, we can expect the general tastes, interests, and activities, and even values with respect to a multitude of nonreligious matters, to be more like those found in corresponding organizations among non-Catholics.

Moreover, with the present search for values to render life in the affluent society significant, Catholic values may even gain a new respectability. This has already happened in some circles. Yet here a note of caution is in order. Secularist commitments and, on a larger scale, prejudices among the educated remain strong. That Catholic ideas often run diametrically counter to general positions may be seen in the reception of the statement of the bishops in the United States on birth control and foreign aid issues. How the new problems that life in bureaucratic, affluent, and socially mobile America will raise may or may not polarize Catholic and secularist positions on value problems, we cannot say. But Catholicism will remain Catholicism despite important sociological transformations, and older conflicts may well assume new and unforeseen forms. Moreover, older residues will find some form of expression in new situations and often render Catholic responses less than adequate. In some cases they may merge with the new conservatism of middle-class Catholics to supply an ideology justifying these groups to themselves. In others, they will give rise to askewness in relation to non-Catholic cultural developments and become the cause of social and personal disarticulation.

One thing, however, is clear. From now on Catholics will play a larger part in the general organizations of American life and will in many important respects be more like their non-Catholic fellow Americans. They will become more important in the dialogue about foreign affairs and more involved in foreign affairs education.

N O T E S

1. For most purposes it is probably not accurate to speak of one Catholic community in this country. There is, however, a sense in which such a usage is justified in the present case, as we shall suggest in our discussion below of what we shall designate as the "American Catholic experience."

2. Much has been written on immigration. See, for example, Marcus Lee Hansen, *The Atlantic Migration* (Cambridge: 1951), and Oscar Handlin, *Boston's Immigrants, 1790-1865* (Cambridge: 1941).

3. See Ray Allen Billington, *The Protestant Crusade. 1800-1860. A Study of the Origins of American Nativism* (New York: 1938).

4. For an interesting article on quite different European solutions to the problems of religious pluralism and the different point of view they engender, see Erik von Kuchnelt-Leddihn, "A European View: Church-State Relations," *Commonweal*, LXXI (November 27, 1959), 255-258. For an American Catholic comment, see the editorial in the same issue, "Church and State," pp. 251-252.

5. For two books, published in the last decade, important to this subject, see Robert D. Cross, *The Emergence of Liberal Catholicism in America* (Cambridge: 1958), and Colman J. Barry, O.S.B., *The Catholic Church and German Americans* (Milwaukee: 1953).

6. See Abbé Felix Klein, *Americanism: A Phantom Heresy* (Atchison, Kans.: 1951), and Thomas T. McAvoy, C.S.C., "Americanism, Fact and Fiction," *Catholic Historical Review*, XXXI (July, 1945), 138 153.

7. For example, see Walter J. Ong, S.J., *Frontiers in American Catholicism* (New York: 1957), Chapter 2, "An Apostolate of the Business World," pp. 24-34.

8. Abbé Francois Houtart, *Aspects Sociologiques du Catholicisme Americain* (Paris: 1957), p. 37. See also Gerald Shaughnessy, *Has the Immigrant Kept the Faith?* (New York: 1925).

9. Ernst Troeltsch, *The Social Teachings of the Christian Churches*, Olive Wyon, tr., Vols. I and II (London and New York: 1931).

10. I borrow this phrase from H. Richard Niebuhr, *Christ and Culture* (New York: 1951), a book which continues the analysis of Troeltsch on this basic issue.

11. An excellent account of what is in some respects the exemplary case, and one that shows the inadequacy of popular stereotypes, is given in Giorgio De Santillana, *The Crime of Galileo* (Chicago: 1955). But this is but one dramatic example.

12. For example, see such a book as John W. Draper, *History of the Conflict between Religion and Science* (New York: 1873), where we are told, "Roman Christianity and

Science are recognized by their respective adherents as being absolutely incompatible" (p. 303). Or about a generation later, Andrew Dickson White, *History of the Warfare of Science with Theology* (New York: 1896), Vols. I and II. White saw theology as the enemy of both science and capitalism, the two unquestioned sources of progress.

13. With respect to naturalism Merle Curti states, "The most striking fact in the intellectual history of the last third of the nineteenth century was the blow to the historic doctrine of supernaturalism by new developments in the biological and physical sciences." Merle Curti, *The Growth of American Thought* (New York: 1943), Chapter XXI, p. 531.

14. Houtart, *op. cit.,* p. 84. See also John J. Kane, *Catholic-Protestant Conflicts in America* (Chicago: 1955), pp. 70–89.

15. See Ernest Havemann and Patricia Salter West, *They Went to College* (New York: 1952), pp. 187–188.

16. The Act of Supremacy passed in the winter parliament of 1534 was, of course, in English, but the sixty-six bishops, abbots, and others of the clerical Convocation whom we quote here repudiated Rome in Latin!

17. Quoted from Carl Wittke, *The Irish in America* (Baton Rouge: 1956), p. 185. Of course there were many Irish revolutionaries in America in this period, such as Thomas D'Arcy McGee, John Mitchel, and Thomas F. Meagher. Meagher, for example, identified himself with the efforts of both Kossuth and Mazzini. And Irish immigrants contributed money to the causes of Irish reform and revolt.

18. Charles A. Beard and Mary R. Beard, *The Rise of American Civilization* (New York: 1930), II, 363–364.

19. Irvin G. Wyllie, *The Self-Made Man in America. The Myth of Rags to Riches* (New Brunswick: 1954).

20. Eric F. Goldman, *Rendezvous with Destiny* (New York: 1956), p. 86.

21. Robert K. Merton, *Social Theory and Social Structure* (Glencoe: 1949), pp. 151–160.

22. Arnold J. Toynbee, *A Study of History* (Somervell abridgment) (New York and London: 1947), p. 307 ff.

23. Of course, response to the symbolic aspects of Communism is not characteristic of conservative Catholics or conservative non-Catholics alone. Many liberals, too, offer an example of symbolic response in the other direction, or did until a few years ago. This response is a mirror image of the response we have been discussing here and just as inappropriate to reality. Thus some people could not react very strongly to the outrageously sham "trial" of Mindszenty in 1949. He was a Cardinal Priest of the Roman Church and hence by the "rules" of symbolic affinity necessarily a "reactionary."

24. *Public Opinion,* 1935–1946. Prepared under the editorial direction of Hadley Cantril by Mildred Strunk (Princeton: 1951), p. 808.

25. Will Herberg, *Protestant, Catholic, Jew* (Garden City, N.Y.: 1955).

26. See David M. Potter, *People of Plenty* (Chicago: 1954)

THREE: The Catholic Immigrant and the American Scene

The Socratic maxim which holds that "the unexamined life is not worth living" remains a basic natural premise of the life of the spirit. An important aspect of what is now often called "authenticity," it requires confrontation of the question "What am I?" This is indeed a question of many dimensions. Socrates, in his own original treatment of it, suggested that he himself was not only the *ephemeros* implied by the Delphic understanding of the slogan "Know Thyself," but also the Greek in contrast to the barbarian, the Athenian who owed so much in terms of his character formation and way of life to the laws of his polis that he preferred to die under their jurisdiction rather than to escape from them to freedom. The Socratic teaching and example indicate the close connection between the "I" and the "We." "What am I?" is a question which can be perceived adequately only when it is seen in the wider context of the question "What are we?"

Recent developments in American life and changes in America's world position have given the perennial problem of self-understanding a new importance. For while the leadership of the struggle for survival which Western civilization faces has been thrust upon the United States, necessitating responses and attitudes and even perceptions of ourselves which are often at variance with those created and preserved by past experience and habits, we have been experiencing on the domestic scene an unprecedented prosperity and the greatest surge of upward social mobility in our history. A homogeneous middle class of vast proportions is emerging from heterogeneous origins. These

From *Thought,* Fordham University Quarterly, XXXI (Summer, 1956), 251–270.

internal developments also contribute to the upsetting of older self-perceptions and require an understanding of just what changes are involved and their implications. In fact, there is being realized in America today a new society compounded of democracy and technology and highly colored by that combination of enterprise and co-operation which has marked our history. The American adventure is in part fulfilling the promise of those who went out into the wilderness; yet the fulfillment involves much that was unforeseen, perhaps some that is disappointing. It is producing a situation and raising problems which cannot be understood in terms of ideologies and approaches that reflect societies of earlier times. The times call for self-examination, and the availability of social science as an instrument of such examination should be more thoroughly utilized.

What has been indicated of Americans as a whole is even more true of American Catholics. They have experienced an even greater transformation. From a despised minority, they have become perhaps a disproportionately large section of the new middle class. From an immigrant church, American Catholicism has "become one of the three great 'religions of democracy,' " recognized as "a genuinely American religious community."[1] Yet the road has not been easy, and it has left a mark on us which is sometimes no longer appropriate to the real situation in which we find ourselves. Moreover, the new success involves new problems, which must be understood before they can be solved. For American Catholics as individuals and as a group, self-examination, to discover the conditions and forces that have shaped and formed us, that may have to some extent distorted us, and that impinge on us at the present, is doubly appropriate. The recent progress of Catholics in the social sciences suggests that these disciplines may prove helpful in the venture. Let us consider first the general nature of the problem and then the way in which social science can contribute to its understanding.

The American Setting

The American nation is the product of voluntary settlement and energetic mastery of the natural environment. Immigration and westward movement on the one hand, and the unprecedented development of agriculture, transportation, commerce, and industry on the other, are the fundamental activities out of which has arisen a large, wealthy, self-governing republic. From 1815 to 1932 there took place a huge transfer of population which followed the paths beaten by the feet of earlier arrivals for over two centuries.[2] In this period about 60,000,000 people emigrated from the Old World to the New. Some 60 per cent of these millions who poured upon the shores of the New World came to the United States, which generally led all other countries, yielding only for a short time to Brazil in the 1820's and to Peru in the 1850's. Up to 1880 immigrants had come to the United States from northern and western Europe, from the British Isles (which provided a majority), from Germany, and from Scandinavia. The "new immigration" added to these after 1880 when additional millions came from Italy, the Balkans, and the other countries of eastern Europe. Many more of these newcomers returned to their native land than is usually realized in this country, since some 30 per cent of those who came to the United States went back between 1821 and 1924. Yet assimilation into the receiving society was the significant result of the great movement.

Transformed and assuming new patterns, this process of population transfer continued on this side of the ocean as other people moved westward across the wilderness, leaving room behind them for the newcomers from Europe.[3] American "westward movement" soon crystallized into a pattern which reflected the requirements for conquering the virgin land and the interests of those groups first attracted to its great expanses. First went the fur traders making contact with the aborigines and extracting from the earth its most available product, the pelts of its living cover. Cattlemen, miners, and pioneer farmers came next, preparing each in his own way for the permanent settlement of the "equipped farmers" who, taking up where the ground-breaking pioneers left off, brought the new country to economic maturity attracting urban trades—the merchant and miller, the editor and educator.

The most striking and in some ways the most important aspects of this great human adventure were not the miracles of transformation wrought in a century and a half, though these were striking and important enough in their own right. More important, however, were the spiritual dimensions. The ideals and values creating and created by, sustaining and sustained by, the settlement and development of America represent a transmutation of beliefs and values and a fulfillment of hopes which immigrants brought across the Atlantic with them. Old ideals and new conditions conspired to enhance the worth of the human individual: old values and new experiences combined to emphasize the efficacy of human effort. Here was a land where a man could improve his condition and where men could affect their destiny.

It was ironical that the America which Turner declared to be "another name for opportunity"[4] should have been settled by Calvinists who took a dim view of man and his potentialities. Yet the new land called forth new attitudes, and the history of American religion is from one point of view the history of a growing belief in free will and in the possibility of self-determination.[5] This transformation appeared at times in terms of a moderated Calvinism, at times as an emphasis on a revivalistic use of emotional and other "means" of preparation for grace, again as acceptance of Arminianism and later of Unitarianism and Universalism, and even took such extreme forms as perfectionism and "Oberlin theology." But in every case optimism triumphed and a more cheerful utopianism blended with or replaced earlier chiliastic notions.

Despite the importance of religion in American colonial settlement, there appears always to have been present a strong drive toward accomplishment in this world, and trade became a leading American concern almost from the first. De Tocqueville found men in America ready to "sacrifice for a religious opinion their friends, their family, and their country," but saw them "seeking with almost equal eagerness material wealth and moral satisfaction."[6] The early sectarian demands which made church membership so difficult and the highly intellectualized sermons of the eastern clergy, together with the rough conditions of settlement and westward movement, contributed further to lessening the emphasis placed on religion by the ordinary man. By the time of the Revolutionary War, despite the dramatic events of the Great Awakening, America was largely unchurched, although religion never became a negligible force and was revived to become a dominant one in the second great revival movement which followed independence.[7] Moreover, the thought of the European Enlightenment was one of the most important intellectual elements transmitted from the Old World to the New. Rationalism in religion, the belief in progress, natural rights, and humanitarianism became salient features in American thinking by the time of the War for Independence, and they were by no means limited to the educated stratum. The Revolution may be said to have incorporated many Enlightenment values into the very fabric of our national life. Biblical religion reacted against deism and "infidelity" and re-established its dominance in the first half of the last century, but the heritage of the Enlightenment remained a permanent acquisition of our culture. Yet the revolt against Calvinist pessimism, the continuation of the Enlightenment on these shores, the development of learning and native science in the first half of the nineteenth century, did in fact continue a trend toward secularization which had characterized the development of the colonies.

Utopianism, optimism, activism, secularism, and revived Protestantism were important ingredients of American culture throughout the century which was to see the millions of Europe come to this land. Perhaps the most important similarity between the older population and the newer arrivals was that both groups could have assented to some version of the interpretation of America given by John Adams in 1765 as "the opening of a grand scheme and design in Providence for the illumination and emancipation of the slavish part of mankind all over the earth."[8] Meanwhile, fueled by such attitudes and manned in the spirit of such activism, science, technology, and business were at work transforming the face of the land and as a consequence the way of life of its citizens.

The Catholic Background

It was to this bustling America, largely Protestant in temper, that Catholic immigrants began to come in large numbers in the third decade of the century. How many had come in colonial days is difficult to ascertain, and of those who did it appears certain that many lost the faith of their fathers. "Catholics by no means had an easy time of it in colonial America," as Herberg has pointed out. "Their church was proscribed in most of the colonies and actively persecuted in some."[9] By the outbreak of the Revolutionary War there were some 25,000 Catholics in the thirteen colonies, a large majority of them in Maryland. When the first American diocese was established with the see of Baltimore in

1789, Catholics made up about 1 per cent of the total population of the new republic.

Catholic immigration was ethnic immigration. That is, Catholics who came to this country were, with the conspicuous exception of the Maryland colonists, products of national backgrounds other than that of the core culture group, whom de Tocqueville called the "Anglo-Americans." Among these new groups two were earliest and most conspicuous, the Irish and the Germans. Relations between the two were not always at the best, and at times their struggle divided the Catholic community. As Maynard has pointed out, "Upon the whole, it is incontestable that the guiding hands of the church in the United States have been Irish."[10] "The Irish in America," says Desmond Fennell, "supplied the numbers that made Catholicism for the first time a major factor in American life. . . . They established the precedents for all future Catholic immigrants."[11] Of considerable importance, then, as background to the problems of Catholicism in America was the position of Catholics in Europe and that of the Irish in particular.

The last hope of an independent Gaelic Ireland died lingeringly at Limerick in 1691 in that twilight between seventeenth-century gentlemanliness and the timeless brutality of survival war during which Patrick Sarsfield sent home the French reinforcements, thereby remaining faithful to his truce with William III and ensuring the final defeat of his cause. The next decades saw the continued reduction of Ireland to peasant status and its decapitation through the emigration of the native aristocracy, mourned and celebrated as the "Flight of the Wild Geese." In the course of time a Presbyterian group of Scottish origin who had settled in the north rose up to challenge Anglican supremacy and seemed for a while destined to establish an independent Ireland as a commercial nation under its own leadership. A century after the ill-starred Truce of Limerick the rumblings of revolution on the Continent caused a deep stirring in the country, and for a brief but promising moment it looked as though old divisions would dissolve in the fires of rebellion and the men of Ireland, Protestant and Catholic, would submerge their differences and unite under the ensign of the new, exciting nationalism. The United Irishmen, however, failed, because of a most unhappy combination of circumstances—"What glorious joy and sorrow fill the name of Ninety-eight!" The vast mass of Catholics continued to exist a submerged population, economically land-less, religiously proscribed, politically helots.

Yet they could not be kept so forever, and in the second and third decades of the new century the struggle for Catholic Emancipation, which had begun in the century before, grew and in 1829 was victorious. The Irish people under the leadership of the great O'Connell began to learn modern parliamentary politics and returned to public life as an important force. This return took place not only in the United Kingdom but also in the far-flung regions of the world to which Irishmen had gone either as transported convicts or as voluntary exiles and emigrants, what Chesterton called "the strange exiled empire of the Irish." They soon became politically important in the British dominions and in the new republic "across the say." Persecution and struggle had sharpened group consciousness, and religion and nationality came to dominate the Irishman's conception of himself. Though the two might, indeed, conflict at times—remember Parnell!—on the whole they sat well together. The split between church and nation, so tragic in its consequences in Continental countries, was sufficiently unimportant in the case of the Irish to be practically negligible. Moreover, in Ireland the established church had not been Catholic, and the exploiting classes had been outlanders. Consequently, here faithful and devout Catholics became revolutionaries. Ireland's only great socialist leader died a martyr to the nationalist cause and went to his execution with a Catholic priest by his side. Moreover, in Ireland the peasant masses, with their democratic impulses and their increasingly middle-class orientations, became the domi-nant influence on the formation of the mentality of the people.

Consequently the Irishman who came to America in the nineteenth century, when the repeal of the corn laws and the failure of nature combined in the form of unrelieved famine to depopulate the country, was plebeian and democratic, antiaristo-cratic and antimonarchical. He was often dreadfully poor. He was grievously alienated from political allegiance at home and ready to become a citizen of his new country without regrets. Though uneducated and unprepared in many ways for life in urban industrialized society, he was soon seen to participate in political and economic action. Irish names became prominent in labor and reform movements. Yet the Irish immigrant was also a devout Catholic; indeed, his Catholicism was even more salient than his sense of nationality with which it so inextricably intertwined. It was this Irishman, whose sense of "Irishness" blended so quickly with an identification with America, who "Americanized" the Catholic Church. This oppressed and submerged peasantry from one of the few Catholic enclaves in a northern Protestant world became the chief instrument in laying the foundation for American Catholic life.

The position of Catholics on the Continent, while more favorable generally, was less fortunate in some respects as preparation for the tasks to be met in America. The development of modern Europe had seen the center of gravity shift from the Mediterranean to the Atlantic. This was precisely the area, with the exception of France, which the Reformation had broken off from the church. In France and throughout Latin Christendom the Renaissance, the Enlightenment, and the Revolution developed a militant secularization of life. As a result the church was forced to embark on a struggle for survival. The posture of defense was not the best way to confront the new civilization, which was developing on the basis of commerce, power politics, science, and lay learning.

One unfortunate aspect of this defensive struggle was that Catholic thought often found itself too exclusively identified with conservative classes. The inevitable result was that causes such as freedom and reform, whose basic conceptions were frequently derived from Christian social teachings, were often inextricably confounded with a militant anti-Christian secularism. There resulted that tragic split between liberty and religion, while much of the Western world achieved its most striking social and economic successes in an atmosphere neutral, or at worst hostile, with regard to genuine Christian values.

In terms of this background, America offered an ambiguous prospect to the development of Catholicism. Certainly the new land offered economic and social opportunity as well as political and religious liberty, and these great goods more than compensated for the struggles and suffering which the new situation inflicted. It is small wonder that Irish immigrants embraced their new homeland with such enthusiasm. As an old Irish woman is reported to have said, "Sure it seems that God has saved this grand country for the poor." Even those immigrants who came desiring to preserve native languages and cultures could not resist the powerful forces making for assimilation and the potent attractions of American life. Yet if America has been a solicitous land, she has also exacted a heavy price down to the third and fourth generation of those that loved her. The history of American Catholics as a group, like that of all immigrants, is a record of assimilation with its conflicts and compromises, its successes and failures, its humor and pathos, and, perhaps above all, its ambiguities.

The Irony of Catholic Experience

Yet despite the difficulties and ambiguities involved, there developed an American Catholicism whose autochthonous quality can be denied only by the excessively partisan or the exceedingly uninformed. In fact, "American Catholicism has successfully negotiated the transition from a foreign church to an American religious community," as Herberg has noted. "It is now part of the American Way of Life."[12] In this undoubted achievement there is contained, however, a great historic irony, one that will long continue to create problems for Catholic adjustment. The basic framework of the great America we know is derived in large part from what W. W. Sweet has called "left Protestantism."[13] Even irreligion and revolt against traditional orthodoxy are to be understood in America as negating or revolting against a Protestantism that was often narrow and one-sided in important respects. The result of this has been that conceptions and categories of thought evolved within or even remotely derived from Protestantism are often not immediately relevant to Catholic conceptions and categories. For example, the dichotomy in Protestantism between liberalism and fundamentalism is, at least in that form, irrelevant to Catholicism. A Catholic position accepts and rejects important aspects of both positions. In New England, Arminianism led to Unitarianism, but quite similar and earlier Tridentine definitions concerning freedom of the will have never carried the slightest suggestion of anti-Trinitarianism in a Catholic milieu.

Ideas concerning human nature, despite great reinterpretation, secularization, and liberalization, still bear the marks of Protestant and Calvinist origin insofar as they retain the *fundamentum divisionis* of their theological ancestors in their basic structure. Such dichotomies as "reason—emotion," "faith—reason," and "freedom—determination," even in the form in which they are often used in intellectual discourse, are some examples. Concepts derived from Catholic origins would be formed along a quite different division and would often join together aspects which Protestant-derived conceptions rend asunder. Since a concept is in part a perspective on reality, such disarticulations between Catholic and general secular American notions further complicate the problems of intellectual communication.

The same differences are to be seen with respect to other aspects of secular thought. The philosophy of John Dewey, for example, insofar as it is a return to concrete existence and a recognition of the whole man and his social nature, finds itself in agreement with traditional Catholic thought on many points, but, insofar as it insists on the ultimacy of its terrestrianism and its instrumentalism, is completely foreign. The attitude of the Catholic toward issues of this kind will thus be complex and arrived at only with difficulty. Communication between Catholics and non-Catholics on such questions will often be subtly confused, while conceptions and definitions of issues currently accepted in the community at large will not infrequently tend to force the Catholic to take sides in a disagreement whose basis of division does some violence to the implications of his Catholicism.

In fact, this fundamental irony of putting the whole into the part lies at the heart of Catholic problems in America. Catholic culture in a larger sense was the greater whole from which Protestantism seceded and out of which secularism, whether in its Renaissance, Enlightenment, or modern forms, is ultimately derived. In adapting itself to American conditions, Catholicism was fitting itself as an embodiment of the older unbroken whole into one of the fragments which had broken away from it. This is still true despite the facts that the part had grown tremendously and the Catholic immigrants who came to America by and large represented only very partially the older whole of Catholic culture. What count here are basic premises and the fundamental sweep of the perspective, not the concrete pieces of information which persons may or may not possess. Of course, the immigrants who came here did not embody the older culture in the sense of explicit intellectual mastery, but their outlooks and attitudes were formed under its influence and were in many and subtle ways its products. Moreover, judging the ignorance of the immigrants is a more difficult question than might be imagined even by some scholars in the field. At any rate, the Catholic immigrants were not necessarily ignorant in the ways suspected by their non-Catholic neighbors. They were certainly different. Yet if their piety looked like superstition, and, among the Irish, their reverence and respect for the clergy appeared to be supine submission to authority, the reasons are to be sought as much in the kinds of association which these suggested to the minds of Protestants as in the actual condition of the immigrant. Moreover, the Catholic Church in one of its most fundamental aspects is a teaching institution, and it brought its larger heritage to bear upon the immigrant in countless ways. The spaciousness of the Catholic frame of reference was not lost on the immigrant church, although it was cramped by immigrant conditions. As Catholic intellectual life developed, the strain resulting from this ironical juxtaposition of whole and part became more obvious and made itself felt more and more.

This disarticulation of Catholic and non-Catholic thinking was made difficult and the former further constricted by the defensive position of the church as a whole in the nineteenth century. Never was Catholic thought less prepared to grapple with the kind of problems involved, for the posture of defense inhibited innovation and encouraged caution. Certainly advance and defense cannot go along together, at least not at the same time and in the same respects.

Social elements added further complexities. The Catholics who came to America from the older mainstream of Christian culture were forced by their circumstances to enter the native society at the lowest occupational, intellectual, and economic levels. They took the lowest position in terms of social prestige, and their religion, already in disfavor by Protestant and secularist standards, took it with them. Catholics became disproportionately hewers of wood and drawers of water, and the disadvantaged social position of the newcomers often strengthened older prejudices on the part of their neighbors which had been inherited from Foxe's *Martyrs* and Jenkins' Ear, Smithfield Market and the Black Legend.

Perhaps most fundamental of all was the fact that the newcomers were new. This was complicated for them, however, by other circumstances of their situation. "American nationalism and democracy had in fact," as Merle Curti has pointed out, "been traditionally identified with Protestantism."[14] Moreover, American democracy had been largely rural in its origins, its roots going back to settlement and frontier conditions. Immigrants in great number did not share that common background. They generally could not grapple with frontier conditions, as Hansen has shown, since they lacked the requisite skills which several generations of breaking the wilderness had developed among native pioneers. Consequently the newcomers stayed in the more settled areas where they often formed enclaves of their own people, culture, and language. These were in part bastions for defense of older culture traits and in part agencies for assimilation of the ethnic group to the general society. Time has shown that the latter was their most important function. Poverty, to which in the case of the Irish must be added some clerical admonition, kept large numbers in the cities. The Irish, who had been entirely rural at home, turned to urban industry in the new land. Political machines, block voting, and bossism in the cities often resulted when the newcomers tried to get a grip on their situation and, attempting to make use of democratic political forms, act therein for their own interests. These developments in turn evoked the fears and increased the suspicions of the older sections of the community. Yet these were by and large but the natural defensive political activity of new groups and their first steps toward integration into American life and were by no means simply and purely reprehensible, as Lincoln Steffens later discovered for himself. While such urban immigrant behavior frightened members of the native middle classes, militant labor activity aroused opposition from business people. Yet at the same time native labor saw in the foreign-born a threat to the American standards of work and wages. Even urban crime, which increased with the process of city growth, was laid at the door of the immigrant. As a result of all these factors the newcomers came to appear to many as un-American, as an alien people clutching strange idols. First the nativistic Know-Nothing movement and later the American Protective Association combined antiforeign with anti-Catholic agitation. Catholicism became for many synonymous with foreignism. This bore heavily on the newcomers, and especially on the Irish, whose native democratic impulses and alienation from British political institutions hastened their identification with the United States, while they remained stanchly loyal to their church and their ancient religious tradition. In the process of becoming American, the immigrants had to face the questioning of their very right to belong.

Cultural developments complicated an already complex picture. Developments in science and learning which amounted to a native Enlightenment resulted in the alienation of large numbers among the intellectual strata from traditional Protestant Christianity. As secularist and scientistic ideas and aspirations replaced and transformed the earlier combination of Christian and worldly hopes and became a frankly terrestrial optimism, the consequent anti-Christian sentiment was often focused on the Catholic Church as the very type of the reactionary religious institution. Yet those who moved away from Protestantism in many cases did not abandon the prejudices of the Protestant past. They especially did not abandon those which were of such long standing and so habitually taken for granted as to be beyond the sphere of conscious examination. Many anti-Catholic prejudices were precisely of this kind. The result was that many de-Christianized Americans still accepted, and acted in, terms of the implicit apprehension of Catholicism which they carried with them out of their Protestant backgrounds. They now combined their older implicit Protestant prejudices with their newer suspicions based on newer intellectual positions. Thus behind the suspicions of Catholicism as the enemy of enlightenment and progress were concealed more vague but more pervasive (and possibly more persuasive) older prejudices against "Babylon" which had "persecuted the Saints of God." To such secularized post-Protestant thinking such figures as Luther, Ridley, Galileo, and even Loisy were often seen as the heroes of a struggle for liberty. It mattered little that none of the figures would have recognized the new historic roles assigned to them, for an uncritically accepted theory of progress made them all successive steps in the upward and onward development of mankind. This myth cast its shadow across the path of the Catholic immigrants whose church was seen as the great obstacle against which such heroes had fought the common battle, while the immigrants themselves attempted to struggle against native prejudice to make available the "blessings of liberty to themselves and their posterity" on these shores. Moreover, such enlightened sentiments, behind which lurked more conventional but possibly more firmly held prejudices, not infrequently contained as well some measure of social condescension based on the social priority and ascendancy of the older population group.

Catholicism, which had presided over the birth of Western civilization when that of antiquity succumbed and fell beneath its own inertial weight and the onslaught of the northerner, found itself in an anomalous position in the United States. Here the whole was being crowded into the part; the older main stream was being poured into one of its tributaries; that which was the old and established had become the new and suspected; those who had come here to escape oppression and find liberty were identified with oppressors and even accused by some of plotting to oppress their older fellow countrymen in their new country; those who were barely tolerated in many cases were themselves accused, or at least suspected, of intolerance. Yet the assimilation process continued and merged with that of upward social mobility. Immigrant group followed immigrant group up the ladder of occupational opportunity, education, and social prestige as one century gave way to the next and as newer technological developments further transformed the face of the land and the outlooks of its inhabitants. As for the Catholic immigrants and their children, and Catholicism itself, both became naturalized: the fundamental congruity between the basic premises of the ancient Faith and those of the new Republic combined with released energies and proffered opportunities to make the newcomers Americans and to make America a nation of many sources and diverse roots, whose progressively greater approximation as time went on to the ideal of liberty and justice for all made it, despite the variety of its origins, one nation indivisible. In this process the Catholic Church proved its adaptability despite the defensiveness forced upon it by its historical position in the world, its defensive requirements in the new country, and the obstacles in its way there. Moreover, as the decades went by, the situation of the church in the world improved, especially since the pontificate of Pope Leo XIII.

In this process of assimilation native attitudes—the utopianism, activism, faith in democracy, and ambition to rise in the economic and social scale—became a part of the outlook of the new groups. In fact, America was always in some sense a utopia for many of the immigrants. If they did not come to build the sectarian Kingdom of God as had early arrivals, they came to achieve the fulfillment of human potentialities which had long been inhibited in the Old World. The immigrants and their descendants took over ready-made the attitudes which this land had already evoked among those who preceded them. Yet they made them genuinely their own and often infused into them their own aspirations and definitions. There has resulted a highly secularized community with a strongly this-worldly emphasis in life goals and values.

Toward a Program of Research

An understanding of ourselves in some depth demands that we see in ourselves precisely those elements which are the products of our history and those which are in part at least conditioned by our present situations. As long as such precipitates in our consciousness, in our angles of vision, in our stable expectations, in our allegiances, and even in our character traits remain obscure, they remain removed from conscious criticism and from the control of intelligence and the judgment of conscience. But a conscious understanding of the forces that have operated on us and which do operate on us, and of the kinds of formative influences which they exert, makes such forces and influences available for conscious acceptance, criticism, or rejection. Such self-analysis and self-understanding can diminish the realm of the conditioned and increase the realm of freedom. Precisely here the social sciences can make an intelligent contribution, through the systematic analysis of cultural and social factors and their influence on the formation of group outlooks and propensities.

Some twenty years ago Christopher Dawson declared, "Most of the great schisms and heresies in the history of the Christian church have their roots in social and national antipathies, and if this had been clearly recognized by the theologians, the history of Christianity would have been a very different one."[15] America has seen few heresies and therefore offers little material for testing Dawson's generalization, but the only recent example of heresy in this country was certainly a product of precisely the kind of social conditioning of cognition and action which sociological analysis brings to light. Perhaps it may be justifiable to paraphrase Dawson's statement in something like the following way: "The history of Christianity in America will be a different one if Christians understand the social forces and circumstances operating upon them." To the needs which interior spirituality has for the examined life may be added the prerequisites for an intelligent carrying out of the Christian apostolate.

In the same article Dawson suggested the importance of sociology in meeting the problem. He called for a "scientific sociology" which would give "a general systematic analysis of the social process." This sociology, said Dawson, would collaborate with history, and historical scholarship from its own side would contribute "a genetic description of the same process in detail." Dawson conceived both history and sociology as "two parts of a single science." He stated, "Material environment, social organization and spiritual culture all help to condition social phenomena, and we cannot explain the social process by one of them alone, and still less explain one of the three as the cause and origin of the other two." In the two decades since Dawson wrote these words the social sciences have made considerable progress toward the goals which he proposed. Nicholas S. Timasheff has recently shown the development in the field of sociology of a whole range of concepts proved useful in empirical research and analysis and accepted by workers in the field who hold widely varying approaches to the field itself.[16] Such concepts, Timasheff has noted, are the product of a genuine convergence from various points of view on tools of analysis which have demonstrated their theoretical fruitfulness and a measure of empirical adequacy. Similar observations could be made about related social science disciplines such as psychology and social psychology. Moreover, an increasing number of people in historical scholarship have shown an interest in working with social scientists, and such co-operation has taken place and been found reciprocally rewarding. The usefulness of such interdisciplinary influences has been officially recognized by learned societies and agencies.

Twenty years ago in his prospectus Dawson was entirely explicit as to the uses to which such scientific social research could be put. He declared, "A scientific method of sociological analysis may serve the same purpose for society as a psychic analysis may accomplish for the individual by unveiling the cause of latent conflicts and repressions and by making society conscious of its real ends and motives of action." One of the most important uses of knowledge, and one to which this chapter has sought to call special attention, is thereby indicated. The agencies for providing such knowledge are obviously those in which research and teaching normally take place. The university is not only a mechanism for the discovery and transmission of knowledge; it is also and by the same token one whose larger social purposes include that fundamental examination which characterizes in Socratic terms "the examined life." The problem of the examined life for the American Catholic community (or communities) becomes, then, the problem of the American Catholic university.

What is called for in the circumstances is nothing less than a large program of research dedicated to scholarly and scientific study of the American Catholic experience. Leadership for such research should lie with graduate departments in history and the social sciences in the leading Catholic universities in the country. Catholics have already recognized the utility of many of these disciplines in solving practical problems, but even more important is the contribution they can make to less immediate and practical matters. Like all knowledge, they also offer much to the contemplative needs of men. This program should be somewhat analogous to those carried out by many universities as American Studies or American Civilization programs, except that the social sciences should be far more integrally involved. A general strategy of research should be planned and agreed upon, one which will introduce chief aims and general directions while leaving considerable room for individual and departmental choice of subject and emphasis within the larger areas. Such a program should be planned and carried out by an interdepart mental committee on which history and the social sciences, as well as other interested disciplines, are represented. Research projects, thesis programs, and the like should be worked out, and important aspects of the program should be put on a foundation-supported basis. It is not suggested that this program replace or jettison other work being done in the respective disciplines themselves. Not at all; yet this program can in all probability contribute to stimulating such older programs. In present-day Catholic sociological research, for example, significant work is being done in parish sociology.[17] Such work continuing in its own right will find a larger and more meaningful context in the framework of an American Catholic Studies Program such as proposed here. Catholic historians have done much good work which would give such a program a considerable background of already available data, as well as the benefit of the research experience of the historians themselves. At present much of this work tends to be known only to specialists. In terms of an ongoing research program such as proposed here, it can be made the common background of a large body of scholars and social scientists.

It would appear that Catholic scholars and scholarly institutions would have some advantages in initiating such a program. First of all, the American Catholic experience is an identifiable spiritual, intellectual, and sociological entity which, although diverse and various in composition, has a basic unity derived from the common values and circumstances of its participants. As such it presents a real and identifiable object for study. Moreover, a common fundamental orientation underlying all apparent differences which the Catholic faith gives to Catholic scholars and investigators should make easier—though not necessarily easy—the difficult communicative process of converging distinct disciplines with various and often opposing perspectives and propensities and focusing them on common problems. The existence of such common problems is guaranteed by the reality of an American Catholic experience itself. Moreover, in a Catholic university setting, such research can have the benefit of a living dialogue with philosophy and theology. This venture alone would make the projected program worth while, for from such a dialogue the benefit derived on both sides would be inestimable.

Such a program would provide a meaningful frame of reference for the development of Catholic scholarship and Catholic scholars and social scientists while at the same time performing an important function in developing better self-understanding by the American Catholic community. The development of research perspectives, work habits, attractive career patterns, and so on among Catholics can be considerably furthered by such a program. In this way the unfortunate numerical inferiority of Catholics in scholarship to which Monsignor John Tracy Ellis has recently called attention can be diminished.[18] Only by building into Catholic institutions a going system which encourages and directs youth to scholarship and rewards them in terms of prestige and social recognition (including financial return) can this inferiority be overcome. Such a program as that proposed here can make an important contribution toward the erection of such institutional forms. Good work is being done, of course, by Catholics in many fields, but such a program will make the example of this work more effective. Monsignor Ellis concluded his article on "American Catholics and the Intellectual Life" by saying that "a unique opportunity . . . lies before the Catholic scholars of the United States, which if approached and executed with deep conviction of its vital importance for the future of the American Church, may inspire them to do great things."[19] An interdisciplinary program of American Catholic Studies which could carry out foundation-supported advanced research on the American Catholic experience is here suggested as one step toward those great things which, in Monsignor Ellis' words, our "oldest, wisest, and most sublime tradition of learning"[20] demands of us.

NOTES

1. Will Herberg, *Protestant, Catholic, Jew* (Garden City, N.Y.: 1955), pp. 175–176.

2. Important aspects of immigration are treated in the works of Henry Pratt Fairchild, Robert Park, Marcus L. Hansen, Irvin Child, Oscar Handlin, and others.

3. A treatment of westward movement can be found in the works of Frederick J. Turner, Frederick Merk, Ray Allen Billington, and others.

4. Frederick Jackson Turner, *The Significance of the Frontier* (New York: 1920 and 1947), p. 37.

5. William Warren Sweet, "Left-Wing Protestantism Triumphs in Colonial America," in *The American Churches* (New York and Nashville: 1947, 1948), pp. 11–33.

6. Alexis de Tocqueville, *Democracy in America*, Phillips Bradley, ed. (New York: 1954), I, 45.

7. On revival movements, a tremendous amount of good material is to be found in the works of William Warren Sweet, Wesley M. Gewehr, Whitney Cross, C. H. Maxson, Catherine Cleveland, and others. Related topics are treated by H. Richard Niebuhr, Liston Pope, and such Europeans as Ernst Troeltsch, Max Weber, R. H. Tawney, Amintore Fanfani, and others.

8. Merle Curti, *The Growth of American Thought* (New York and London: 1943), p. 49.

9. Herberg, *op. cit.*, p. 151.

10. Theodore Maynard, *The Story of American Catholicism* (New York: 1941), p. 507.

11. Desmond Fennell, "Continental and Oceanic Catholicism," *America* (March 26, 1955).

12. Herberg, *op. cit.*, p. 175.

13. Sweet, *op. cit.*

14. Curti, *op. cit.*, p. 493.

15. Christopher Dawson, "Sociology as a Science," quoted from the republication in *Cross Currents*, IV, No. 2 (Winter, 1954), 136.

16. Nicholas S. Timasheff, *Sociological Theory: Its Nature and Growth* (New York: 1955).

17. See Frank A. Santopolo, Joseph F. Scheuer, and Joseph B. Schuyler, "Parish Sociology," *Thought* (Summer, 1955).

18. John Tracy Ellis, "American Catholics and the Intellectual Life," *Thought* (Autumn, 1955).

19. *Ibid.*

20. *Ibid.*

FOUR: The Ideologists and the Missing Dialogue

Oscar Cullmann stated recently that the prerequisite for Protestant-Roman Catholic conversation is "complete openness." Actually this aim, achievable among some groups in Europe, is too high for American conditions. The best we can do is to work for a growing openness as we build some basis in mutual trust and friendship. Our bridges are very weak. They bear a warning—"Capacity: not too many tons"—and we are all quite good at implicitly reading such signs.

Thus, Protestant-Catholic dialogue in this country does not take place in an atmosphere of relaxation and interior freedom. It is usually characterized by a kind of distant and respectful restraint expressing a kind of etiolated good will. Only real and fairly continuous association can bring relaxation of such attitudes. While individuals achieve this, representative individuals in religious or semireligious dialogue usually fall far short of it. And the two great religious bodies certainly do not attain anything like this.

One result of this general absence of Christian dialogue is that one receives the impression—rather a caricature of the facts—that the reciprocal attitudes of the two groups are quite antagonistic. This impression arises from the statements and actions of the noisier elements on each side, who may be characterized loosely in terms of two identifiable groups.

Let us call them, for want of better terms, Catholic hyper-integralists and Protestant hyper-reformationists. Both find a marked satisfaction in carrying out, quite inappropriately in the contemporary setting, religious conflicts of the past. The source

From *Christianity and Crisis* (June 8, 1959), pp. 81–84.

of this satisfaction deserves deep study. All that can be done here is to suggest some elements that must be included in any adequate hypothesis.

The Hyper-Integralists

The Catholic hyper-integralists want two incompatible things at once. They want some kind of Catholic ghetto, and at the same time they seek to identify Catholicism with America and Americanism, understanding the latter especially in terms of right-wing political opinions. They see no need for any larger expression of Christian solidarity nor any useful end in genuine dialogue with Protestants or others about fundamental value problems. Their viewpoint is an ideology in the sense that it displays a marked economy in relation to the ambiguities of reality. It is a set of stereotypes and is given to blacks and whites, rights and wrongs, fors and againsts.

Ideologies are embraced because they serve some function—often implicit and unrecognized—for their adherents. They fulfill needs and allay anxieties.

Hyper-integralists suffer from two strains, both derived from their historical experience. They experience the defensiveness of all Christianity before the rapid secularization of culture. This is aggravated by the defensive posture that much of post-Tridentine Catholicism has inherited from the Counter Reformation.

Another closely related set of strains derives from the American Catholic experience. Immigration and assimilation were difficult processes for those involved, and they precipitated attitudes that did not simply fade away when the most palpable difficulties no longer existed. Catholics were not well received at first. This is a fact; one that Protestants perhaps do not ponder enough. Many of them were Irish and brought with them bitter memories of oppression by a Protestant ruling class in Ireland. Thus certain symbols and their attendant feeling tones are often differently experienced by Catholics and Protestants, who in fact may be equally "democratic."

Consequently Catholics as a group have developed a complex relationship to America, and the complexity lies precisely in areas not easily understood by the ordinary man. The American Catholic feels himself an American, wants to be and is glad he is an American, takes over American middle-class values, and joins the social mobility merry-go-round alongside his Protestant fellows.

To the extent that he remains Catholic, he often finds it difficult to relate himself to some aspects of American culture, especially to intellectual areas of life that derive from a Protestant substrate and show pronounced secularization and to other areas more closely related to Protestantism proper.

When Catholics become middle-class they take over many of the general fears and anxieties of the middle class—fears of aggrandizement of other groups at their expense. Since Catholics derived recently from lower-class status, their new middle-class attitudes may involve some degree of guilt.

Moreover, since Catholic values have stressed social ethics, the new political and social attitudes may involve guilt on this score. The unevenly assimilated Catholic needs something to enable him to handle these problems, something to give him a new conception and legitimation of himself and to supply him with the basic security that is derived in less mobile societies from social solidarity and tradition. This function is served by the ideology of hyper-integralism.

This is done by making a strident identification of Catholicism with America and Americanism, which also exorcises the heritage of the Enlightenment and its modern leftist derivatives. Not only is Catholicism equated with genuine Americanism, but secularism is rendered un-American, and criticism of bourgeois values becomes anti-American and anti-Catholic. America, the business system, and the Catholic Church stand together, attacked by a common enemy. Their defense is a single task.

The earlier defensiveness invites a militant response, and the bothersome problems—difficult to make explicit and to evaluate rationally—are translated into bogeys to be combated. Thus a lot of anxiety-provoking problems are given some kind of formulation, and therapists tell us that any kind of definition offers a measure of relief. Furthermore, identification of the problems makes an attack on them possible, albeit only a symbolic one. But the symbolic attack provides the self-definition that is needed and acts as a catharsis for built-up tensions.

Three marks of ideology may be distinguished: stereotyped oversimplification of reality, militancy, and rigidity. The last reveals the presence of anxiety, and the presence of aggressiveness is an obvious response to strain. We have here a historically conditioned social and cultural syndrome involving displacement and projection. I do not mean that it is a neurosis in the individual sense, though in some cases it may be. It is an instance of social pathology.

The Hyper-Reformationists

The hyper-reformationists—the Protestant equivalents of the Catholics just described—also are reacting in terms of historical conditioning to contemporary strains. Protestants and Protestantism today are having to accept something less than the central and dominant position they have long had in American culture and society. The social mobility of other groups, among whom the Catholics are prominent, makes this the case.

Once securely identified with the core of American culture and society, Protestants now must move over a bit. That men do not move over graciously is one of the few undeniable generalizations from history. This adjustment is not yet clearly explicit in Protestant thinking, but the nudge is felt and is responded to.

When upsetting social developments, such as industrialization and urbanization, shook American society in the nineteenth century, it was fairly standard for many Protestant groups to respond in terms of anti-Catholic clichés. The great and honorable tradition of Protest has had the unfortunate by-product of supplying the man in the street with a ready set of counters from Foxe's *Martyrs* and the Black Legend with which to organize experience. Such clichés serve similar purposes today.

Catholics are certainly nervous in the face of the rapid secularization of culture, but Protestants are, often enough, inundated by it. A curious aspect of this development, which does not aid the inner security of Protestant church groups, is that some secularized Protestants tend to identify Catholicism with the older orthodox tradition of Christianity, something certainly in no way encouraged by official Protestantism. When such people feel guilt—often not very consciously—for no longer believing what they were brought up to believe, they tend to project it outward and to aggress Catholicism as the external visible surrogate of their former beliefs.

The hyper-reformationists see as their chief religious and civic task the carrying forward of the counter-Catholic aspects of the Reformation in today's world. In fact, the very weakening of their Protestantism by secularization makes them more and not less anti-Catholic for the reasons I have suggested, and also because it is the one aspect of the long and honorable tradition of the Reformation that is meaningful to them in their present situation.

More pressing problems, such as the very problematic future of all religion in American culture, do not bother them despite their close relation to rational Protestant interests. By saving America from "Catholic aggression," this ideology once again identifies Protestantism with America and symbolically reaffirms the older, central role of Protestantism in our society.

This is, in fact, a symbolic counterattack against the social rise of Catholics and the inevitably concomitant increasing visibility and influence of Catholicism. In some cases, at least, it is also a way of handling guilt over an older, abandoned Protestant orthodoxy. This ideology, too, shows itself as employing a truncating stereotyping and as exhibiting militancy and rigidity. Like its Catholic counterpart, it goes in heavily for verbal realism.

Reality and Fantasy

Some will object that there is certainly some truth in what hyper-reformationism says about "Catholic authoritarianism," or in what hyper-integralism says about liberalism and Protestant "connivance" with secularism. Yes, of course. If they were not built on some reality, ideologies would not serve their function. The real bases exist in the complicated social developments we have briefly indicated and in the real and important faith and value differences that exist between Catholics and Protestants.

The neurotic individual who reacts to his boss in terms of unsolved infantile problems in relation to his father does not imagine that his boss is an authority figure who creates problems for him. This is part of the real situation. What he does is to perceive this realistic element in a context derived from earlier and now inappropriate experiences. He adds unreal elements. In part he does this by schematizing the current situation in terms of the dimension of the earlier one. The perception is a distorted one, and the reaction is overdetermined. In the same way, these ideologists respond to their present predicaments with older and now inappropriate organizing ideas and actions. In both cases this is a disguised way of handling anxieties, wishes, and aggressions.

These ideologies provide for each group a simplified and manageable definition of the situations in which they find themselves. They provide the self-image needed in a time of rapid transition to replace the older conventional images and definitions now being rendered obsolete by social change. The plight of the individual in a progressively complicated society also finds some fantasy expression, as do frustrations and aggressions of more purely personal origin.

It should be stressed that the anti-Romanism of the one and the antiliberalism of the other are the sociological equivalents of the anti-Semitism of the German conservative classes who proved so vulnerable to Nazism. Why these ideologies appeal only to some elements among both religious groups and not to all is deserving of serious research. Undoubtedly some groups are more securely anchored in reality.

There are three reasons why I have considered at length these groups that are not representative of the typical Catholic or Protestant. First, they should not be underestimated; they are not a lunatic fringe. There are hard cores on both sides, and around them cluster all shades of affected opinion.

Second, these groups should be a problem to intelligent Catholics and Protestants. It is important that they do not come to act as focuses for the crystallization of American opinion.

Third, these ideologies play an important part in structuring the framework in which a great deal of exchange of ideas takes place. The exchanges are often marked by considerable intensity. Issues like education, birth control, an ambassador to the Vatican, or a Catholic President arouse the hyper-reformationists.

Their Catholic counterparts are, in fact, likely to remain calmer and more rational on these issues, which they see more realistically and less symbolically. They tend to get triggered off by such symbolic counters as Communism, which plays the role of master symbol for many of them, criticism of the FBI, or Alger Hiss speaking at Princeton, over which a Catholic chaplain becomes so exercised. Some symbols are shared in common, and in local contexts any of the long list may become the catalyst to set things off.

Fortunately, these two ideologies are not organized around the same symbols, and their adherents do not face each other as two quite polarized groups reacting with equal intensity to the same issues. The loosely integrated character of American society and culture helps account for this fact.

It is ironical that neither group seems aware that both constitute striking examples of the secularization of their religious ethos. If the hyper-integralists see no inconsistency in championing a Catholicism that has centered its ethic on *caritas* ("charity," cf. I Cor. 13) and, at the same time, in embracing Joseph McCarthy as a sterling defender of the cause, the hyper-reformationists see nothing anti-Protestant in the crude secularism of Paul Blanshard on so many ethical issues. Each confuses religion and secular nationalism in its own way.

Thus the hyper-integralists tend to merge loosely into rightist secular political groupings, a fact that reaffirms their Americanism for them. The hyper-reformationists also merge loosely, in some cases at least, with quite militant secularizers.

Certain conservative Protestant groups today appear to be taking up a line like the hyper-integralists. As recent events in the South have shown, the identification of conservative and defensive religion with right-wing causes is not a Catholic monopoly. Will the hyper-reformationists reconcile themselves with their Catholic equivalents on the basis of a secular rightism and find themselves combating fellow Protestants?

Reality Testing via Dialogue

An important effect of the existence of these ideologies is, as I have noted, that they tend to define the universe of discourse for more moderate people. The result is a great lack of reality testing about controversial issues. To give but one example: it is surprising to what a great extent the discussion of a possible Catholic President is marked by tenseness and lack of sense of proportion. The symbolic elements outweigh the real in the thinking of many otherwise sensible people.

It seems clear to any political realist that no Catholic President would or could alter the American Constitution, either as a document or as a body of practices embodying and interpreting that document. Certainly this is one area where formal and informal control seem quite effective.

Indeed, anyone with an ounce of political shrewdness knows that the Catholic Church as a religious group would have far less influence on a Catholic President than on almost any other conceivable administration. The social controls are such that he would lean over backward to avoid even the suggestion of influence. In France members of the clergy were much freer in approaching high government officials under distinctly secular cabinets than they were when MRP, a liberal Catholic party, had formed the government.

Every issue of this kind picks up connotations that find resonance in Catholic and Protestant souls, reactivating memories of our unfortunate and most un-Christian history of fighting and persecuting one another—triggering off our often unconscious and, too often, equally un-Christian anxieties about our present predicaments. These foreshortened attempts to handle a reality we have not really faced are, in fact, an unwary abandonment of reality. Nonrational fears and aggressions replace Christian action: symbolic concerns replace real ones.

Reality testing must be developed, but reality testing is not an individual process. It is a social affair in which the slants of men with different perspectives partly correct and partly supplement each other, eliminating fantasy and enlarging the range of the real. It requires communication, the basis of which should exist in a common Christian heritage.

In isolation, each group finds it difficult to recognize in its own view the elements of fantasy and projection that creep in. That is why Protestant-Catholic dialogue is so important. It has already started in theological discussions and in biblical studies. There is much room for creative thinking in extending it. Only dialogue will deliver us from the spell of the ideologists.

SECTION II

THE SOCIOLOGY OF MORMONISM: FOUR STUDIES

FIVE: A Comparative Study of the Role of Values in Social Action in Two Southwestern Communities

With Evon Z. Vogt

It is one of the central hypotheses of the Values Study Project that value orientations play an important part in the shaping of social institutions and in influencing the forms of observed social action. By value orientations are understood those views of the world, often implicitly held, which define the meaning of human life or the "life situation of man" and thereby provide the context in which day-to-day problems are solved.¹ The present chapter is an outgrowth of one phase of the field research carried out in western New Mexico. It presents the record of two communities composed of people with a similar cultural background and living in the same general ecological setting.

The responses of these two communities to similar problems were found to be quite different. Since the physical setting of the two villages is remarkably similar, the explanation for the differences was sought in the manner in which each group viewed the situation and the kind of social relationships and legitimate expectations which each felt appropriate in meeting situational challenges. In this sphere of value orientations a marked difference was found. Moreover, the differences in response to situation in the two cases were found to be related to the differences between the value orientations central to these communities.

From *American Sociological Review*, XVIII, (December 1953), 645–654. Reprinted by permission of the journal and the American Sociological Association.

We do not deny the importance of situational factors. Nor do we intend to disparage the importance of historical convergence of value orientations with concrete situations in explaining the centrality of some values as against others and in leading to the deep internalization of the values we discuss. But the importance of value orientations as an element in understanding the situation of action is inescapably clear. All the elements of what Parsons has called the action frame of reference—the actors, the means and conditions which comprise the situation, and the value orientations of the actors—enter into the act.[2] The primacy of any one in any individual case does not permit generalization. Yet the present study testifies to the great importance of the third element—the value orientations—in shaping the final action which ensues.

Focus of the Inquiry

The inquiry is focused on a comparison of the Mormon community of Rimrock[3] with the Texan community of Homestead, both having populations of approximately 250 and both located (forty miles apart) on the southern portion of the Colorado Plateau in western New Mexico. The natural environmental setting is virtually the same for the two villages: the prevailing elevations stand at 7,000 feet; the landscapes are characterized by mesa and canyon country; the flora and fauna are typical of the Upper Sonoran Life Zone with stands of pinyon, juniper, sagebrush, and blue gramma grass and some intrusions of Ponderosa pine, Douglas fir, Englemann spruce, and Gambel oak from a higher life zone; the region has a steppe climate with an average annual precipitation of 14 inches (which varies greatly from year to year) and with killing frosts occurring late in the spring and early in the autumn.[4] The single important environmental difference between the two communities is that Rimrock is located near the base of a mountain range which has elevations rising to 9,000 feet, and a storage reservoir (fed by melting snow packs from these higher elevations) has made irrigation agriculture possible in Rimrock, while in Homestead there is only dry-land farming. Today both villages have subsistence patterns based on combinations of farming (mainly irrigated crops of alfalfa and wheat in Rimrock and dry-land crops of pinto beans in Homestead) and livestock raising (mainly Hereford beef cattle in both villages).

Rimrock was settled by Mormon missionaries in the 1870's as part of a larger project to plant settlements in the area of northern Arizona. Rimrock itself, unlike the Arizona sites, was established as a missionary outpost, and the intention of the settlers was the conversion of the Indians, a task conceived in terms of the *Book of Mormon*, which defines the American Indian as "a remnant of Israel."

The early settlers were "called" by the church, that is, they were selected and sent out by the church authorities. The early years were exceedingly difficult, and only the discipline of the church and the loyalty of the settlers to its gospel kept them at the task. Drought, crop diseases, and the breaking of the earth and rock dam which they had constructed for the storage of irrigation water added to their difficulties, as did the fact that they had merely squatted on the land and were forced to purchase it at an exorbitant price to avoid eviction. The purchase money was given by the church authorities in Salt Lake City, who also supplied 5,000 pounds of seed wheat in another period of dearth. The original settlers were largely from northern Utah, although there were also some converts from the southern states who had been involved in unsuccessful Arizona settlements a few years earlier.

As the emphasis shifted from missionary activities to farming, Rimrock developed into a not unusual Mormon village, despite its peripheral position to the rest of Mormondom. Irrigation farming was supplemented by cattle raising on the open range. In the early 1930's the Mormons began to buy range land, and Rimrock's economy shifted to a focus on cattle raising. Today villagers own a total of 149 sections of range land, about four sections of irrigated or irrigable land devoted to gardens, and some irrigated pastures in the immediate vicinity of the village. The family farm is still the basic economic unit, although partnerships formed on a kinship basis and devoted to cattle raising have been important in lifting the economic level of the village as a whole. In recent years some of the villagers—also on the basis of a kinship partnership—purchased the local trading post, which is engaged in trading with the Indians as well as local village business. In addition to twelve family partnerships which own 111 sections of land, there is a village co-operative which owns 38 sections. Privately owned commercial facilities in the village include two stores, a boardinghouse, two garages, a saddle and leather shop, and a small restaurant. With this economic variety there is considerable difference in the distribution of wealth.

The church is the central core of the village, and its complex hierarchical structure, including the auxiliary organizations which activate women, youth, and young children, involves a large portion of the villagers in active participation. The church structure is backed up and impenetrated by the kinship structure. Moreover, church organization and kinship not only unify Rimrock into a social unit; they also integrate it into the larger structure of the Mormon Church and relate it by affinity and consanguinity to the rest of Mormondom.

Rimrock has been less affected by secularization than most Mormon villages in Utah and is less assimilated into generalized American patterns.[5] Its relative isolation has both kept such pressures from impinging on it with full force and enhanced its formal and informal ties with the church, preserving many of the characteristics of a Mormon village of a generation ago.

Homestead was settled by migrants from the South Plains area of western Texas and Oklahoma in the early 1930's. The migration represented a small aspect of that vast movement of people westward to California which was popularized in Steinbeck's *Grapes of Wrath* and was the subject of investigation by many governmental agencies in the 1930's and 1940's.[6] Instead of going on to California, these homesteaders settled in a number of semiarid farming areas in northern and western New Mexico and proceeded to develop an economy centered around the production of pinto beans. The migration coincided with the period of national depression and was due in part to severe economic conditions on the South Plains which forced families to leave their Texas and Oklahoma communities, in part to the attraction of land available for homesteading which held out the promise of family-owned farms for families who had previously owned little or no land or had lost their land during the depression. The land base controlled by the homesteaders comprises approximately 100 sections. Each farm unit is operated by a nuclear family; there are no partnerships. Farms now average two sections in size and are scattered as far as twenty miles from the crossroads center of the community which contains the two stores, the school, the post office, two garages, a filling station, a small restaurant, a bean warehouse, a small bar, and two church buildings. Through the years, farming technology has shifted almost completely from horse-drawn implements to mechanized equipment.

With the hazardous farming conditions (periodic droughts and early killing frosts) out-migration from Homestead has been relatively high. A few of these families have gone on to California, but more of them have moved to irrigated farms in the middle Rio Grande Valley and entered an agricultural situation which in its physical environmental aspects is similar to the situation in the Mormon community of Rimrock.

The Mormon Case

In broad perspective these two villages present local variations of generalized American culture. They share the common American value orientations which emphasize the importance of achievement and success, progress and optimism, and rational mastery over nature. In the Mormon case, these were taken over from the nineteenth-century American milieu in western New York, where the church was founded, and reinterpreted in terms of an elaborate theological conception of the universe as a dynamic process in which God and men are active collaborators in an eternal progression to greater power through increasing mastery.[7] The present life was and is conceived as a single episode in an infinity of work and mastery. The result was the heightening for the Mormons of convictions shared with most other Americans. Moreover, this conception was closely related to the belief in the reopening of divine revelation first through the agency of Joseph Smith, the original Mormon prophet, and later through the institutionalized channels of the Mormon Church. The Mormons conceived of themselves as a covenant people specially chosen for a divine task. This task was the building of the Kingdom of God on earth, and in this project—attempted four times unsuccessfully before the eventual migration to the west—much of the religious and secular socialism of the early nineteenth century found a profound reflection. The Mormon prophet proposed the "Law of Consecration" in an attempt to reconcile private initiative with co-operative endeavor. Contention led to its abandonment in 1838 after some five years of unsuccessful experiment. Yet this withdrawal did not limit, but indeed rather enhanced, its future influence in Mormon settlement. The Law of Consecration was no longer interpreted as a blueprint prescribing social institutions of a definite sort, but its values lent a strong co-operative bias to much of later Mormon activity.[8] In the context of the notion of peculiarity and reinforced by out-group antagonism and persecution, these values became deeply embedded in Mormon orientations. The preference for agriculture combined with an emphasis on community and lay participation in church activities resulted in the formation of compact villages rather than isolated family farmsteads as the typical Mormon settlement pattern.[9]

While Rimrock and Homestead share most of the central value orientations of general American culture, they differ significantly in the values governing social relationships. Rimrock, with a stress on community co-operation, an ethnocentrism resulting from the notion of their own peculiarity, and a village pattern of settlement, is more like the other Mormon villages of the West than it is like Homestead.

The stress on *community co-operation* in Rimrock contrasts markedly with the stress on *individual independence* found in Homestead. This contrast is one of emphasis, for individual initiative is important in Rimrock, especially in family farming and cattle raising, whereas co-operative activity does occur in Homestead. In Rimrock, however, the expectations are such that one must show his fellows or at least convince himself that he has good cause for *not* committing his time and resources to community efforts, while in Homestead co-operative action takes place *only* after certainty has been reached that the claims of other individuals on one's time and resources are legitimate.

Rimrock was a co-operative venture from the start, and very early the irrigation company, a mutual nonprofit corporation chartered under state law, emerged from the early water association informally developed around—and in a sense within—the church. In all situations which transcend the capacities of individual families or family combinations, Rimrock Mormons have recourse to co-operative techniques. Let us examine four examples.

THE "TIGHT" LAND SITUATION

Rimrock Mormons, feeling themselves "gathered," dislike having to migrate to non-Mormon areas. However, after World

War II the thirty-two returned veterans faced a choice of poverty and underemployment or leaving the community. This situation became the concern of the church and was discussed in its upper lay priesthood bodies in the village. It was decided to buy land to enable the veterans to remain. The possibilities of land purchase in the area were almost nonexistent, and it appeared that nothing could be done, when unexpectedly the opportunity to buy some 38 sections presented itself. At the time, the village did not have the needed $10,000 for the down payment, so the sum was borrowed from the Cooperative Security Corporation, a Church Welfare Plan agency, and the land was purchased. The patterns revealed here—community concern over a community problem, and appeal to and reception of aid from the general authorities of the church—are typically Mormon. However, Mormon co-operation did not end here. Instead of breaking up the purchased land into plots to be individually owned and farmed, the parcel was kept as a unit, and a co-operative Rimrock Land and Cattle Company was formed. The company copied and adapted the form of the mutual irrigation company. Shares were sold in the village, each member being limited to two. A quota of cattle per share per year to be run on the land and a quota of bulls relative to cows were established. The cattle are privately owned, but the land is owned and managed co-operatively. The calves are the property of the owners of the cows. The project which has not been limited to veterans, supplements other earnings sufficiently to keep most of the veterans in the village.

THE GRAVELING OF THE VILLAGE STREETS

The streets of Rimrock were in bad repair in the fall of 1950. That summer a construction company had brought much large equipment into the area to build and gravel a section of a state highway which runs through the village. Before this company left, taking its equipment with it, villagers, again acting through the church organization, decided that the village should avail itself of the opportunity and have the town's streets graveled. This was discussed in the Sunday priesthood meeting and announced at the Sunday sacrament meeting. A meeting was called for Monday evening, and each household was asked to send a representative. The meeting was well attended, and although not every family had a member present, practically all were represented at least by proxy. There was considerable discussion, and it was finally decided to pay $800 for the job, which meant a $20 donation from each family. The local trader paid a larger amount, and, within a few days after the meeting, the total amount was collected. Only one villager raised objections to the proceedings. Although he was a man of importance locally, he was soon silenced by a much poorer man who invoked Mormon values of progress and co-operation and pledged to give $25, which was five dollars above the norm.

THE CONSTRUCTION OF A HIGH-SCHOOL GYMNASIUM

In 1951 a plan for the construction of a high-school gymnasium was presented to the Rimrock villagers. Funds for materials and for certain skilled labor would be provided from state school appropriations, providing that the local residents would contribute the labor for construction. The plan was discussed in a Sunday priesthood meeting in the church, and later meetings were held both in the church and in the schoolhouse. Under the leadership of the principal of the school (who is also a member of the higher priesthood), arrangements were made whereby each able-bodied man in the community would either contribute at least 50 hours of labor or $50 (the latter to be used to hire outside laborers) toward the construction. The original blueprint was extended to include a row of classrooms for the high school around the large central gymnasium.

Work on the new building began in late 1951 and was completed in 1953. The enterprise was not carried through without difficulties. A few families were sympathetic at first, but failed to contribute full amounts of either labor or cash, and some were unsympathetic toward the operation from the start. The high-school principal had to keep reminding the villagers about their pledges to support the enterprise. But in the end the project was successful, and it represented an important co-operative effort on the part of the majority.

THE COMMUNITY DANCES

The Mormons have always considered dancing to be an important form of recreation—in fact, a particularly Mormon form of recreation. Almost every Friday evening a dance is held in the village church house. These dances are family affairs and are opened and closed with prayer. They are part of the general church recreation program and are paid for by what is called locally "the budget." The budget refers to the plan under which villagers pay $15 per family per year to cover a large number of entertainments, all sponsored by the church auxiliary organization for youth, the Young Men's Mutual Improvement Association, and the Young Women's Mutual Improvement Association. The budget payment admits all members of the family to such entertainments.

Observation of these dances over a six-month period did not reveal any tension or fighting. Smoking and drinking are forbidden to loyal Mormons, and those who smoked did so outside and away from the building. At dances held in the local school there has been evidence of drinking, and at times fighting has resulted from the presence of nonvillagers. But on the whole the Rimrock dances are peaceful family affairs.

Rimrock reveals itself responding to group problems *as a group*. The economic ethic set forth by Joseph Smith in the Law of Consecration is seen in the dual commitment to private individual initiative (family farms and family partnerships in business and agriculture) and to co-operative endeavor in larger communal problems (irrigation company, land and cattle company, graveling the streets, and construction of school gymnasium). For the Mormons, co-operation has become second nature. It has become part of the institutionalized structure of expectations, reinforced by religious conviction and social control.

The Homesteader Case

The value stress on individual independence of action has deep roots in the history of the Homesteader group.[10] The Homesteaders were part of the westward migration from the hill country of the Southern Appalachians to the Panhandle country of Texas and Oklahoma and from there to the Southwest and California. Throughout their historical experience there has been an emphasis on a rough and ready self-reliance and individualism, the Jacksonianism of the frontier West. The move to western New Mexico from the South Plains was made predominantly by

isolated nuclear families, and Homestead became a community
of scattered, individually owned farmsteads—a geographical
situation and a settlement pattern which reinforced the stress on
individualism.

Let us now examine the influence of this individualistic value
orientation on a series of situations comparable to those that
were described for Rimrock.

THE "TIGHT" LAND SITUATION

In 1934 the Federal Security Administration, working in conjunction with the Land Use Division of the Department of
Agriculture, proposed a "unit re-organization plan." This plan
would have enabled the Homesteaders to acquire additional
tracts of land and permitted them to run more livestock and
hence depend less on the more hazardous economic pursuit of
dry-land pinto-bean farming. It called for the use of government
funds to purchase large ranches near the Homestead area which
would be managed co-operatively by a board of directors
selected by the community. The scheme collapsed while it was
still in the planning stages, because it was clear that each family
expected to acquire its own private holdings on the range and
that a co-operative would not work in Homestead.

THE GRAVELING OF THE VILLAGE STREETS

During the winter of 1949–1950 the construction company
which was building the highway through Rimrock was also
building a small section of highway north of Homestead. The
construction company offered to gravel the streets of Homestead
center if the residents who lived in the village would co-
operatively contribute enough funds for the purpose. This community plan was rejected by the Homesteaders, and an alternative plan was followed. Each of the operators of several of the
service institutions—including the two stores, the bar, and the
post office—independently hired the construction company truck
drivers to haul a few loads of gravel to be placed in front of his
own place of business, which still left the rest of the village
streets a sea of mud in rainy weather.

THE CONSTRUCTION OF A
HIGH-SCHOOL GYMNASIUM

In 1950 the same plan for the construction of a new gymnasium was presented to the Homesteaders as was presented to the

Mormon village of Rimrock. As noted above, this plan was accepted by the community of Rimrock, and the new building was completed. But the plan was rejected by the residents of Homestead at a meeting in the summer of 1950, and there were long speeches to the effect that "I've got to look after my own farm and my own family first; I can't be up here in town building a gymnasium." Later in the summer additional funds were provided for labor; and with these funds adobe bricks were made, the foundation was dug, and construction was started—the Homesteaders being willing to work on the gymnasium on a purely business basis at a dollar an hour. But as soon as the funds were exhausted, construction stopped. Today a partially completed gymnasium, and stacks of some 10,000 adobe bricks disintegrating slowly with the rains, stand as monuments to the individualism of the Homesteaders.

THE COMMUNITY DANCES

As in Rimrock, the village dances in Homestead are important focal points for community activity. These affairs take place several times a year in the schoolhouse and are always well attended. But while the dances in Rimrock are well-co-ordinated activities which carry through the evening, the dances in Homestead often end when tensions between rival families result in fist fights. And there is always the expectation in Homestead that a dance (or other co-operative activity such as a picnic or rodeo) may end at any moment and the level of activity be reduced to the component nuclear families which form the only solid core of social organization in the community.

The individualistic value orientation of the Homesteaders also has important functional relationships to the religious organization of the community. With the exception of two men who are professed atheists, all the Homesteaders define themselves as Christians. But denominationalism is rife, there being ten different denominations represented in the village: Baptist, Presbyterian, Methodist, Nazarene, Campbellite, Holiness, Seventh Day Adventist, Mormon, Catholic, and Present Day Disciples.

In the most general terms, this religious differentiation in Homestead can be interpreted as a function of the individualistic and factionalizing tendencies in the social system. In a culture with a value stress on independent individual action combined with a "freedom of religion" ideology, adhering to one's own denomination becomes an important means of expressing individualism and of focusing factional disputes around a doctrine and a concrete institutional framework. In turn, the doctrinal differences promote additional factionalizing tendencies, with the result that competing churches become the battleground for a cumulative and circularly reinforcing struggle between rival small factions in the community.[11]

To sum up, we may say that the strong commitment to an individualistic value orientation has resulted in a social system in which interpersonal relations are strongly colored by a kind of factionalism and in which persons and groups become related to one another in a competitive, feuding relationship. The Homesteaders do not live on their widely separated farms and ignore one another, as it might be possible to do. On the other hand, they do not co-operate in community affairs as closely as does a hive of bees. They interact, but a constant feuding tone permeates the economic, social, and religious structure of the community.

Relationship between the Two Communities

Although there is some trading in livestock, feed, and other crops, the most important contacts between the two communities are not economic, but social and recreational. The village baseball teams have scheduled games with each other for the past two decades, and there is almost always joint participation in the community dances and in the summer rodeos in the two communities. Despite Mormon objections to close associations with "gentiles," there is also considerable interdating between the two communities among the teen-age groups, and three intermarriages have taken place.

In general, the Homesteaders envy and admire the Mormons' economic organization, their irrigated land, and more promising prospects for good crops each year. On the other hand, they regard the Mormons as cliquish and unfriendly and fail completely to understand why anyone "wants to live all bunched up the way the Mormons do." They feel that the Mormons are inbred and think they should be glad to get "new blood" from intermarriages with Homesteaders. They add, "That Mormon religion is something we can't understand at all." Finally, the

Homesteaders say that Mormons "used to have more than one wife, and some probably still do; they dance in the church, they're against liquor, coffee, and tobacco, and they always talk about Joseph Smith and the *Book of Mormon*."

The Mormons consider their own way of life distinctly superior to that of the Homesteaders in every way. Some will admit that the Homesteaders have the virtue of being more friendly and of "mixing more with others," and their efforts in the face of farming hazards are admired, but Homestead is generally regarded as a rough and in some ways immoral community, especially because of the drinking, smoking, and fighting (particularly at dances) that take place. They also feel that Homestead is disorganized and that the churches are not doing what they should for the community. For the past few years they have been making regular missionary trips to Homestead, but to date they have made no conversions.

Comparisons and Conclusions

In the case of Rimrock and Homestead, we are dealing with two communities which are comparable in population and ecological setting and are variants of the same general culture. The two outstanding differences are: *(a)* irrigation versus dry-land farming and associated differences in settlement pattern, compact village versus isolated farmstead type;[12] *(b)* a value stress on co-operative community action versus a stress on individual action. The important question here involves the relationship (if any) between these two sets of variables. Is the co-operation in Rimrock directly a function of an irrigation agriculture situation with a compact village settlement pattern, and is the rugged individualism in Homestead a function of a dry-land farming situation with a scattered settlement pattern? Or did these value orientations arise out of earlier historical experience in each case, influence the types of communities which were established in western New Mexico, and later persist in the face of changed economic situations? We shall attempt to demonstrate that the second proposition is more in accord with the historical facts as we now know them.

Nelson has shown that the general pattern of the Mormon

village is not a direct function (in its beginnings) of the requirements of irrigation agriculture or of the need for protection
against Indians on the frontier. Rather, the basic pattern was a
social invention of the Mormons, motivated by a sense of urgent
need to prepare a dwelling place for the "Savior" at "His Second
Coming." The "Plat of the City of Zion" was invented by Joseph
Smith, Sidney Rigdon, and Frederick G. Williams in 1833 and
has formed the basis for the laying out of most Mormon villages,
even those established in the Middle West before the Mormons
migrated to Utah.[13]

It is very clear that both the compact village pattern and the
co-operative social arrangements centering around the church
existed before the Mormons engaged in irrigation agriculture
and had a strong influence on the development of community
structure not only in Utah but in the Mormon settlements like
Rimrock on the periphery of the Mormon culture area. There is
no objective reason in the Rimrock ecological and cultural setting
(the local Navahos and Zunis did not pose a threat to pioneer
settlements in the 1880's) why the Mormons could not have set
up a community which conformed more to the isolated farmstead type with a greater stress on individualistic social relations.
Once the Mormon community was established, it is clear that the
co-operation required by irrigation agriculture of the Mormon
type and the general organization of the church strongly reinforced the value stress on communal social action.

It is of further significance that as the population expanded
and the Rimrock Mormons shifted from irrigation agricultural
pursuits to dry-land ranching in the region outside the Rimrock
Valley, the earlier co-operative patterns modeled on the mutual
irrigation company were applied to the solution of economic
problems that are identical to those faced by the Homesteaders.
Moreover, in midwestern and eastern cities to which Mormons
have recently moved, church wards have purchased and co-
operatively worked church welfare plan farms.

In Homestead, on the other hand, our evidence indicates that
the first settlers were drawn from a westward-moving population
which stressed a frontier type of self-reliance and individualism.
They were searching for a place where each man could "own his
own farm and be his own boss." Each family settled on its
isolated homestead claim, and there emerged from the beginning
an isolated farmstead type of settlement pattern in which the
nuclear family was the solidary unit. The service center which

was built up later simply occupied lots that were sold to store-keepers, filling station operators, the bartender, and others by the four families who owned the four sections which joined at a crossroads. Only two of these four family homes were located near the service center at the crossroads. The other two families continued to maintain their homes in other quarters of their sections and lived almost a mile from "town." In 1952 one of the former families built a new home located over a mile from the center of town and commented that they had always looked forward to "getting out of town."

There is no objective reason in the Homestead ecological setting why there could not be more clustering of houses into a compact village and more community co-operation than actually exists. One would not expect those farmers whose farms are located fifteen or twenty miles from the service center to live in "town" and travel out to work each day. But there is no reason why those families living within two or three miles of the village center could not live in town and work their fields from there. In typical Mormon villages a large percentage of the farms are located more than three miles from the farm homes. For example, in Rimrock over 31 per cent, in Escalante over 38 per cent, and in Ephraim over 30 per cent of the farms are located from three to eight or more miles from the center of the villages.[14]

It is clear that the Homesteaders were operating with a set of individualistic property arrangements (drawn, of course, from our generalized American culture) and that their strong stress on individualism led to a quite different utilization of these property patterns (than was the case with the Mormons) and to the establishment of a highly scattered type of community. Once Homestead was established, the individualism permitted by the scattered dry-land farming pattern, and encouraged by the emphasis on the small nuclear family unit and on multidenomi-nationalism in church affiliation, reacted on and strongly rein-forced the value stress on individual independence. It is evident that the Homesteaders continue to prefer this way of life, as shown by their remarks concerning the "bunched up" character of a Mormon village and the fact that a number of families have recently moved "out of town" when they built new houses.

Of further interest is the fact that when Homesteader families move to irrigated farms in the middle Rio Grande Valley, the stress on individual action tends to persist strongly. They do not readily develop co-operative patterns to deal with this new setting, which is similar to the situation in the irrigated valley of the Mormons at Rimrock. Indeed, one of the principal innovations they have been promoting in one region along the Rio Grande where they are replacing Spanish-Americans on the irrigated farming land is a system of meters on irrigation ditches. These meters will measure the water flowing into each individual farmer's ditches, effectively eliminating the need for more highly organized co-operative arrangements for distributing the available supply of water.

In conclusion, we should like to reiterate that we are strongly cognizant of situational factors. If the Rimrock Mormons had not been able to settle in a valley which was watered by melting snow packs from a nearby mountain, providing the possibilities for the construction of a storage reservoir, they certainly could not have developed an irrigation agricultural system at all. In the case of Rimrock, however, the actual site of settlement was selected from among several possible sites in a larger situation. The selection was largely influenced by Mormon preconceptions of the type of village they wished to establish. In fact, Mormons chose the irrigable valleys throughout the intermontane west. On the other hand, the physical environmental features for the development of irrigation were simply not present in the Homestead setting, and the people had no alternative to dry-land farming. There is no evidence to suggest that had they found an irrigable valley, they would have developed it along Mormon lines. In fact, the Homesteaders' activities in the Rio Grande Valley suggest just the opposite. It is clear that the situational facts did not *determine* in any simple sense the contrasting community structures which emerged. Rather, the situations set certain limits, but within these limits contrasting value orientations influenced the development of two quite different community types. It would appear that solutions to problems of community settlement pattern and the type of concrete social action which ensues are set in a value framework which importantly influences the selections made with the range of possibilities existing in an objective situation.

NOTES

The authors are indebted to the Rockefeller Foundation (Social Science Division) for the financial support of the research reported in this chapter as part of the Comparative Study of Values in Five Cultures Project of the Laboratory of Social Relations at Harvard

University. We also wish to express our appreciation to Ethel M. Albert, Wilfrid C. Bailey, Clyde Kluckhohn, Anne Parsons, and John M. Roberts for criticisms and suggestions in the preparation of the chapter.

1. Clyde Kluckhohn, "Values and Value-Orientations in the Theory of Action: An Exploration in Definition and Classification," in Talcott Parsons and E. A. Shils, eds., *Toward a General Theory of Action* (Cambridge: 1951), p. 410.

2. Talcott Parsons, *The Structure of Social Action* (Glencoe: 1949), pp. 43–86; *Essays in Sociological Theory* (Glencoe: 1949), pp. 32–40; *The Social System* (Glencoe: 1951), pp. 3–24.

3. "Rimrock" and "Homestead" are pseudonyms used to protect the anonymity of our informants.

4. For additional ecological details on the region, see Evon Z. Vogt, *Navaho Veterans: A Study of Changing Values,* Peabody Museum of Harvard University, Papers, XLI, No. 1 (1951), 11–12; and John Landgraf, *Land-Use in the Rimrock Area of New Mexico: An Anthropological Approach to Areal Study,* Peabody Museum of Harvard University, Papers, 1953.

5. Lowry Nelson, *The Mormon Village* (Salt Lake City: 1952), pp. 275–285.

6. See especially the reports of the Tolan Committee, U.S. Congress, "House Committee to Investigate the Interstate Migration of Destitute Citizens," 76th Congress, 3rd Session, Volume 6, Part 6, 1940.

7. The data from Rimrock are based on seven months' field experience in the community during 1950–1951. Additional data on this community will be provided in O'Dea's forthcoming monograph on *Mormon Values: The Significance of a Religious Outlook for Social Action,* published (Chicago: 1957) as *The Mormons.*

8. The Law of Consecration became the basis of the Mormon pattern of co-operative activity also known as "The United Order of Enoch." Cf. Joseph A. Geddes, *The United Order among the Mormons* (Salt Lake City: 1924); Edward J. Allen, *The Second United Order among the Mormons* (New York: 1936).

9. Nelson, *op. cit.,* pp. 25–54.

10. The data from Homestead are based on a year's field work in the community during 1949–1950. Additional data on this community are provided in Vogt's forthcoming monograph on *The Homesteaders: A Study of Values in a Frontier Community* published (Cambridge: 1955) as *Modern Homesteaders.* See also Vogt, "Water Witching: An Interpretation of a Ritual Pattern in a Rural American Community," *Scientific Monthly,* LXXV (September, 1952).

11. This relationship between churches and factionalizing tendencies has also been observed by Bailey in his unpublished study of a community in west Texas, in the heart of the ancestral home region of the present residents of Homestead. Cf. Wilfrid C. Bailey, "A Study of a Texas Panhandle Community; A Preliminary Report on Cotton Center, Texas," Values Study Files, Harvard University.

12. Cf. Nelson, *op. cit.,* p. 4.

13. *Ibid.,* pp. 28–38.

14. See *ibid.,* pp. 99 and 144, for data on Escalante and Ephraim.

SIX: Mormonism and the Avoidance of Sectarian Stagnation: A Study of Church, Sect, and Incipient Nationality

One of the many churches founded in the region south of the Great Lakes in the first half of the nineteenth century, the Church of Jesus Christ of Latter-day Saints, or the Mormon Church, alone avoided the stagnant backwaters of sectarianism. Founded in New York State in 1830 by a small group of men, it has today more than a million members in the United States and in its mission countries of Europe and the South Seas. It is the only religious body to have a clear majority of the population in a single state (Utah), and it has been the central and strategic group in the settlement of the intermountain West. Of its numerous dissident bodies, five survive, the largest of which has 100,000 members; the smallest, 24. The former, the Reorganized Church of Jesus Christ of Latter-day Saints, is an important denomination in parts of the Middle West.[1] From its founding the Mormon Church has set out to establish the Kingdom of God on earth and had created—once in Ohio, twice in Missouri, and once in Illinois—settlements in which this ideal was to be realized, only to see them consumed by external conflict and internal dissent. Finally, in 1847, the Mormons, harassed and persecuted, dispossessed of all but faith, leadership, and superb organization, crossed the plains and settled in the Utah desert. There, relying on these spiritual and sociological assets, they

From *American Journal of Sociology*, LX (November, 1954), © 1954 by the University of Chicago Press.

established a regional culture area bearing the pronounced imprint of their peculiar values and outlook.

This chapter attempts to answer two questions: (1) What enabled the Mormon Church to avoid sectarianism? (2) If the Mormon Church did not become a sect, is it, then, an ecclesiastical body or "church" in the sense in which that term has been understood in the sociology of religion since Ernst Troeltsch?[2] In answering these two questions, two others—of more general interest—suggest themselves; the first of interest to sociological theory, the second to the growing concern with interdisciplinary research: (3) Is the accepted dichotomy, church or sect, conceptually adequate to handle the empirical data in the sociology of religion? (4) Can sociological analysis alone adequately explain the emergence of one type of social structure as against another?

Presented here are the findings of a larger study of Mormon values and Mormon social institutions[3]—a study which involved an analysis of Mormon theology and religious teaching, the development of Mormon social institutions—ecclesiastical, political, economic, and educational—and a community study based on participant observation in a rural village, the characteristic product of Mormon efforts at settlement in the West.[4]

Church and Sect

Ernst Troeltsch and Max Weber define a sect as a body of believers based on contracted or freely elected membership in contrast to the institutional ecclesiastical body or church in which membership is ascribed. "Born into" and "freely chosen" signify the vital distinction. Park and Burgess, Simmel and von Wiese, and, following them, Becker elaborate this definition.[5] For them a church or *ecclesia* is characterized by the following: (1) membership on the basis of birth; (2) administration of the means of grace and its sociological and theological concomitants—hierarchy and dogma; (3) inclusiveness of social structure, often coinciding with ethnic or geographical boundaries; (4) orientation to the conversion of all; and (5) a tendency to compromise with and adjust to the world. The sect, on the contrary, is characterized by (1) separatism and defiance of or withdrawal from the demands of the secular sphere, preferring isolation to compromise; (2) exclusiveness, expressed in attitude and social structure; (3) emphasis on conversion prior to membership; and (4) voluntary election or joining.

The sect is often persecuted and is always ascetic. It usually rejects hierarchy and endeavors to implement the "priesthood of believers" in an egalitarian if narrow social organization. As H. Richard Niebuhr has observed, sectarianism, strictly defined, cannot outlast the founding generation[6] and, as Liston Pope has shown, often does not last it out.[7] The birth of children to the freely electing sectaries and the worldly success which so often crowns sectarian frugality and industry result in that adjustment to the world which Weber has called "the routinization of charisma." To cover this phenomenon, von Wiese and Becker introduce a third type, as does Niebuhr—the denomination. "Denominations are simply sects in an advanced stage of development and of adjustment to each other and the secular world."[8]

There have been attempts—often highly suggestive—to characterize the sectarian personality.[9] Von Wiese and Becker introduce a fourth type—the cult in which religion is private and personal; and Wach introduces another—the independent group. This latter is a semiecclesiastical body which starts out resembling a sect and through slow transformation and organizational differentiation becomes much more like a church. Wach's chief example is the Mormon Church. This classification is perceptive, but arguments will be given below to show that it is inadequate.

Wach also points out the impossibility of applying any of the above-mentioned criteria with rigor. Accepting the importance of sociological criteria and of theological and philosophical doctrines in differentiating sects from other religious bodies, he concludes that the characteristic attitude is most pertinent—an attitude which claims to be "renewing the original spirit of the absolute or relative beginnings" of a religious movement.[10] In what follows the criteria of von Wiese and Becker and of Wach are applied to Mormonism.

The Avoidance of Sectarianism

The Mormon Church claimed to be a divine restoration of the Apostolic Church after centuries of apostasy. The mark of the new dispensation was contemporary revelation. Through the prophet Joseph Smith, the Lord was believed to have called the elect. The result was the church which was founded in western New York, at the time a near frontier and the scene of a great religious enthusiasm.[11] To its converts it offered security—a resolution of the outer conflict and inner turmoil of denominational confusion and one which claimed the sanction of divine revelation. Convinced of a covenant to build the Kingdom of God on earth, the Latter-day Saints attempted to establish their settlements on the basis of the Law of Consecration, or United Order of Enoch, a plan announced by the prophet-founder which reconciled Christian socialism with private initiative and management.[12] This law was withdrawn in 1838 after some seven years of experiment marked by contentions and jealousies, and tithing was substituted for it.

The Mormon Church placed great emphasis on the restoration of Hebrew ideals and on the revival of Old Testament practices and institutions. The Saints were, they believed, a modern Israel: called by God, party to the covenant, and about to be gathered unto Zion. Polygamy was but one, although the most notorious, example of such revivals. In restoration and peculiarity, two important aspects of the Mormon gospel, the attitudes of renewal and exclusiveness characteristic of sects, were palpably present.

While commitment to building the Kingdom was sectarian insofar as it required withdrawal from the world and refusal to accommodate to the routine demands of secular life, it certainly had other possible implications. The idea of a Christian commonwealth was capable of quite nonsectarian interpretation. Moreover, the withdrawal from "Babylon" did not involve a repudiation of worldly pursuits, for in the City of God, the New Jerusalem, business, family life, government, and even armed defense would be acceptable and accepted. Nature was not seen as corrupted, and the vitiating effect of original sin on preternatural virtue was denied—a most unsectarian doctrine. Work and recreation were both accepted and sanctified. Against the sectarian notions of renewal and exclusiveness must be placed the nonsectarian possibilities of building a Christian society and the doctrine of human goodness—of total "undepravity."

Yet other groups had set out to build the Kingdom, and whatever nonsectarian possibilities lie hidden in the idea of a Christian commonwealth were never made apparent. How many sects built isolated little communities where prosperity followed upon the sectarian ascetic of work and thrift? Such settlements often reached a membership of a thousand and then stopped growing. Others experienced "swarming"; that is, excess numbers, usually in excess of a thousand, migrated and established a new settlement emulating the mother community but independent of its authority. This was the common sectarian fate. How were the Mormons to avoid it and realize the nonsectarian possibilities of their vision?

The Kirtland attempt to build the Kingdom failed because of internal dissent, external opposition, and economic distress—the last the most important. The Saints then migrated to Missouri and there at two points—Jackson County and Far West—endeavored to construct the New Jerusalem. Their strange doctrines claiming contemporary converse with God, their frugality and industry and consequent prosperity, their talk of making the region a "promised land," and their northern manners accentuated by rumors of abolition sentiments aroused the animosity of their neighbors. Consequently, they were driven from the land, and, crossing the Mississippi, the only eastward move in their long wanderings, they entered Illinois, where they built another city. Nauvoo, on the east bank of the river, saw the arrival of converts in great numbers, the first fruits of the European harvest. But there, too, hostility followed the Saints, and rumors that the leaders were practicing polygamy—rumors that turned out to be true—and a more defiant attitude from the Mormon leadership increased gentile antagonism. In 1844 Joseph Smith was murdered at Carthage jail, and in the next three years the Saints were driven from Nauvoo. In 1847, after a period of disorganization and hardship, they migrated to Utah under the leadership of Brigham Young.

In the West the church gained the respite needed for its internal recovery and at the same time the relative isolation required for establishing a civilization whose institutions would be informed by Mormon conceptions and Mormon values. In the 1880's and 1890's, however, the Mormon-gentile conflict broke out anew with considerable acuteness, the issues now being polygamy and the admission of Utah to the Union. After harsh federal legislation and prosecution of Mormon leaders, the church abandoned polygamy and accommodated itself to the demands of the larger American community into which it was reintegrated. Yet relative isolation had done its work: Utah and the surrounding region remained a Mormon culture area, although the implicit claim to it as an exclusive homeland was given up. Moreover, Mormon peculiarity and self-consciousness remained.

In this early period of Mormon history many marks of sectarianism were present: not only the attitude of renewal and exclusiveness but voluntary election as the basis of membership, withdrawal from the secular community, asceticism which placed a high value on hard work, persecution which increased in-group cohesion, and the conception of the priesthood of believers. The last doctrine, however, was not interpreted in terms of an egalitarian congregationalism. Rather it found expression in a hierarchical priesthood organization, authoritarian in structure and function. As the church grew, as its early charismatic leadership became more institutionalized in the leading offices, and as it had to stand against external threats, the early congregationalism gave way more and more to authoritarian rule.

What factors militated against the development of a typical sect in this situation? Two have already been mentioned: (1) *the nonsectarian possibilities of building the Kingdom which could require so much subtle accommodation* and (2) *the doctrine of natural goodness, by way of which nineteenth-century American optimism entered Mormon religious consciousness to blend there with the chiliastic expectations of a restorationist movement.* Yet the former alone could not effect the avoidance of sectarianism, as the record of many other groups makes clear; nor could the latter; although, when combined with other factors effective in the concrete situation, both could affect the issue in a powerful and pervasive manner. These two factors combined with the following eight to effect the issue:

3. *Universal missionary understanding of the notion of "gathering the elect."* The Mormon notion of peculiarity was exclusive, but it was not necessarily sectarian in the strictest sense. It was rather committed to missionary work: to calling the elect from the world. This was of great consequence when taken together with several other factors, despite its being a rather sectarian idea of missionary work.

4. *The temporal appropriateness of the doctrine in the late 1830's.* A generation before, the "gathering of the elect" might have been understood in terms of calling the elect from the neighboring counties. But in the second decade of the nineteenth century, American Protestantism had discovered a bigger world. The Mormons came upon the scene in time to inherit the newer

and broader definition. The universal understanding of calling the elect, combined with the new worldwide definition of the mission field, worked against a sectarian issue.

5. *The success of missionary work.* The ability of the Mormon gospel to bring meaning and hope to many, in America and in Europe, especially England and Scandinavia, resulted in thousands of conversions. With increased numbers, the notion of the holy city which the Saints were called to build now took on dimensions hardly compatible with sectarianism. Nauvoo had a population of 20,000 when Chicago had 5,000.

6. *The withdrawal of the Law of Consecration.* Had the Law of Consecration worked, the Mormons might have built another one of the successful communitarian settlements of which our history has seen so many. The failure of the Law, on the other hand, deprived them of a blueprint, rigid conformity to which could have been interpreted as the only permissible economic ethic, thereby lending a sectarian narrowness to their activities and inhibiting growth. Moreover, the Law was withdrawn by Joseph Smith in a revelation which still held up its ideals as the will of God. As a result, the flexibility of charismatic leadership was transmitted to the institutionalized church in economic matters, and its spirit vivified economic experiment for the next century, while a killing economic literalism was successfully eschewed. This is all the more striking, since in scriptural interpretation Mormons have generally been literalists.

7. *The failures and consequent necessity of starting again.* The need to start over again four times in sixteen years also contributed to flexibility, preventing a set routine from developing which could then have been imposed on new problems, thereby limiting growth and contributing to a sectarian atmosphere and structure. Combined with the withdrawal of the Law of Consecration, this made a dogmatism of minutiae impossible.

8. *The expulsion from the Middle West.* The Middle West, the continent's most attractive ecological area, was destined to draw large numbers of non-Mormon settlers. In such a situation it would have been quite impossible for the Mormon Church to maintain any hegemony, spiritual, political, or economic. Instead, it would in all likelihood have become one of a number of denominations accommodating to each other and to the secular world and thus would be reintegrated into the general American community with which it shared many common roots as another small and unimportant Protestant group.

9. *The choice and the existence of a large, unattractive expanse of land in the West.* The Mormon leadership deliberately chose an unattractive region to gain the necessary respite that isolation would give and resisted the seductions of more pleasant prospects. The existence of this arid region was something over which they had no control. It was unquestionably a prerequisite for the future form of their community. The result was the opening up of a huge area waiting to be converted from desert, supporting a scant nomadic population, to a Mormon culture area based on irrigation farming. This also gave the necessary time in isolation for Mormon social institutions to emerge and to "set."

10. *The authoritarian structure of the church and the central government which it made possible.* The existence of a charismatic leader in the early stages of Mormon Church history whose right to rule was believed to be based on divine election and the consequent authoritarian and hierarchical structure of church government permitted scattered settlement in the West under central direction. Such authoritarian characteristics were strengthened by the external conditions of conflict and hardship. Centrifugal tendencies in the West were restrained when not completely inhibited. The priesthood structure and the routinization of prophetic rule might in other circumstances have been completely compatible with sectarianism; yet in the western settlement they combined with open and relatively empty and isolated land, and missionary success and consequent emigration, to make large-scale settlement possible under central government. This combination ruled out the last chance of sectarianism.

These last eight factors, then, combined to militate against a sectarian issue to the Mormon experiment and to bring into existence the Mormon Church of the present day. Instead of becoming a sect, the church became the core of a large culture area. In these eight factors and their combination we have the answer to our first question.

Neither Church Nor Sect

The Mormon Church is excluded by definition from the category of church or *ecclesia,* unless it has become one in the course of its development. Similarly with regard to the category of denomination: since we have defined denominations as "routinized sects," Mormonism, having avoided sectarianism, at the same time avoided denominationalism. However, to be of genuine interest, these two statements must be true in more than a formal sense: they must be more than mere analytical inferences from definitions. The question is, then: Has the Mormon Church become an ecclesiastical body in the course of its evolution?

Despite the avoidance of typical sectarian structure and isolation, the Mormon Church has displayed and retained many sectarian characteristics. Most important are: (1) a sense of peculiarity, of election, and of covenant, which is reinforced by explicit theological doctrine; (2) a tendency to withdrawal from the gentile world (this is now most frequently expressed in admonition and symbolic practices; yet it found large-scale expression in the Church Welfare Plan with which the Mormon Church sought to meet the Great Depression as a separate body capable of considerable autarchy); (3) a commitment to "warning the world" and "gathering the elect," the implications of which have been more routine and less dramatic since the accommodation which followed the defeat of the church on the polygamy issue; and (4) chiliastic expectations, still important not only among rural groups but in the writings of some leaders of the church.

While the Mormons have never identified group membership with peculiarity of dress as sectarists have frequently done, the strict interpretation of Joseph Smith's no-liquor, no-tobacco counsel serves an analogous function today and has become the focus of the expression of exclusivist sentiments. Moreover, although persecution has stopped, the memory of it preserves ingroup solidarity and strengthens loyalty.

Yet despite the *notae* of the sect, the basic fact in Mormon history since 1890 has been the accommodation of the church to the demands of the larger gentile community. The abandonment of polygamy—that camel at which many strained but which became so identified with loyalty that all were willing to suffer in its defense—was the surrender of what had become the typical Mormon institution. Economic experimentation—the communism of the United Order, for example—became less characteristic of Mormon activities, and, in general, the secular demands of Babylon displaced the earlier enthusiasm for the New Jerusalem. Even the successes of earlier fervor strengthened the trend to accommodation. Having become the dominant group over a large culture area, the Mormon Church experienced the conservatism of the successful, which was not likely to upset a working equilibrium. The involvement of church leadership in established political, economic, and educational institutions, the education of children, the comparatively long-established hierarchy and dogma—all display ecclesiastical features of Mormon organization. The demand for conversion and the aversion to the ecclesiastical practice of infant baptism were soon institutionally compromised in the baptism of the eight-year-old children of Mormon families.

This combination of sectarian characteristics with structure, policy, and circumstances similar to many *ecclesiae* suggests that the Mormon Church is a mixture of the pure categories outlined in our typology. Joachim Wach, recognizing this problem—specifically about the Mormons and generally in such typologies—has characterized the Mormon Church as an independent group with semi-ecclesiastical organization.[13] It is, for Wach, neither church nor sect; it is an independent group through whose organization its members have access to the necessary means of salvation.

In terms of theology and group structure there is considerable justification for Wach's classification. Yet, in larger terms, there is more to be said. The Mormon restoration was not only a Christian renewal; it was a Hebrew revival. Mormondom conceived itself as a modern Israel. This alone is not uncommon in Christian experience, and we are likely to take it for granted. Yet in the Mormon case, contemporary conditions of life were to give the revival of Hebrew ideals a more genuine content than would have been possible in smaller groups in less demanding circumstances. The acceptance of a model is always important in the patterning of subsequent behavior, and in the Mormon case the model of the chosen people could not but affect Mormon belief and behavior: polygamy is but the most notorious example.

Guided by this model, the Saints withdrew from the modern Babylon to build the modern Zion. Owing to circumstances over which they had little control, they found themselves wandering in the wilderness. They had sought but part of the Israelitish parallel; circumstances had provided the rest. For sixteen years they were driven about, attempting four times to build their city. Their size, the extent and duration of their suffering, and the way in which defeat several times crowned the most palpable successes combined to transform the bread and water of sectarian

affliction into the real presence of national potentiality. Common
effort in success and in failure, common suffering from elemental
and human adversaries, even common struggle with arms against
common enemies—all these lent to the symbolic emulation of
ancient Israel an existential reality which devoted sectaries in
more (or less) fortunate circumstances could hardly surmise.
Mormonism lived its Exodus and Chronicles, not once but many
times. It had its Moses and its Joshua. Circumstances had given
it a stage on which its re-enactment of biblical history was
neither farce nor symbolic pageant.

Throughout this intense group experience—an experience
which produced a genuine folk tradition in a decade and a half—
Mormon family life and Mormon economic and political activity
continued. During this time the Mormons courted and married,
begat children and reared them, and established ties of consanguinity and affinity—made more numerous and complex by
polygamy—which reinforced and impenetrated those of membership in the church. Economic activity, both co-operative and
private, and political necessities established further bonds. Moreover, in the years of wandering the Saints spent their lives in
largely Mormon surroundings. This was even more true in the
years that followed 1847, when geographical reinforced social
isolation.

Fellowship in the Gospel became—and remains today—supported by and imbedded in a matrix of kinship. The circum-
stance of enforced nomadism and of successive resettlement,
brought about by no design of the Saints and yet in close
emulation of their Hebraic model, was experienced in a manner
that would guarantee its transmission as informal family history
as well as the more formally taught church history. In each
attempt at settlement a group increasingly conscious of itself as a
chosen vessel established its holy city—its spiritual and temporal
homeland—only to be driven out under circumstances that
strengthened in-group loyalty and increased self-consciousness.
In Utah a homeland was finally found where "the desert would
blossom as the rose," and all previous Mormon history was
reinterpreted as precursory of this final fruition in "the place
which God for us prepared." The death of Joseph on the eastern
side of the Mississippi was the final act of the first stage, as was
that of Moses on the borders of the land of Canaan. It was the
first stage in the development of incipient nationhood. The

members of the Church of Jesus Christ of Latter-day Saints had become—to use the significant term often used most casually by the Mormons themselves—the "Mormon people." Moreover, the Mormon people had found a homeland. The ties of religious faith were reinforced by those of blood and marriage, of common group memories often involving suffering and heroism, of common economic and cultural aspirations—and now by a region whose very physiognomy would become symbolic of another and perhaps greater group achievement, the successful settlement in the desert.

The Mormons were not completely unaware of what they had become. It is true that their American patriotism, which was an article of faith with them, inhibited any movement for national independence, and they tended to see their own religious homeland as part of a secular manifest destiny. Yet the latter was certainly subordinate to a religious conception of Zion in the mountaintops. In 1850 the Mormons established the state of Deseret—much larger than present-day Utah—and applied for admission to the Union. The covenant people would become an American state rather than an independent nation. In Nauvoo they had been virtually a state within a state through grant of a special charter from the Illinois legislature, and all previous attempts to build the city were characterized by considerable autonomy. The Civil War had not yet settled certain limitations of autonomy, nor had postwar developments in politics, economics, and technology made autonomy seem so far-fetched as one might imagine in today's conditions. Moreover, it must be recalled that, in moments of passion in the Mormon-gentile conflict, separatism and secession were openly considered and that armed, if inconclusive, conflict with federal forces did take place.

The Mormons had gone from near sect to near nation. The Zionism of the nineteenth-century Mormons stopped short of the national fulfillment of the Jewish Zionism of the twentieth century. Yet the Saints had in large part realized the implications of the model which had guided them in such auspicious circumstances. If their own patriotism combined with their defeat in the Mormon-gentile conflict to inhibit the full fruition of national sovereignty, Mormondom, nevertheless, became a subculture with its own peculiar conceptions and values, its own self-consciousness, and its own culture area. The Mormons, in a word, had become a people, with their own subculture within the larger American culture and their own homeland as part of the American homeland.

Conclusion

We have now answered the first two questions. A peculiar concatenation of ten factors—ideal, matters of conceptions and values; historical, matters of unique concomitance or convergence in time; and structural, matters of social structure—combine to explain how the Mormon Church escaped sectarianism. In avoiding the fate of an isolated sect which had been the nemesis of so many other restorationist religious groupings, it did not become either a denomination or a church in the sense of the accepted definitions, although it displayed characteristics of both. Rather, the emulation of the Old Testament Hebrews in the unsettled conditions of the nineteenth-century Middle and Far West resulted in the emergence of a Mormon people—a phenomenon not unlike the emergence of nations and empires from religious groups in the past or in our own day. The development of nationhood, such as we have seen in contemporary Jewish Zionism, or in the fulfillment of the aspirations of Indian Islam, was inhibited by American patriotic convictions on the part of the Latter-day Saints themselves and by the integrating power of the larger American community; yet the flare-up of separatist sentiment in the heat of conflict suggests the possibilities of development, had circumstances been different.

What of the third and fourth questions asked above?

The dichotomy of church and sect and their derivatives—independent group and denomination—do not exhaust the possibilities which are offered by empirical research in the sociology of religion. The development of a people with a peculiar culture and with developed self-consciousness as well as a native region identified with themselves and their group "myth" is another possibility as was realized in the history of Mormonism.[14]

The final question is whether sociological analysis alone can adequately explain the emergence of one type of social structure as against another. Ten factors have been given as preventing the Mormon Church from becoming a sect despite a theological and sociological tendency in the sectarian direction. Eight of these have been presented as particularly effective. It should be noted that, of these, all but the third and tenth factors are matters of historical contingency. That is, in the cases of factors 4 through 7 unique convergence of specific events must be considered in any adequate explanation. These matters could hardly have been predicted from, or be explained in terms of, a purely sociological frame of reference. It would seem that sociology in the uncontrolled field situation—and most significant problems are still in that category—must not attempt to solve its problems in terms of abstract schemata which do not take account of historical contingency and which abstract from time. From another point of view it may be said that intellectual analysis of the content of conceptions and values often gives a much richer understanding and a much safer lead concerning their implications for social action than do categorizations in terms of highly abstract schemata. Yet this difficulty seems less formidable than the historical. The inability of sociological analysis alone to predict or explain the emergence of one type of social structure as against another must be granted, at least in the present example.

This concession has great significance for sociology, whether in the planning of research or in the training of specialists. It proves again the importance of interdisciplinary co-operation. This may be either what Linton used to call several disciplines under one skull or collaboration between social scientists and scholars across departmental lines. In larger research it must certainly mean the latter.

NOTES

1. Elmer T. Clark, *The Small Sects in America* (New York: 1937). Clark gives the following dissidents besides the Reorganized Church: Bickertonites, Hedrickites, Strangites, and Cutlerites. None of these groups had over 1,500 members; the Cutlerites had about two dozen and practiced community of property.

2. See Joachim Wach, *The Sociology of Religion* (Chicago: 1944), pp. 195 ff.

3. This research was done as part of the Values Study Project of the Laboratory of Social Relations of Harvard University and was supported financially and otherwise by the project. It will be published in the forthcoming monograph by the writer entitled "Mormon Values: The Significance of a Religious Outlook for Social Action," published (Chicago: 1957) as *The Mormons*.

4. See Lowry Nelson, *The Mormon Village* (Salt Lake City: 1953).

5. Robert Park and Ernest W. Burgess, *Introduction to the Science of Sociology* (Chicago: 1921), pp. 50, 202–203, 611–612, 657, 870–874; Howard Becker, *Systematic Sociology: On the Basis of the "Beziehungslehre und Gebildelehr" of Leopold von Wiese: Adapted and Amplified* (New York: 1932), pp. 624–628.

6. H. Richard Niebuhr, *The Social Sources of Denominationalism* (New York: 1929), pp. 17 ff.

7. Liston Pope, *Millhands and Preachers: A Study of Gastonia* (New Haven: 1942).

8. Becker, *op. cit.*

9. See John L. Gillin, "A Contribution to the Sociology of Sects," *American Journal of Sociology*, XVI (1910), 236 ff.; Robert P. Casey, "Transient Cults," *Psychiatry*, IV (1941), 525 ff.; and Ellsworth Faris, "The Sect," in *The Nature of Human Nature* (New York: 1937), Chapter V.

10. Wach, *op. cit.*, pp. 194–196. For an excellent discussion of the church-sect problem, see *ibid.*, pp. 195–205, and especially his later "Church, Denomination, and Sect," Chapter IX in *Types of Religious Experience* (Chicago: 1951), pp. 187–208.

11. Whitney Cross, *The Burned-over District* (Ithaca: 1950).

12. See Doctrine and Covenants 42:30–36; also 51:1–16; 70:3, 9; 104; 82; and 92. This is a standard scriptural work of the Mormon Church and contains the revelations of Joseph Smith. See also Leonard Arrington, "Early Mormon Communitarianism," *Western Humanities Review*, VII, No. 4 (Autumn, 1953), 341–369; and also Arthur E. Bestor, Jr., *Backwoods Utopias: The Sectarian and Owenite Phases of Communitarian Socialism in America: 1663–1829* (Philadelphia: 1950).

13. Wach, *The Sociology of Religion*, pp. 194–197.

14. After I had worked through my data to the conclusion that Mormonism developed into something like an incipient nationality I found the following paragraph in Park and Burgess, *op. cit.*, pp. 872–873: "Once the sect has achieved territorial isolation and territorial solidarity, so that it is the dominant power within the region that it occupies, it is able to control the civil organization, establish schools and a press, and so put the impress of a peculiar culture upon all the civil and political institutions that it controls. In this case it tends to assume the form of a state, and become a nationality. Something approaching this was achieved by the Mormons in Utah." Although Park did nothing more with the idea, its statement here leaves little to be desired in clarity—a strong argument in favor of more familiarity with the masters of American sociology.

SEVEN: The Effects of Geographical Position on Belief and Behavior in a Rural Mormon Village

In his analysis of Mormon settlement in Alberta, Canada, Lowry Nelson indicates the contribution of religious institutions and religious beliefs to successful settlement in frontier conditions.[1] Especially concerning the village of Orton, Nelson shows that religious institutions held the settlers to their community when the physical difficulties were extreme. Religious beliefs and institutions enabled the Latter-day Saints to conquer difficult frontiers not only in Canada but also in Utah and the Southwest. Equally interesting to sociology, however, is the reverse relationship: the role of frontier conditions, that is, of peripheral situation, in the perseverance of religious institutions themselves. As in so many matters of interest to sociologists, there is a two-way relation, a feedback, here also. Not only did religion act as an important factor enabling the Mormons to subdue forbidding areas but the isolation and "peripheralness" of these areas also contributed to strengthening Mormon religious sentiments and institutions.

The present study, unfortunately, is not a planned and controlled one. It is rather an attempt to subject material collected for other purposes to comparative examination. Nelson's study is an analysis of the Mormon village as a pattern and technique of land settlement. It includes an examination of the most striking trends to be seen in rural Mormon villages today. Three villages

From *Rural Sociology*, XIX (December, 1954), 358–364.

in Utah, all studied originally in the mid-twenties, are resurveyed, and these in particular provide a base point from which to measure change and a re-examination point at which to observe it. The present study is of a Mormon village in northwestern New Mexico and is a part of a larger analysis of Mormon values and their influence on settlement and social institutions.

The most striking difference between the village to be discussed here and the villages studied by Nelson is one of geographic position. Let us take this characteristic as the independent variable and assume that in all other important particulars these villages are drawn from a homogeneous universe. This is by no means a rigorous statement; yet, if taken in a general way, such an approach to comparison is highly suggestive. All the villages here were founded as part of a deliberate and conscious Mormon effort to establish settlements which would embody, and provide a proper setting for, the Mormon way of life. From an economic point of view, there do not appear to be any more serious differences between Nelson's three villages and the writer's one than among Nelson's three alone. There is an important difference in size, but this chapter will attempt to show that size in this case is a function of geographical position, which is here taken as the independent variable.

There are two additional supporting theses which may be submitted in defense of this procedure. It is, although not rigorous, in the tradition of comparative studies which have added much to sociological knowledge, Weber's larger—but also not rigorous—study of comparative religion being the most illustrious example. Moreover, the hypothesis—that isolation and peripheral position tend to strengthen distinctive in-group social institutions and beliefs—is supported by a larger study of Mormon history.[2]

Rimrock—A Village on the Periphery of Mormondom

Rimrock,[3] located in northwestern New Mexico, was settled in the late 1870's as part of a larger Mormon project to plant settlements in the region of the Little Colorado River. Even at the time of settlement, it was on the periphery of Mormon pioneering efforts. It was originally set up as an outpost for missionary work among the Indians to whose conversion the Mormons were especially dedicated, believing them, as they did, to be descendants of apostate Hebrews. Although there was some polygamy practiced in the early settlement, it was definitely not established as a refuge for those prosecuted under federal antipolygamy legislation, as was the case with the first wave of Canadian Mormon settlement. The first settlers in Rimrock were "called" by the church; that is to say, they were chosen and sent on their task by the church leadership.

The settlement was located in the southern part of the Colorado Plateau at an elevation of approximately 7,000 feet, in country characterized by mesas and canyons and with flora and fauna typical of the Upper Sonoran Life Zone. The village was placed at the base of a mountain range which rises as high as 9,000 feet, a site purposely chosen by the Mormon pioneers because it offered the possibility of collecting winter water by means of a storage dam and thus making irrigation farming possible. Average annual precipitation is about 14 inches, but varies greatly from year to year. Water, even with the present excellent storage reservoir, is an ever-present problem. The early years were difficult, indeed. Drought, rust, and the breaking of the rock-and-earth dam which the settlers had constructed added to the troubles of the pioneers. Moreover, the Mormon settlers had squatted on land which was owned by a land company, and they were forced to buy it at an exorbitant price to avoid eviction. In these crises they received substantial aid, in cash and seed, from the general authorities of the church in Salt Lake City. One Mormon leader called this settlement the "toughest proposition in the Church." Like Orton,[4] Rimrock would have been abandoned without the religious motivation and the religious institutional framework which kept its settlers at their tasks.

In 1950, when the data for the present study were collected, Rimrock was a Mormon village of about 250 inhabitants. With the passing of the years, emphasis had shifted from missionary work to farming, especially cattle raising. Irrigation farming provided alfalfa, wheat, and garden vegetables. The church, with its hierarchically structured priesthood and its auxiliary organizations which activate women and youth, is the central core of the village. Local co-operatives, such as the cattle company, the irrigation company, and the water company, grew out of church activities. The church provides today the basic structure not only for religious life but also for civic life and much of economic life. The village embodies the classic Mormon design.[5] Its pattern of life and social relations reflects the basic ideal of Mormon settlement throughout the West. Its physical layout is based on the Nauvoo revision of Joseph Smith's plat for the City of Zion.

Nelson's Conclusions

In his definitive study, Lowry Nelson has demonstrated the existence of two trends among the villages of the Mormon area. The first is a tendency away from the compact village pattern of settlement that has been characteristically Mormon and derives from the policy of the church in the settlement period. This tendency was by no means uniformly found. Nelson says that "the persistence of the village pattern among the Mormons depends upon the character of the physical environment in which particular communities are located."[6] Dispersion was not found in Escalante or in Ephraim, either in the mid-twenties or in the resurvey made in 1950. It was found in American Fork in both periods. Nelson states that "there is little question that dispersion on farms will continue in the valleys along the front of the Wasatch Range from Utah County on the south to Cache County on the north."[7] He documents this trend further by the data of a study of four villages in Cache County and four villages in Utah County made by the Bureau of Reclamation.[8] Nelson notes that a "line village pattern is emerging in Utah, Davis and Weber counties."[9] Nelson's second tendency, and probably the more important in relation to the present study, is secularization of life in the Mormon villages. He gives some seven criteria of secularization, all of which he found in the three Utah villages:

> In some respects, if not most, the villages described in this volume represent in microcosm the changes that are transpiring in American rural life in general. Urbanization, or as some sociologists call it, secularization of life is proceeding at a rapid pace. Communication and transportation devices which characterize contemporary life place the remotest corners in instantaneous contact with the world. The diffusion of urban traits to the countryside is everywhere apparent. Farming is becoming more mechanized and efficient.

Farmers are declining in numbers and farms increasing in size. Life becomes more impersonal, mutual aid declines, and contractual forms of association increase. Formal organizations multiply as new interests arise—economic, social, recreational, educational. New occupations come into being as specialization and division of labor grow more elaborate. Homogeneity of the population gives way to increasing heterogeneity. Attitudes change. The sense of *community* suffers as cleavages develop around special interests. These developments are clearly evident in the Mormon villages today, as they are in the communities of the United States elsewhere.[10]

Rimrock Compared with Nelson's Villages

PERSISTENCE OF THE VILLAGE PATTERN

In Utah, Nelson found the persistence of the village pattern dependent on the physical environment of the communities. In some areas, the trend was definitely away from the village pattern and toward either dispersed dwelling on farms or a line village pattern. In Rimrock, the village pattern appears secure. In 1950, there were 31 families and 172 individuals in Rimrock out of a total of 41 families and 244 individuals who lived in the blocked area of the village. If one accepts living within a half-mile of the village center as the definition of village dweller, there were 38 village-dwelling families out of the total of 41. Moreover, a town lot was divided into eight house lots in the winter of 1950 and placed for sale by the local church ward, which had purchased it from the estate of a deceased former resident. Thus, while there is some expansion along two roads leading out of the village—one toward the nearest large town and shopping center, and one to the storage reservoir—there is immediate likelihood of residential building in the village itself.

Since two of the Utah villages studied by Nelson are comparable to Rimrock in regard to persistence of the village pattern, this characteristic does not distinguish Rimrock in any significant way from villages nearer the center of the Mormon domain. Yet some comment deserves to be made. One questions if physical terrain is an important factor in keeping the village pattern in Rimrock. The peripheral location of Rimrock, whose inhabitants are very conscious of their Mormonism, sets up a situation where a move from Rimrock is a move away from the Mormon area. This would not be true in the same sense in any of the Utah villages studied and reported in Nelson's research. The most that can be said as a result of the comparison made here is that Rimrock is maintaining its Mormon character, in terms of persistence of the village pattern, as well as any village reported in Nelson's work. Six months of participant observation in the village suggest that the fact of being culturally peripheral is more important than the physical characteristics in making this so.

SECULARIZATION

Certain aspects of urbanization have been felt in Rimrock as they have been in rural villages, Mormon and non-Mormon, throughout the country. Moving pictures are shown every week in the local "churchhouse." Almost every house has a radio. Nonchurch publications are subscribed to and read. There is a local elementary and high school, which is part of the county and state school system. Many automobiles are owned in the village, and trips of forty-five miles to the nearest large town for shopping and recreation are common. Moreover, employment outside the village has been fairly common since early days of settlement when Mormon pioneers took jobs in temporary lumber camps throughout the region. Thirty-two Mormon youths from the village were called into the service in World War II, and all returned to dwell in the village. Thus connections with and influence from the outside non-Mormon world are frequent and common.

Yet if we understand "secularization of life" to indicate a departure from certain earlier Mormon standards of rural village community life, Rimrock has not been affected to anywhere near the degree indicated by Nelson's study of the Utah villages. Four indices of secularization, or trends away from earlier Mormon ideals, which Nelson found "clearly evident" in the Utah villages are discussed below as to their presence in Rimrock.

1. *Decline in the number of farmers.* While farms have increased in size in Rimrock as in the other Mormon villages, there has not been a drop in the proportion of farmers in the population. The Mormon preference for agriculture keeps farming *a* preferred, and often *the* preferred, form of earning a livelihood. Also, those who are employed outside the village remain engaged in part-time agriculture.

2. *Multiplication of formal organizations (outside the church).*
Rimrock is still an old-fashioned Mormon village, in a structural
sense. That means that the church and its auxiliary organizations
make up the organized center of village life. Priesthood councils
play the role of civic bodies elsewhere. There is an irrigation and
a land-and-cattle company, both co-operatively organized and
both emerging from the church organization. The only organization in the village of a purely secular origin (outside of political
bodies like the school board) is the Parent-Teacher Association.
It was formed within the last few years. Its main moving spirits
were a non-Mormon woman married to a Mormon husband and
a Mormon woman married to a gentile husband. It is definitely
marginal so far as strategic influence on village life is concerned,
although it has enlisted wide community support. There have
been formed no other voluntary organizations outside the
church. The local Boy Scout troop is part of the church youth
movement.

3. *Increase in impersonality and contractual relationships.* There
are contractual, that is to say, business relationships between
residents. Yet they are embedded in a larger context of face-to-
face relationships. The villagers are all conscious of their fellowship in the Mormon gospel and are all active in the local
organizations of the church. Moreover, this religious and social
bond is backed up and impenetrated by the bonds of consanguinity and affinity. Most of the villagers are related in one way
or another and are, moreover, connected by ties of blood and
marriage to the rest of Mormondom. Family lineage and religious fellowship are so close and so important that it would be
impossible for sheerly impersonal relationships to become of
dominant importance in social relations.

4. *Homogeneity gives way to increasing heterogeneity; the sense
of community suffers as cleavages develop around special interests.*
The loss of a sense of community and the decline in homogeneity
have not progressed far in Rimrock. Six months of close participant observation revealed a deep sense of community. Reactions
to current problems, repair of streets, volunteer work to construct
a new high school, and the like evoked a response which bears
testimony to a vital sense of community. Special interests there
are, but they have not split the village into contending factions.
There is a great discrepancy in the distribution of wealth. Some
villagers are quite wealthy, while others have had to depend on

aid from church relief. In 1950, a year of great prosperity in the cattle market and therefore a good year for many Rimrock farmers, seven families received aid from church relief. These included some older couples. Yet there are not two communities—one of the rich and one of the poor. There is village solidarity both in consciousness and in action. Moreover, since the foundation of the village there have been family cleavages. These persist, although they may, in fact, be weaker now than at an earlier period. Yet these do not prove themselves divisive in a larger sense of village unity and especially in dealings with outsiders, where complete solidarity is usually shown.

On these four criteria, Rimrock shows itself to be far less secularized than the villages studied by Nelson. In this sense, Rimrock is more like a Mormon village of a generation ago in Utah than like the present villages reported in Nelson's resurvey.

Summary and Conclusion

Rimrock, by the criteria of Nelson's study, is far less secularized and far more congruent with the ideal of the Mormon village as established by the pioneers throughout Mormondom than any of the Utah villages studied by him. The chief difference between this northern New Mexico village and those of Nelson's study is that Rimrock is located on the periphery of the Mormon culture area. Except for size, there are no other outstanding facts about or factors influencing Rimrock social and economic development which distinguish it from the villages in Nelson's sample. Yet size is in large part a result of the geographic location of Rimrock on the periphery of the Mormon area. Most of the land around the village is owned by non-Mormons, and much of it is part of an Indian reservation. Thus, position has made it impossible for the village to expand in the last fifty years. On the other hand, its peculiarity and relative isolation have kept it from being assimilated into any other larger groupings.

Isolation and peripheral location appear to deepen and make more important the ties of Rimrock with the rest of Mormondom. Church conferences in the stake (Arizona) and in Salt Lake City are attended by Rimrock people. Alone, the only village of its kind in the area, Rimrock feels its peculiarity. The highly developed educational system of the Latter-day Saints Church inculcates into the villagers the belief that they are "gathered unto Zion," that they are "a peculiar, a covenant people." Their own position on the edge of Mormondom makes it possible for them to experience their own distinction, both in their consciousness of themselves as a group apart with its own history and in the attitudes of outsiders toward them. Removed from the center of Mormondom, they cannot take it for granted. Alone and needing the consciousness of membership in the larger whole as well as the tangible financial aid the church has given them from time to time, the Rimrock Mormons still experience their own distinctness from the gentile world—from Babylon—in a way reminiscent of the earlier generations of Mormon pioneers. All Mormons are rightly aware of the distinction involved here, but residence on the periphery—where the contrast of Saint and gentile, mine and thine, is a continual and constant reminder—never permits the memory to become merely a memory.

Moreover, located on the edge, Rimrock Mormons contact the Mormons of the center only under the most auspicious circumstances and in the most favorable representatives. Traveling apostles of the church and others of the kind come from time to time to Rimrock. Rimrock Mormons see the best side of the church when they attend stake and general conferences in Arizona and at Salt Lake City. In this they are like converts in mission countries who see only the exemplary conduct of the missionaries, and not the sins of the fellow members at home. Isolation thus not only enhances the ties with the church but also makes the interaction of periphery and center a kind which will enhance Rimrock's respect for the church still more.

The Mormon consciousness of Rimrock has the alertness of the outpost about it. This is to be gathered from attitudes expressed in church attendance and activities, or in oral declaration at sacrament meetings or in conversation. Moreover, an application of the criteria of Nelson's study reveals that the social relations, the social attitudes, and the social organization of the village have not felt, in any very noticeable way, the impact of the secularizing tendencies felt elsewhere.

This comparison suggests one answer. Peripheral position cannot create strong belief; but given strong belief, peripheral position and isolation can act to strengthen belief and the in-group solidarity based on the consensus of common belief. This will be reflected in the social organization evolved in the development of group life. Isolation will tend to remove the group from outside influences and to make it resistant to those which impinge on it. In the latter, especially, geographic position has been of great importance in Rimrock.

NOTES

1. Lowry Nelson, *The Mormon Village: A Pattern and Technique of Land Settlement* (Salt Lake City: 1952), pp. 213–272.

2. This problem will be dealt with in greater length in the writer's forthcoming monograph, *Mormon Values: The Significance of a Religious Outlook for Social Action,* published (Chicago: 1957) as *The Mormons.*

3. Data on this village were gathered by the writer in six months of field work in the community in 1950–1951 as a part of a comparative study of five cultures financed by the Rockefeller Foundation. This research was done through the support of the Values Study of the Laboratory of Social Relations, Harvard University. The forthcoming monograph (note 2) represents research done under the auspices of the Values Study. Rimrock is a pseudonym, in keeping with project policy.

4. Nelson, *op cit.,* pp. 249–260.

5. *Ibid.,* pp. 23–54. Also see Joseph A. Geddes and Carmen D. Fredrickson, *Utah Housing in Its Group and Community Aspects.* AES Bull. 321, Utah State Agricultural College (Logan, Utah: 1945), pp. 73–77.

6. Nelson, *op cit.,* p. 275.

7. *Ibid.,* p. 276.

8. Carl C. Taylor, assisted by Walter Goldschmidt and Glen Taggart, *Patterns of Rural Settlement,* Columbia Basin Joint Investigations, Bureau of Reclamation, Department of the Interior (Washington, D.C.: 1947), p. 26.

9. Nelson, *op. cit.,* p. 276.

10. *Ibid.,* pp. 276–277.

EIGHT: Mormonism and the American Experience of Time

I

"We live our lives forward," said Kierkegaard, "although we understand them backwards." And Cassirer has noted that we cannot describe organic processes without reference to the future. It is even more true of those historical processes which, involving the interactions of men, are to be understood only in terms of thought and ambition. This is to say that human life, both on the biological level and on the level of meaning, involves development and growth, realization and fulfillment. The human condition is characterized by what Aristotle called the reduction of potency to act, accounting for man's ability to conceive the merely possible—an ability which Kant considered constitutive of human intelligence—and at the same time testifying to man's transcendence above the processes of his own historical and biological existence. Man is both in and out of time. As a result he is capable of forming an attitude toward his own temporality; he develops a *conception* of time, and conceptions of time differ from society to society and from culture to culture.

Most societies, primitive and civilized, seem to have conceived the future as part of a circle to be experienced by human subjects, but to be experienced *again*. Life is an eternal procession and an eternal return. History is a cycle. "Men in their generations are like the leaves of the trees. The wind blows and one year's leaves are scattered on the ground: but the trees burst into bud and put on fresh ones when the spring comes round. In the same way one generation flourishes and another nears its

From *Western Humanities Review,* VIII (Summer, 1954), 181–190 end."[1] In the Orient, the way of the mystic promised escape from this round, but as for time itself, its direction was circular.

Western civilization is based on a different conception of time, in fact on a unique conception of time. The Judeo-Christian tradition is the bearer of a conception of time which is no longer circular, but proceeds toward fulfillment—toward accomplishment. For in the Messianic hopes of Jewry was a new conception of realization, which was freed from organic incorporation into ecological or biological rhythms. Spinoza observed that the genius of the Jews was not in philosophy, but in prophecy. It is, indeed, in terms of prophecy that the new conception of time is to be understood. Prophecy is not simply, nor even primarily, prediction; it is expectation. It is expectation impenetrated with aspiration—a state of tension in the face of the future which Christians call hope. Christianity representing the accomplishment of Israel, the fullness of time, with its doctrine of the unique historical event, the Incarnation of the *Logos,* freed Western thought from the tyranny of the cycle. "St. Augustine in his *City of God* was the first to develop that Christian concept of history according to which mankind as a whole is to actualize a purpose in the world throughout the succession of generations. Thus history has a teleological structure: every nation may hope to fulfill its own mission through the development of its particular religious, political, or scientific faculties."[2]

With the secularization of Western thought in the modern period, the notion of Christian hope and expectation has been replaced by the idea of progress. With such a shift of view, the utopia—the classical literary product of man's transcendence over his historical specificity—becomes more believable. Plato knew that the commonwealth set forth in the *Republic* would not work—until philosophers became kings or kings, philosophers. Nor was More a victim of what we might call "utopian illusions." With secularization, however, the fulfillment of history, which in Christian terms was to mark the end of history, was more and more conceived as an event to take place within history. It is not just the rude facts of the human situation and the frailties of the human condition that make every utopian viewpoint rationally indefensible. It is the inherent contradiction of the very conception itself. The idea of a fulfillment of time within time—of an accomplishment within the realm of becoming—is what is implied by the notion of utopia. It is, on sober analysis, unthinkable. In our present world of contention and

disorder, Marxism and the evangelical call it utters to the
oppressed of the world is a typical example of dechristianized
eschatological aspiration. It is not to be deduced from scientific
principles or inducted from empirical experience. It is believed
by men because it appeals to something far deeper than
demonstration.

Marxism is at the same time the child of the Enlightenment,
for it is through the rational application of science and technique, including scientific socialism, that the fulfillment of
human destiny within the context of history will be brought
about. Yet science is here a means and an instrument; the
fundamental appeal is to deeper resonances of the human spirit.
In these two respects Marxism and its contemporary products are
not alone, for they are but a later and more desperate manifestation of an aspect of Western thought which became apparent
earlier, and of which we are ourselves a product. America is the
product of European aspirations toward fulfillment and accomplishment. In the words of the Mexican classicist Alfonso Reyes,
"America is a utopia." The discovery of the New World, its
settlement and exploitation by generations of emigrants and
immigrants, is the most dramatic and self-conscious of utopian
movements which Western civilization has ever known.

II

Nowhere as in the New World, and nowhere in the New World
as in the United States, has utopia been institutionalized as part
of the legitimate expectations of a whole society. America was
made up of Europeans who turned their backs upon the Old
World and came to the New in hope. As a former President
declared, "We are all descended from immigrants and revolutionaries." Here in the new environment individual initiative, hard
work, and a special blessing of providence or of history would
conspire together for the accomplishment of the aspirations of
centuries. This sentiment was common to Americans and Europeans who came to America. In fact, it was shared by many who
stayed home. No less a figure than Goethe felt that America had
escaped from the past of European man, seeing in the new
continent "nature and man equally free from the burden of an
unhealthy past." As Lincoln said, the "sentiment in the Declara

tion of Independence . . . gave liberty not alone to the people of this country, but hope to all the world, for all future time. It was that which gave promise that in due time the weight would be lifted from the shoulders of all men and that all should have an equal chance."[4] And as Whitman confirmed, "All the pulses of the world, Falling in, they beat for us. . . ."

What this fulfillment would be like *in concreto,* no one could say. But the indefiniteness—the indefinableness—of American expectations did not detract from the powerful attraction of the undefined ideal. America was the accomplishment of European history; it was this in a small as well as in a great manner; it was a fulfillment to be traced in every family history. It was by the same token a transcendence of historicity. The weight that would fall from all men was the weight of Europe and of history. America was utopia—constantly in the process of birth, since to combine extrahistoricity with history was to prolong becoming indefinitely. This sentiment may be strained by recent developments, but it is far from gone. Commenting on the meeting of the American Association for the Advancement of Science then being held in Boston, the Boston *Herald* of December 28, 1953, said: "Our explorers and pioneers gave us a new world in which to create a democracy. Our scientists are giving us the tools with which to create a utopia."

America with its roots in Europe—the Europe of historic Christendom, the Europe of the Renaissance, the Europe of the Enlightenment, and the Europe of the Revolution—was to be the fulfillment of aspirations associated with all these aspects of European culture. America would produce itself within itself—would produce in microcosm the mirror of its own internal composition. In the "burned-over district" of New York, western at the time but not a crude frontier, experiencing the achievement of American democracy, and deeply disturbed by religious problems, the new movement that mirrored America came into existence.[5] Significantly it moved westward almost immediately and almost continually for over half a century. Its problem was, in a sense, "What did Christian salvation mean in America?" and heroically it attempted for over a century to write its answer across the pages of American history.

Christian salvation had always meant some sort of divinization of man. "To as many as received him, to them gave he the power to become the sons of God." But in America this would be accomplished in a more Pelagian manner. Man's own effort would be an important agency in its realization. Moreover, it would be accomplished within the context of time and in the present life. Time was here and now, and there would be no here and now outside of time. America meant what his Concord birthplace meant to Thoreau: the most estimable place in all the world and in the nick of time. All this was given religious and theological expression by the Church of Jesus Christ of Latter-day Saints. The Mormons are the typical American religious movement. As such, Mormonism presents a heightening, a more explicit formulation, and a summation of the American experience of time and of America's timeliness. In order to see this more clearly, let us examine three aspects of Mormonism: its conception of God and the cosmos, its notion of sacred and secular history, and its apprehension of the relationship between America and Europe. In all of these the conception of time will be of central interest.

<h2 style="text-align:center">III</h2>

In classic Christian metaphysics, God is Pure Act. In Him there is neither potency nor deficiency, and consequently He is outside of time; the divine life is an eternal present.[6] Time and the world of creatures come into existence together; both are creations of the timeless uncreated God.[7] It is precisely this conception which Mormonism has challenged. Writing in 1855, Parley P. Pratt declared: "In contemplating the works of Creation, then, the student must not conceive the idea that space, or time, or element, or intelligence, was originated, but rather that these are eternal, and that they constitute the energies which act, the things acted upon, including the place and time of action."[8] For Mormonism the world is uncreated and God and men are winning mastery over other uncreated elements. The radical transcendence of God, his radical otherness from his creation, has disappeared. God has become a demiurge once again. Philo in the *De Somniis* contrasts the Old Testament with Plato's *Timaeus* in the following words: "God, when He gave birth to all things, not only brought them into sight but also made things which before were not, not just handling material as a demiurge, and artificer, but being Himself its creator."[9] For the same reason the Jewish translators of the Septuagint did not make use of the word "demiurge," which means one who works on existing material, a craftsman, but rather chose the word *ktistes,* which means founder and was applied to the founder of a city. Mormonism, on the other hand, declares that uncreated intelligence is gaining mastery over other uncreated elements of the universe. God is seen as the most advanced, most intelligent, and most powerful of such intelligences.

> In "the beginning" which transcends our understanding, God undoubtedly exercised his will vigorously, and thus gained great experience of the forces lying about him. As knowledge grew into greater knowledge, by the persistent efforts of the will, his recognition of universal laws became greater until he attained at last a conquest over the universe which to our finite understanding seems absolutely complete.[10]

Plato in the *Timaeus* had said: "The god took over all that is visible—not at rest, but in discordant and unordered motion—and brought it from disorder to order."[11]

Yet the Mormon belief in the uncreated character of the universe and the corresponding denial of anything outside of and beyond time,[12] is *not* a return to the older belief in the cyclical conception of human history caught in the grip of *ananké* or *até.* The liberation of man from the ecological cycles of antique and Asiatic thought is preserved. The Judeo-Christian notion of progressive change, of the uniqueness of historic events, and of teleological development toward a goal is preserved. Even God is now conceived as a developing being, himself fully within the context of time and development. Joseph Smith declared in the King Follett discourse: "God himself was once as we are now, and is an exalted man, and sits enthroned in yonder heavens." Eternity in Mormon thought has become indefinitely prolonged time. All that is, is in process, and it is a process that is marked by two main characteristics: it is becoming increasingly more complex, and intelligent beings, God and men, are collaboratively gaining increasing mastery over it. Man's life on earth is seen as one of an infinity of episodes characterized by increasing development and mastery over the other elements of nature. Summing up Mormonism's conception of man's existence, the late Dr. John A. Widtsoe declared: "The law of progression is then a law of endless development of all the powers of man in the midst of a universe becoming increasingly more complex. No more hopeful principle can be incorporated into a philosophy of life."[13]

Two aspects of this view of man deserve our attention. It is first of all a conception of man's endless development toward godlike status, yet within the context of time and development. It is, in the second place, a view that denies that man's nature is in any way vitiated by original sin. History is thereby transcended while time remains. Mormonism, in this context, places the greatest stress on the freedom of the will. "The Church holds and teaches as a strictly scriptural doctrine, that man has inherited among the inalienable rights conferred upon him by his divine Father, absolute freedom to choose the good or the evil in life as he may elect."[14] Joseph Smith had declared in the Articles of Faith "that men will be punished for their own sins, and not for Adam's transgression." "It is evident that the Fall was foreordained, as a means whereby man could be brought face to face with both good and evil; that of his own agency he might elect the one or the other."[15] Man capable of infinite development is not vitiated by the effects of original sin.

Mormonism preserves and reinterprets the doctrine of the fall of man and of the redemption of man through Christ. There is no space for a consideration of that doctrine here. Yet what we must note in this context is that the Mormon conception of man, free, unburdened by the sins of the past, and facing a vista of limitless development, is expressive of the deepest and often implicit premises and aspirations of American utopianism. Man is a collaborator with God in winning mastery over the universe. In the beginning—which was not a beginning—God stood in a relationship to the other uncreated elements of the universe similar to that of American man to the undeveloped possibilities of this continent. God is conceived as within the context of time, while man emerges from out of the context of history. Both become partners in development. The prospect is endless progression, a genuine development without a goal, a teleology without a *telos*.

IV

The Mormon Church defines itself as a restoration in the latter days of the original Gospel of Jesus Christ which had been corrupted and lost in part for the previous fifteen centuries. Its restoration is conceived in terms of Christian history. A unique prophet and a unique and timely moment, as well as a uniquely appropriate place, are part of this conception. Mormonism holds itself to have been revealed in the fullness of time—a fullness of time which involves the destiny of the western hemisphere and the American nation. The discovery of America and the development of the political institutions of the United States are seen as prepared by divine guidance for the restoration which was made through the agency of the original Mormon prophet, Joseph Smith. Within this larger framework of world and American history, the Church of Jesus Christ of Latter-day Saints has its own history, a record of wandering and persecution, of construction and conquest over hostile elements coming to fruition in the building of Zion in the mountaintops.

Mormonism sees America as a chosen land and holds that the second coming of Christ will be to this continent and that it is here that Christ will reign during the millennium. America is a divinely preferred country, and the previous periods of history were preparatory for its appearance on the human scene, just as all that went before was preparatory for the Mormon restoration. Thus the Mormons, while exalting America and exulting in it, could at the same time feel called out of Babylon to build the city of God. The city would be built here in America, and it would fulfill America as America had fulfilled Europe. The conquest of America after the escape from Europe was placed in a Christian setting. Both were in preparation for the building of Zion.

Within a decade after its founding, the Mormon Church sent missionaries to Europe to gather the elect and bring them to America. Later the church organized the Perpetual Emigrating Fund Company to aid converts to emigrate.[16] European converts came in large numbers to Nauvoo, Illinois, in the early forties of the last century and later to Utah. For such immigrants America offered an escape from Europe and from the limitations which European civilization had placed on the destiny of human individuals. In America and in the Mormon gospel a new horizon was opened up, a new world spread before them. The Mormon missionaries, indeed, had good news to preach. The evangelical and chiliastic aspects of Mormonism consecrated and heightened the utopian attraction of America for the European. As America offered an indefinable utopian future to work and effort, Mormonism added unto it the conviction of divine choice, of a redeeming covenant with God and a promised land.

America offered an escape from history and from the historicity of Europe in which men, especially common men, were embedded. Mormonism offered in place of the older historical matrix the vista of limitless development, of time as the potentiality of endless individual development.

The Mormons saw themselves as a covenant people, divinely called by God through the agency of Joseph Smith and the church he established to build the kingdom of God on earth. The Mormon gospel was nothing short of a reopening of the heavens to Americans. The Mormons were an American people, already delivered from Europe, or delivered out of it then and there by the Perpetual Emigrating Fund Company, called to build the kingdom here in America, an accomplishment to be achieved in the face of hardship, but for which God had prepared the continent and the nation from the beginning and which would be its fulfillment. How remarkably familiar are the basic elements of the Mormon gospel! How remarkably like the general apprehension of America by other Americans when it sheds its theological poignancy! The fulfillment was to come through hard work, and it was about to begin. All past history and all present effort were directed to its coming. It was in itself indefinite, but the present was full with it, and it would soon be upon us.

Mormonism here too sums up much American experience. Speaking of earlier immigration, de Tocqueville had said that the arrivals were seeking "with nearly equal zeal for material wealth and moral good."[17] Yet he was keenly aware of the importance of the religious element in the foundation of America and feared its weakening which would result in a "headlong thrust into the single doctrine of interest." Mormonism, however, represents a retheologizing of much that had already been quietly and perhaps imperceptibly secularized. The redemptive and utopian elements in America, which had for most Americans remained parallel to Christian feelings and ideas, gradually superseding them in some cases, had in Mormonism been reincorporated into a new interpretation of Christianity itself. What is striking about this new interpretation of Christianity is that it made the American apprehension of history and time, the utopian and transcending elements, the emergence out of Europe, out of history, and out of time within time—the paradox of the American experience of time—its central insight. From this follow optimism, hard work, patriotism, a predisposition for the use of science and technology, and a belief in the special position of America.

V

Mormonism is important to Latter-day Saints on religious grounds. It is important to the West because it is the viewpoint of a movement which made inestimable contributions to the settlement of the West and to planting there a viable and vital American civilization. But it is of importance to the student of human culture for additional reasons. Mormonism, for all its peculiarity—even that theological peculiarity which has been its particular mark—presents a distillation of what is peculiarly American in America. The urge which brought millions of Europeans to the new country, the optimism and effort which characterized their own and their children's activities here after they came, the hope and aspiration for the indefinite fulfillment in terms of which all their efforts gained meaning, and the conviction of a difference (a genuine emergence to another plane of existence in America), of American peculiarity, and American destiny which in a sense transcends Europe and history—all these are found integrally incorporated into the Mormon reinterpretation of Christianity. It is a transcendentalism within the context of time itself. The apprehension of time, the experience of time, is of key importance here. Time is not a limitation from which man is to be delivered; it is a challenging vista. It is not experienced as a process of which we are integrally a part, but rather as one over which we are gaining mastery. The Mormon conception of time is an eschatological conception without an end. It is the prolonged moment of becoming—the moment of fruition never quite but always about to be realized. What Comte had perceived in his Law of Three Phases, what Engels had called the leap from the kingdom of necessity to the kingdom of freedom, America was experiencing in her own present. Mormonism in turn took this experience and made it central to the apprehension of Christianity itself.

By making the American conception of time articulate and by making it central to its theology and to its practical ethic, Mormonism answered the question which presided over its inception. There was a peculiarly American answer to the problem of Christian salvation. While the challenge and opportunities of America led to the spread of this-worldly attitudes, which though not openly anti-Christian at least gave a practical primacy to ends and goals in the context of a secular understanding of the human situation, Mormonism, by incorporating the goals of the present world into a vision of eternal progression, succeeded in annihilating for its followers the line of demarcation between time and eternity in quite a new way.

This was not a sacramental obliteration of the line by the notion of Presence—of eternity being here in the bosom of time, yet somehow not of time—but rather by a notion of integral causation. In his next life beyond the earth, the Mormon holds, man will start off from where his efforts here in this life have brought him. Mormonism is radically unsacramental; it is preeminently practical. Yet the difference between spiritual and secular is gone for the believing Mormon. With the apprehension of eternity as indefinitely prolonged time—the disappearance of the earlier metaphysical apprehension of eternity—there can be no conflict between the temporal and that which transcends time. All human endeavors are temporal, and all transcend time. There is only a question of which goal or end is nearest in the causal chain which binds them all together and over which the will and the intelligence of man are gaining mastery. Thus does Mormonism articulate the transcendentalism of American practicality.

NOTES

1. *Iliad,* Book VI, Rieu translation, p. 121.

2. Erich Frank, *Philosophical Understanding and Religious Truth* (London, New York, Toronto: 1945), p. 136, n. 9. For an excellent discussion, see Frank's Chapter V, "History and Destiny," pp. 116–147.

3. Wolf Frank, "Goethe for America," *American Scholar,* Vol. XX (Spring, 1951).

4. Quoted from F. S. C. Northrop, *The Meeting of East and West* (New York: 1946), p. 70.

5. Cf. Whitney Cross, *The Burned-over District* (Ithaca: 1950).

6. Cf. St. Thomas Aquinas, *Summa Theologica,* I, Q. 2–11.

7. Frank, *op. cit.,* Chapter III, "Creation and Time." See also Josef Pieper, "On the 'Negative' Element in the Philosophy of Thomas Aquinas," translated from *Hochland* (February, 1953), in *Cross Currents,* Vol. IV (Fall, 1953).

8. Parley P. Pratt, *Key to the Science of Theology* (Liverpool and London: 1855), p. 44.

9. Quoted from Frank, *op. cit.,* p. 75.

10. John A. Widtsoe, *Rational Theology* (Salt Lake City: 1915), p. 24.

11. *Plato's Cosmology,* Francis M. Cornford, tr. (New York: 1937), p. 22.

12. Orson Pratt declared in 1848: "What could be more unphilosophical, contradictory and absurd, than to assume that something can exist that is 'unextended'—that 'occupies no room, fills no space'—has no parts." "The Kingdom of God," No. 2 (Liverpool: 1848).

13. Widtsoe, *op. cit.,* p. 22.

14. James E. Talmage, *Articles of Faith* (Salt Lake City: 1901), p. 54.

15. *Ibid.,* p. 71.

16. See Gustive O. Larson, *Prelude to the Kingdom* (Francestown, N.H.: 1947).

17. "Democracy in America," quoted from Joachim Wach, *Types of Religious Experience* (Chicago: 1951), Chapter 8, "The Role of Religion in the Social Philosophy of Alexis de Tocqueville," pp. 171–186.

IDENTITY AND COMMUNITY

NINE: The Changing Image of the Jew and the Contemporary Religious Situation: An Exploration of Ambiguities

Charles Herbert Stember's study, Part One of *Jews in the Mind of America,* based on polls taken between 1937 and 1962, records a marked change in American gentiles' expressed attitudes concerning Jews. According to his findings, both predispositions to anti-Semitic activity and expressions of anti-Semitic sentiment have declined. Specifically, four features of the traditional hostile image of the Jew have lost much of their currency: unscrupulousness and consequent success in money matters; "pushiness" or aggressiveness in the pursuit of careers and in social relations; clannishness or excessive in-group loyalty outweighing allegiance to the general community; and uncleanliness or uncouthness. Certain ostensibly favorable ideas about Jews which, on closer inspection, turn out to be variants of the unfavorable ones just noted also are less widely accepted than they were.

The last fifteen of the years covered in the polls have not been without occasions of a kind which in earlier times probably would have given rise to anti-Semitism: the phenomenon of McCarthyism; the arrest of Soviet spies with Jewish names and Jewish backgrounds, at a time of strong anti-Communist feeling; the emergence of the State of Israel, vigorously supported by many American Jews; and the rise of a militant movement for Negroes' rights. Yet none of these developments elicited an anti-

Reprinted by permission from *Jews in the Mind of America* by Charles H. Stember and others, ⓒ 1966 by the American Jewish Committee (New York: Basic Books, 1966), pp. 302–322.

Jewish response. Indeed, it was precisely during these years that anti-Semitism underwent its sharp decline.

No data are presented in Stember's study for the years since 1963—a period of increased rightist activity and influence, culminating in the taking over of the Republican party by its extreme right wing during 1964, and of some hostile reaction ("backlash") on the part of whites against the growing agitation and protest among Negroes. Evidence other than polls, however, affords little reason to think that the extremist trends of these years at last produced the "usual" rise of anti-Semitism which the experience of many generations might have led us to expect. On the contrary, a man of Jewish antecedents (though himself a member of the Episcopal Church) became the spokesman, symbol, and standard-bearer of the new vociferous right, the very movement that refused to repudiate "extremism."

The question thus arises whether anti-Semitism in America is dying—whether some deep and permanent alteration has begun in the public's outlook on this vexed problem. The polls, together with recent events, might be taken to indicate that such is the case. Yet, we cannot discount the possibility that the observed changes of attitude and sentiment may be merely superficial fluctuations, which might be canceled out at any time by abrupt and far-reaching shifts in the opposite direction.

We do not doubt that the polls accurately reflect the expressed attitudes of the moment; that is, that the populations sampled were representative and the persons interviewed sincere. We question, rather, whether survey responses can be accepted as evidence of deeper sentiment when they deal with a phenomenon of the psychological depth and historical longevity of anti-Semitism. To put it bluntly: Dare we trust the plain evidence of the polls? Do the attitudes voiced by the respondents faithfully reflect the deeper ground of the public's sentiment?

To help answer these crucial questions, we shall first seek to appraise the reported decline of anti-Semitism in the light of the religious situation in America, past and present. As we do so, we shall discover significant differences between European and American traditions in the relationships between Christians and Jews. We shall also observe important changes apparently taking place in American religious life today. But these investigations will leave us with merely tentative conclusions. They will not tell us definitely to what extent current changes on the American religious scene are actually religious in nature, or just what the distinctively American tradition in Christian-Jewish relations proves for the meaning of Stember's poll data.

For deeper insights into the meaning of reported changes in public opinion, we shall have to enter a second, far larger area of inquiry: the long-term sociological and historical significance of anti-Semitism. Our explorations in this field will first define the nature and the overt causes of modern political anti-Semitism as it has manifested itself since the late nineteenth century. Later, we shall go back over the long centuries of Jewish history, tracing to its origins the accumulated heritage of animosity and bias from which modern anti-Semitism stems and to which it appeals.

It may be well to state at the outset that our investigations will be studies in ambiguity. We have no choice but to proceed cautiously to highly tentative conclusions; for not only do the poll findings themselves permit more than one reading, but so do some of the events and conditions against which the findings must be viewed. In particular, the present-day religious situation in America, as throughout the world, is equivocal. The ambiguity that prevails in this area is reflected in a series of questions which the American Jewish Committee prepared as a set of agenda for the present chapter:

> Are the shifts in attitude toward the Jew related to a growing secularism, which frees older individuals from traditionally held notions about the Jew which have their origin in religious teaching or practice, and prevents younger individuals from learning these notions?
>
> Or can the shifts be explained by a growing religiosity on the part of the American public—a religiosity which influences people toward holding a benign attitude toward religious differences?
>
> Why in fact has the Jew fared so well during a period of religious revival? Must one take the position that this revival has, in effect, been a secular revival and it is because of this secular element that the Jewish position has changed?
>
> How has Judaism come to be regarded as one of the three major faiths and how has this conception reduced hostility?

The hypothesis on which we proceed and which we hope to confirm may be summarized as follows. We believe that relationships of Christians and Jews throughout the long centuries of European history have remained similar in their basic structure, changing only on the surface, and that out of this experience a rich and varied hostile imagery was precipitated in the minds of Christians. These images furnished the terms in which the Jew was usually perceived and defined; in addition, they were capable of arousing emotions, serving as symbolic organizers of feeling and triggers of action. Jews, for their part, developed a complementary imagery of gentiles that was perhaps less rich, but no less unfavorable.

This background of hostile imagery, we submit, was transmitted from generation to generation as a subtle ingredient in cognition, value orientation, and attitudes. It was constantly reinforced and "proved" in encounters between Jews and Christians, occurring as they almost always did in essentially analogous situations. Inevitably, the accumulation of emotion-laden hostile images grew ever deeper, more elaborate, and less amenable to counterinfluences. This, we believe, is why anti-Semitic ideas have been such a long-lived and psychologically vigorous phenomenon in Western civilization.

It follows that traditional hostile images of Jews can be destroyed only when the context from which they sprang is changed; that is, when the unhappy Christian-Jewish relationships typical of the European past are replaced by more auspicious kinds of interaction. What concerns us in this chapter is whether this has actually occurred or can be counted on to occur in America.

The American Religious Background: Protestantism Plus Secularism

Seen in the long range, Western history shows an undeniable trend toward secularization. From the thirteenth century to the twentieth, more and more people became more and more concerned with worldly values, goals, and pursuits. Unbelief increased; important, indeed dominant, spheres of life—government, industry, commerce, education—were largely removed from the sacral context in which they had been embedded during the Christian Middle Ages. Intermittent periods of religious revival caused the trend to fluctuate, but failed to alter its general direction.

For a century and a half, roughly from 1770 to 1920, secularization coincided with a great improvement in the condition of the Jew; in fact, the two developments were intimately related.

Yet, nativist reactions against secularization at times gave anti-Semitism a new prominence during this era; and the years that followed—a time when Western civilization seemed more secularized than ever—saw the worst outbreak of anti-Jewish fanaticism in the history of Europe.

In this country, secularism has been a major force and has affected the condition of the Jew since early days. It played a significant role in the adoption of the Bill of Rights, the first legal document in the West to grant full emancipation to the Jew—emancipation on grounds so broad that he was not even mentioned by name. The Jew's equality and security in America were guaranteed, not by special legislation, but by constitutional safeguards for the rights of all. In an ethnically diverse new nation, his ethnic identity was treated like that of any other group, at least as far as the law was concerned. His actual experience proved less clear-cut; but until social mobility enabled Jews in sizable numbers to become rich, while large-scale immigration from eastern Europe brought masses of additional, almost uniformly poor, Jews to these shores, his condition was quite tolerable. Compared with most of his experience in the preceding centuries, it was unbelievably good. Thus it seems to us that, from the nation's beginnings onward, relations between Jews and Christians were not the same here as in Europe: they were such as to make the background of traditional hostile attitudes less relevant. That, in our opinion, is why anti-Semitism, though usually alive in the American imagination and at times widespread, never assumed the same proportions or significance here as in Europe.

Nor were the religious and social conditions of the United States in the nineteenth century suited to make the Jew an appropriate target for animosity, as were those in Europe. True, Civil War America was less secular, more markedly religious and manifestly Protestant, than revolutionary America had been; unbelief was less widespread or at least less popular. But in the decades after the Civil War, many areas of American life, notably the universities and intellectual life generally, once more became markedly secularized; and, most important, group hostility and distrust on the part of the nation's Protestant majority were finding a target more suitable than the Jews.

Both before and after the Civil War, Catholic immigrants from Ireland and Germany arrived in large numbers, setting off a hostile (at times violent) reaction. It was these Catholic newcomers who were destined to become the prime objects of hostile nativism—not the Jews, who were a smaller, less ubiquitous group and who seemed to fit in better, if only because their values were more like those of Americans. During the nineteenth and early twentieth centuries, anti-Catholicism came to fill the role in America which anti-Semitism played in Europe after 1870. As late as the 1920's, hatred of Catholics was a more important part of the revived Ku Klux Klan's message than hatred of Jews; it appealed more genuinely and more deeply to nativist sentiments.

The Catholic was a significant symbolic figure in the Protestant imagination. Anti-Catholic sentiment and its attendant imagery, dating from the period of the Reformation and the Wars of Religion which followed, formed an important set of inherited attitudes in the American Protestant preconscious. This hostility found a tremendous resonance among the older elements of the American culture. The Reformation had been the great event of the European past; "No Popery" had been an important slogan during the American Revolution, in response to Britain's Quebec Act of 1774, with its favorable terms for the Catholic Church in North America. Thus, mass immigrations of Catholics could easily be interpreted in terms of an already accumulated apperceptive symbolism.

Moreover, in many places from about 1850 on, the Catholic was typically an Irishman; the words "Catholic" and "Irish" became nearly synonymous in common speech. This meant that he was perceived in terms, not only of religious difference, but also of outright religious conflict. The Irish came to America from the scene of the perennial struggle with their English rulers—a struggle which had reached its full bitterness as a result of the Reformation. In America, residues of this Old World battle between Catholics and Protestants became the chief organizing symbols of thought and sentiment in what Ray Allen Billington has called a "Protestant crusade."[1]

The immigrant from Ireland, in short, was apperceived in terms of certain long-inherited, widely current modes of cognition and feeling, which had become incorporated with the imagery of American Protestant popular tradition. Furthermore, he responded to the hostility and suspicion with which he was received according to ready modes of thought and feeling which *he* had brought with him and which his entire previous history had precipitated into *his* consciousness. Thus, his relations with the dominant Protestant group were essentially analogous to those he had known in Europe, with the same deep substratum of mutually hostile images and attitudes.

The Jew, as we have seen, was in a different position. An America compounded of denominational Protestantism and secularism offered a significantly altered context for his relations with gentiles—a context more favorable than he had known in Europe. The contrasting nativist reactions to the Irish and the Jews thus support our hypothesis that intergroup hostility is likely to persist where relations are structurally analogous to those which prevailed when the emotion-laden imagery of the conflict was originally precipitated into the culture.

The American Religious Situation Today

Today more Americans, absolutely and proportionately, are affiliated with churches than ever before. Polls as well as membership rolls reveal this fact: in surveys, more than 75 per cent of Americans call themselves church members. Moreover, between 95 and 97 per cent say they believe in God; some 73 per cent claim to believe in an afterlife and in God as the judge of human behavior. An overwhelming majority hold religion to be something of importance, most believe in prayer, and some 90 per cent say they pray on some occasions in their lives. As Franklin H. Littell points out, America is more churched today than ever before in her entire history.[2] These facts might be taken to mean that a religious revival has occurred in the last decade or two.

Whether the recent growth of church membership and attendance really represents an increase in belief is another question.[3] In the polls just cited, 80 per cent of the respondents also stated that they were most serious, not about the otherworldly concerns of the religions in which they said they believed, but in living as well and comfortably as possible in this world. When those who had described religion as something very important were asked, "Would you say your religious beliefs have any effect on your ideas of politics and business?" 54 per cent replied that such beliefs had no real effect, while 37 per cent said they had and 7 percent gave no answer. In contrast, 91 per cent of the respondents declared they were really trying to lead a good life, 78 per cent thought they measured up more than halfway to their own standards of goodness, and over half said they completely obeyed the counsel to love their neighbors as themselves. If, as Edward Sapir observed four decades ago, genuine religion is everywhere the enemy of self-satisfaction, such findings suggest that perhaps there has been no religious revival at all.[4]

Seymour M. Lipset, mustering the relevant statistics, has shown that increases in church membership and practice have been at best moderate and that among some groups there has been an actual decline.[5] He and many others suggest that the apparent increase in religiosity masks what is in fact advancing secularization. In a somewhat related vein, Littell concludes that while the churches in America have achieved a new popularity, they still face the task of Christianizing and converting their new members. What took place in the 1950's, he holds, was only a "pre-religious revival": a renewed interest in churches, occasioned by a quest for values and community, but not yet a resurgence of religion.

Will Herberg has proposed the hypothesis that Americans, now three or more generations removed from their European cultural backgrounds, and often third-generation city dwellers, have turned to religion in their search for identity in our mass society with its characteristic social mobility. The old ethnic identities are being outgrown; the nation as a whole is too large, and the fact of being an American too indefinite, to serve as meaningful sociological reference points. According to Herberg, religious affiliation comes to fill this need, providing the individual with a significant reference group. To be an American today means to be identified with one of the "three great religions of democracy": Protestantism, Catholicism, or Judaism. Religious identification and membership in the religious group have taken over what used to be the ethnic group's role as intermediary between the individual and the nation as a whole.

That the theory interprets correctly much that we see about us would seem clear enough. Gerhard Lenski reports that it was tested in Detroit and, with some modification, held up: increasing church attendance was found positively correlated with increasing Americanization. Yet all this merely points up the ambiguousness of the situation. Robin Williams notes that religion in America has been losing its otherworldly character, and Herberg himself sees little deepening or intensification of genuine faith. The new religiosity which he thinks is developing does not seem to him to be deeply infused with the spirit of prophetic Judaism or New Testament Christianity.

Beneath the distinctive creeds of the three "religions of democracy" lurks a consensus on secular values, according to Herberg. America, he suggests, really has a common religion in the "American way of life"—the familiar constellation of beliefs and values based on the Constitution, so-called free enterprise, a formal egalitarianism (accompanied by a belief in competition and social mobility), respect for the individual, and a commitment to striving and achievement. It is an idealistic but not an otherworldly creed, compounded of beliefs and values that have long been operative among the American people. As affluence increases, as structural changes in business, education, and technology create new opportunities, as the dying away of ethnic differences and the expansion of the mass media strengthen egalitarianism, these values seem destined to achieve wider currency and an ever more central position on the American scene.[6]

We may reasonably assume that these developments are affecting the position of the Jew and the structure of Jewish-Christian relations. To the degree that adherence to a particular creed becomes less important than membership in one (any one) of the three religious "establishments," Judaism attains an equivalence with Christianity which it has not achieved elsewhere; the dichotomy between the two religions loses some of its salience, and acceptance of Jews is facilitated. The process parallels changes in other areas: for example, the fading of the Old World ethnic awareness that used to make Jewishness appear as something alien and uncouth, or the new social mobility fostered by education, which is breaking down the Jews' concentration in certain socioeconomic sectors and thus weakening the notion of the Jew as a money man. In this fashion, the common American way of life wears down the stereotypes of the old inherited imagery.

Whatever its spiritual state, religion in present-day America seems to have achieved a new respectability among intellectuals, while a serious concern with contemporary issues appears to have significantly increased in religious circles. One of the most striking illustrations of this trend is the rise of an articulate intelligentsia among Catholic laymen—a development closely related to the *aggiornamento* initiated by Pope John XXIII. How developments like these might affect the public's attitude toward the Jew is a matter for speculation. They certainly would seem suited to make Christians increasingly aware of the horrors of anti-Semitism; the memory of the Nazi era presumably would be a major factor, perhaps the leading one, in any such sensitizing process. Albert Schweitzer has suggested that both Catholics and Protestants "became guilty, by simply accepting the terrible, inhuman fact of the persecution of the Jews." This guilt is felt in many places, as can be seen in the statement on the Jews adopted by the Second Vatican Council.

Some observers nonetheless foresee continuing religious conflict in America. Thus, Earl Raab suggests that, even though religious bigotry has considerably declined, religious controversies may actually have become sharper.[7] Issues such as state aid and bus service for parochial schools, or Christmas celebrations, Bible reading, and prayers in public ones have provoked widespread discussion in the years since the war—a by-product of new social mobility and suburbanization. The record clearly shows that such controversies provide occasions for revived anti-Semitism, at least in the short run. Whether they will increase or subside, persist or disappear, remains to be seen.

Finally, international developments no doubt will continue to bear indirectly on Christian-Jewish relations in this country. During recent times, American solidarity has been strengthened by the existence of a hostile alien ideology and a hostile foreign power complex. Foreign policy issues have become much more significant for America than formerly and far more salient in the consciousness of the public. As a result, frustrations and aggressions which formerly would have found an outlet in anti-Catholicism or anti-Semitism have been achieving catharsis through the symbols and imagery of anti-Communism.

To sum up: We noted earlier that Christians and Jews in America have from the beginning confronted each other in situations which, unlike those traditionally found in Europe, did not continually reinforce traditional hostile images and sentiments. Since World War II, the conditions of Christian-Jewish encounter have been further broadened and diversified by social change—especially by alterations in the significance of religion, such as the replacement of ethnic by religious identity in the popular consciousness; the weakening concern with creed and with differences in creed; the emergence of a single, more or less secular consensus within the framework of varied religious groupings; and the recognition of Judaism as one of the nation's major faiths. Combined with other trends, such as the growing role of education in fostering social mobility, these developments may be creating a structural basis for genuinely new intergroup learning.

That such a process has actually been going on can hardly be doubted; yet it would seem neither sound nor safe to assume that the resulting changes have lasted long enough or reached deep enough to assure the demise of anti-Jewish hostility. Before we can draw a firmer conclusion, we must consider the sociological meaning of anti-Semitism itself.

The Sociological Significance of Manifest Political Anti-Semitism

Modern political anti-Semitism began in Germany and Austria during the 1870's. In Russia and elsewhere in eastern Europe, it found an echo almost at once; in France, somewhat later. During the twentieth century, it was to become a major political force. The end of World War I, which saw formal emancipation of Jews enjoined by treaties and covenants, also marked the beginning of a large-scale growth in anti-Jewish agitation—a growth destined to culminate in the rise of Nazism and the horror of Hitler's "final solution."

The anti-Semitic outbursts in various parts of Europe during this era were usually related to events that upset domestic tranquillity, economic prosperity, or general stability. They were often part of pronounced nativist reactions to change. The eruption in Germany and Austria during the 1870's followed on the heels of the ruinous financial crisis of 1873. The beginning of the Russian pogroms in the early 1880's had for its background the economic effects of the emancipation of serfs barely a generation earlier; at the same time, Slavophile sentiment and ideology were rising in a Russia uncomfortably confronted with the culture of western Europe. The French outbreaks of the 1890's, centering on the case of Captain Alfred Dreyfus and his monarchist and militarist foes, occurred soon after the scandalous bankruptcy of the Panama Company, which had ruined half a million members of the middle class. And the tragedy of Hitlerism began in a Germany afflicted successively by defeat in World War I, disastrous inflation, and the Great Depression.

As has often been pointed out, a scapegoat was a functional necessity on these occasions, and a manifest connection between the Jews and the crisis was easily established. In Russia, Jews played an important economic role in the Pale of Settlement, the western provinces to which they were confined. In France, Jewish agents had helped bribe Parliament to authorize a bond issue that was to stave off the Panama Company's collapse; the net effect had been to enlarge the ranks of the ruined when the company foundered after all. In Germany, Jews had long been involved in state finance and in a few industries; furthermore, they were prominent in the arts and sciences and were entering public service careers in somewhat increasing numbers under the Weimar Republic.

Yet, do the surface events explain adequately why in each case the Jew was chosen to be the scapegoat and why anti-Semitism, once aroused, was so virulent? One cannot but agree with Hannah Arendt that the reaction in these and similar situations has been so out of scale with the actual involvement of Jews as to affront common sense. Distrust of cultural and religious differences and buttressing of in-group loyalty by hostility against others are fairly constant human phenomena, however reprehensible they may be; though they outrage any enlightened conscience, they do not surprise the social scientist. But even the expert is shocked by political anti-Semitism's savage terror against a powerless minority, which was not guilty and would not have deserved such frightful treatment if it had been.

If we are to understand modern political anti-Semitism, we must go below the level of manifest events to the underlying sentiments. Forces deeper than momentary excitement were at work when Wilhelm Marr gained notoriety in 1873 with his pamphlet *The Victory of Judaism over Germanism*; when a fight in a provincial Russian tavern could set off anti-Jewish riots that engulfed 167 towns and villages in a few weeks; when the cry of "Kill the Jews" echoed through the streets of enlightened Paris; when a democratic Germany handed the reins of power to a racist demagogue.

In each instance, emotionally charged images and attitudes concerning Jews lay beneath the surface of the collective consciousness, waiting to be activated. That deeper level of cultural reality was the product of a long, still seemingly relevant history. Christians and Jews in Europe, like Protestants and Catholics in America, were facing each other from the vantage points of their respective experiences. They lacked a common background, a common interpretation of the past, and thus could not arrive at common viewpoints in the present.

To what extent emancipation failed to create such a common ground between Christians and Jews is further illustrated in the peculiar nature of friendships between them. Such friendships have occurred for at least two centuries, but they have frequently exhibited a peculiar gingerliness, a well-meaning stereotypy. For example, when Jews first gained entree to some of Germany's fashionable salons during Moses Mendelssohn's time, they were received as specimens of the "universal humanity" which the Romantic age thought it had discovered; and a century later, the *haut monde* of Paris—the society described by Marcel Proust— welcomed the Jew as an intriguing representative of a kind of spiritual underworld. In neither case were the members of the majority ready to accept the Jewish visitor simply as an individual, to be viewed and judged by the same standards as others.

Nor has America, for all its greater progress toward mutual acceptance between Jews and Christians, remained free of this self-consciousness among the well-disposed. One striking example is a peculiar taboo current as recently as the postwar years among presumably objective sociologists and social psychologists. It was then unthinkable to suggest that anti-Semitism must be studied in a reciprocal context; that all stereotypes are products, however distorted, of historical experience; that it is fruitless to seek the key to anti-Semitism in gentile "pathology" alone, neglecting the attitudes of Jews. In this hands-off policy, as in the arm's-length acceptance practiced by European high societies of yesteryear, a residue of the old mutual alienation still lingers.

Underlying Images: The Pagan and Early Christian Eras

We must now trace the historical origins of the various emotion-laden images of the Jew, the components of the latent substrate of feeling which makes manifest anti-Semitism possible. In what follows, we schematically distinguish four phases: (1) the pagan centuries of the Roman Empire and the emergence of Christianity; (2) the Christianized Empire and the Middle Ages; (3) the era of rising secularism and nationalism; and (4) the epoch of modern political anti-Semitism.

Throughout the early years of Imperial Rome, Palestine was torn by a nationalist struggle. The Roman rulers dealt severely with this movement; their policy of repression reached a climax in 70 A.D., when the Second Temple was destroyed and Jerusalem was barred to Jews. Long before these events, however, large numbers of Jews had left Palestine. They established communities in many of the Empire's urban centers, lived much like other ethnic minority groups, and apparently experienced the same conditions of accommodation and conflict. The Roman authorities usually treated the scattered Jewish communities with forbearance, even granting them such unusual concessions as exemption from military service and recognition of their Sabbath. From time to time, public disturbances upset or reversed these policies; thus, in 19 A.D., the Emperor Tiberius expelled the Jewish community from Rome, and in 38 A.D., at Alexandria, a visit by Agrippa I, the King of Judea, occasioned what can fairly be called a pogrom. But the Constitution of Caracalla (212 A.D.) gave Jews the privileges and responsibilities of citizenship, and from that time on their position seems to have been better than that of other dissenting religious groups.

Considerable cultural assimilation took place in pre-Christian antiquity; witness the Septuagint (the oldest Greek translation of the Hebrew Bible), which dates from this period. Yet, in the general thinking of the pagan era, Jews were viewed largely in terms of their ethnic differences, of which their religion formed an important constituent. Social segregation developed at this time, and with it a sense of cultural and religious otherness. Gentiles began to feel suspicious of, or superior to, Jews and to perceive them as mysterious aliens. In centuries to come, these sentiments were to be reinforced by ever richer imagery.[8]

Meanwhile, Christianity was starting out on its meteoric rise. Though the church began as a Jewish sect, it was to bring about a significant change in the Jews' status. Hostility between Christians and Jews began early. At first, controversy centered on the question whether or not Jesus of Nazareth was the Messiah—a conflict fought in terms of the implications of the Jewish Scriptures. Soon the Jews came to be perceived as the leading challengers of the claim that Christianity was "the true, original, universal religion of humanity, that it predated and outshone all that the poets, philosophers and lawgivers of Greece and the East could offer. It could make such a claim only on the basis of the possession, as exclusively part of its own history, of the story of Israel as revealed in the Old Testament."[9]

From the beginning of their relationship, then, the Christian perceived the Jew as a living rejection of, and challenge to, his faith. A new image came into being: the Jew as doubter. Indeed, the Christian, viewing the Old Testament through the interpretive prism of the New, saw him as the descendant of those who had slain the prophets and put Jesus to death. The scorn which Roman satirists like Petronius and Juvenal had heaped upon Jews as a cultural minority was thus augmented by religious animosity. St. Ambrose, for example, denounced their synagogue as a home of insanity and unbelief, condemned by "God whom they have insulted . . . Christ whom they have crucified."[10] Minority alien, distrusted and resented; repudiator of the true faith; doubter and deicide—the accumulation of hostile imagery had begun. Begun in circumstances, moreover, where real interests were involved and where the images could be learned again and again, acquiring ever deeper connotations. The foundation for differential apperception, mutual suspicion, antagonism, and institutionalized segregation had been laid.

The Growth of Imagery in Christian Europe

The Edict of Milan (313 A.D.) recognized both Christianity and Judaism as lawful religions; in effect, however, it heralded the official Christianization of the Empire. The Jews' condition now suffered a radical transformation and deterioration. The later Christian emperors conceived it as their civic and religious duty to combat infidelity and heresy; their edicts described Judaism as a *secta nefaria* (nefarious sect) and Jewish religious gatherings as *sacrilegi coetus* (sacrilegious meetings).

In the disordered centuries that followed, the Christian faith became the official religion of the European culture, the church, the central institution of the society, and Christian thought the dominant source of ideas on the meaning of human existence. Christendom as a cultural entity, the Catholic Church as an ecclesiastical organization, and the civil community, including the state, all became interpenetrating elements of a single cultural and societal fabric. Under these conditions, unbelievers constituted a challenge to the needed consensus of the society and to the very conception that gave human life its accepted meaning.

Unbelievers who were heretical Christians were exterminated wherever practicable, heresy being seen as an evil to be eradicated, rather than as a mere error that might have been embraced in good faith. The Jews were placed in a different category:

> The Church, conscious that Christianity is founded on Judaism, recognized their right to live and to practice their religion without interference. . . . This right, however, was conditioned by the stipulation, which the Fathers of the early Church had often emphasized, that they were to live in a state of misery and degradation. The sons of the bondwoman must be kept in subjection to the sons of the freewoman.[11]

Accordingly, Jews were hedged about with restrictions and disabilities. The idea that their "natural rights" were inviolable was a theoretical concession of limited significance; in practice it was frequently transgressed.

Popes, bishops, and princes often protected Jews from the fury of popular attacks, but the uncertainty of that protection illustrates the ambiguity and difficulty of the Jews' position. For example, according to Gratian's *Decretum,* the 57th canon of the fourth national Council of Toledo in 633 declared that Jews who had been compelled to become Christians and had received the sacraments should remain Christians; the validity of these compulsory conversions was not to be questioned. In the future, moreover, no one was to be constrained to believe: "The Jews are not to be saved in spite of themselves, but freely, so that all justice be safeguarded. Conversions are to be made by consent, not constraint, by persuasion, not force." Yet only five years later, another council gave thanks to God that the King had ordered the Jews to leave Spain, so that there be none but Christians in the country.[12]

Half a millennium later, in 1120, Pope Calixtus II issued a *Constitutio pro Judaeis* to stop Crusaders from massacring Jews in their own regions; Pope Innocent III reissued it in 1199. The second version of this much-hailed document states: "Although the Jewish perfidy is in every way worthy of condemnation, nevertheless, because through them the truth of our own faith is proved, they are not to be severely oppressed by the faithful."[13] In 1190, moreover, Pope Clement III forbade "anyone to compel the Jews to receive baptism against their will." Thus, St. Thomas Aquinas appears to have spoken for the custom and general mind of the church when he forbade the baptism of the children of Jews without the consent of their parents.[14] However, no less a thinker than Duns Scotus disagreed with St. Thomas on involuntary conversion; and the very fact that the subject was discussed over such an extended period is suggestive of the psychological atmosphere that surrounded the relations of Christians and Jews throughout the Middle Ages. Moreover, whatever their theological status, in their civil conditions the Jews were considered "serfs of the Church" and "bondsmen of the princes by civil bondage."

Malcolm Hay has said: "The Popes of the Middle Ages often intervened, not always effectively, to defend Jews against personal violence, but seldom wrote a line to condemn the ill-will which made such violence inevitable."[15] At the deeper level of psychological reality, religious imagery filled with hostile sentiments accumulated throughout these centuries, and no institution in the culture attempted to counteract the accumulation. What had begun in the early Christian period continued and deepened: the image of the Jew as perfidious doubter and deicide became ever more fixed. In the sacral society of the Middle Ages, the Jews were sacral outcasts, possessed of what Durkheim would call an impure sacredness.

Simultaneously, the Jew's economic role provided an entire new dimension for animosity. In the classical period, urban minorities had subsisted by commerce and craftmanship, and these had been the Jew's usual pursuits in early Christendom. During the Middle Ages, the Jew was kept out of political life and most other fields. Amid an agrarian society he remained associated with commerce; in Carolingian times the words "Jew" and "merchant" were synonyms. Agrarian societies tend to distrust merchants, and, as Tawney and Fanfani have shown, medieval Europe was particularly prone to do so, because Christian morality viewed commerce with misgivings. Thus, the Jew, already cast as an ethnic and cultural alien, doubter and deicide, was also invested with the suspect role of merchant—in a society where spontaneous dislike of commerce was reinforced by religious sanction.

With the rise of a Christian mercantile class during the twelfth century, the Jews were gradually driven from commerce. They now entered the only activity still open to them: moneylending, an occupation specifically forbidden to Christians (though not with complete success) by the church. Moneylending, or usury, as it was called, was a necessity in the medieval economy, but its role was not the same as in the expanding industrial societies of later ages. Given the conditions of the period, the usurer appeared all too often as one who took advantage of his fellow men's calamity and distress, becoming "one of the most thoroughly despised and hated members of the medieval community."[16] Forced into this despised though necessary function, the Jew became detested for a new reason—one that exhibited, even more than commerce, the negative sacral character with which he was already associated. "Here was a vicious circle from which there was no escape for the Jew. Society conspired to make him a usurer—and usury exposed him to the cupidity of feudal overlords and to the embittered hatred of the people."

Joshua Trachtenberg has shown how the words "Jew" and "usurer" became synonymous at a time when the church condemned usury much as it did heresy. A new order of imagery arose, in which the Jew was associated with Judas Iscariot and ultimately with the devil.

> Thus the Jew was obliged to bear the brunt of popular feeling against the moneylender from the outset, and long after his short-lived prominence in the field had been preempted by others, he still remained *the* usurer in the mass memory and had to suffer for the sins of his successors. . . . The Jew-heresy-usury equation became a medieval cliche; not even the terminology suffered change. Christian moneylenders were forced to hear themselves slandered as "those other Jews, called Christians," or simply *Kristen-Juden,* in the fifteenth century Christian usury became known in Germany as *Judenspiess,* the "Jews' spear." At a time when Jews as such had been unknown in England for several centuries, Sir Francis Bacon recommended in his essay "Of Usury" (1612) that all usurers "should have tawny orange bonnets, because they do Judaize."[17]

In the sixteenth century Luther referred to the Jews as usurers and the "devil's saints."

Thus, the historical experience of more than a millennium created, in what Trachtenberg calls the "mass memory," a complex image which represented the Jew as an ethnic and cultural alien, a mysterious outsider, a doubter and deicide, the repudiator of God and the killer of Christ, a merchant among farmers, a usurer, a Judas in league with the devil. And during all that time, the structural conditions of society were perfectly fitted to preserve these conceptions; indeed, to enlarge their psychological depth and emotional impact.

Responding to this experience, Jews became increasingly separate and alien in their self-definition, accepting the institutionalized state of war implicit in their position. They tried to convert Christians on a number of occasions and were commonly accused of seeking to subvert Christianity. A passage in Jean de Joinville's *Chronicle of the Crusades* speaks volumes concerning such animosities during the thirteenth century: St. Louis of France, so admirable in most respects, is said to have called for running a sword through a Jew who spoke with disrespect of the Virgin Mary.

The Jews certainly did become, if anything, even more attached to their faith than before; moreover, they organized themselves into separate communities, which were legally recognized in the corporate medieval state. These communities were autonomous, enjoying a considerable degree of self-government, though on a precarious base. The laws they framed were often quite comprehensive, regulating business, religious life, dress, even pleasures and amusements, in such a way as not to arouse the jealousy of gentiles. Institutions of social welfare and education were carefully maintained.

Thus, the Jew and his life became ever more ingrown and alien, providing a more and more plausible basis for charges of clannishness. His visibility—heightened at times by the compulsory wearing of a badge or distinctive dress—further accentuated his otherness. The cultural coexistence under these institutionalized conditions was well suited to deepen the psychological substratum of hostility which Europe was to retain until modern times. Indeed, this discrete yet shared experience of long-lived, institutionalized reciprocal hostility forms the common core of the Jew's and the gentile's histories.

From the time of the First Crusade on, Jewish life was racked by periodic mass onslaughts. The first of the many pogroms that make up this unhappy chronicle occurred in the Rhineland in 1096. Later, mass violence culminated in expulsion, a policy that began in England under Edward I, in 1290, and continued until 1591, when the Jews were driven from the Duchy of Milan, newly occupied by Spain. Western Europe, by and large, gradually became closed to the Jews. There were exceptions: some

were allowed to stay, under ever-tightening restrictions, in parts
of northern Italy, certain regions of Germany, and the papal
possessions in the south of France; and nominal converts to
Christianity, the so-called Marranos, for some time remained in
the Iberian Peninsula, practicing their old religion in secret. But
the bulk of European Jewry went east during the age of expulsion: to Russia, Poland, or the domains of the Turkish Sultan.
These events coincided in large part with the period known as
the Renaissance, so that what to gentiles is the beginning of
enlightened modern times is the start of a new dark age for Jews.

In the imagination of Christians, the Jew had long figured,
inter alia, as an eternally homeless wanderer—a fate allegedly
visited on him for his rejection of Christ. Before and during the
Renaissance, Christian Europe turned this image into reality;
and as if to confirm it, massacres in the East about the middle of
the seventeenth century set off a new wave of Jewish migration
back to the West.

The Imagery of the Nationalist Era

With the rise of secularism and the modern national states,
following the Renaissance, the condition of the Jews became
slowly more bearable. From the sixteenth century on, rulers and
thinkers showed them growing tolerance. Simultaneously, however, Jews became associated with state finance; and the court
Jew of the period, with his international connections and his
ability to supply capital to needy monarchs and princes, added
new sinister dimensions to the Jewish image.

In a Europe slowly developing national consciousness, the Jew
was an international figure; in a society that was mostly poor, a
few Jews were rich. Already, the Jew was unfavorably associated
in the public's mind with money; now the role of international
financier was added to these images. Notions of Jewish solidarity
and clannishness, inherited from the earlier periods, were accordingly reinterpreted: the Jew was alleged to possess international
power based on wealth and later to harbor designs for dominat-
ing the world. To the extent that the Jews of the period were not
identified with particular nationalities and that some of them
engaged in large financial operations, this new modification of
the old stereotype had a basis in reality. Still, it is curious that

gentiles should have perceived Jews as plotting for political power. The Jews' mentality was then quite apolitical, and such designs were entirely foreign to them.[18]

Some Jews, usually rich ones, received privileges during this era which in practice amounted to civil rights. Simultaneously, the spread of liberal ideas and natural religion, together with new interpretations of the medieval idea of natural law and natural rights, contributed to a gradual improvement in the condition of Jewry as a whole—an improvement which continued into the Enlightenment. Voltaire, whom we may take as representative of the Age of Reason, disliked Jews, but encouraged civil freedom for all men; Montesquieu and Rousseau condemned the traditional treatment and persecution of the Jews; the revolutionist Abbé Grégoire and others advocated their emancipation.

Both in fact and in the minds of gentiles, the Jew and his cause became identified with liberalism. Liberal thought appealed to persons of pro-Jewish sentiment and to the Jews themselves; its profound effect on the Jewish intellectuals of the period is exemplified by the ideas of Moses Mendelssohn. In the imagination of conservatives, activated during periods of reaction, this liberal bent fitted well with traits long attributed to Jews: with the roles of doubter and dissenter. Later, in the nineteenth century, most of Russia's Jews became submerged in the proletariat, because of the restrictions placed on their mobility and occupational activities; some joined revolutionary movements. One result was that Jews as a group were now seen as radicals, a notion congruent with their earlier representation as liberals. Finally, in the 1920's and 1930's, the notion of the "Jewish Bolshevik" was added to the abundant imagery laid up over the centuries.

Political Anti-Semitism and Its Imagery

The pseudo-scientific theories of modern anti-Semitism, from the 1870's until its culmination in the holocaust, pictured the Jew as a political and racial menace—an image which gained wide circulation first through such fantastic propaganda as the forged *Protocols of the Learned Elders of Zion* and later through Hitler's teachings.

Nazi anti-Semitism was more extreme and more horribly thorough than anything that had preceded it (no previous enemy of the Jews in the long history of Europe had advocated or attempted their total annihilation); yet the images Hitler drew were only superficially new. Thus, when he condemned the Jew as racially inferior, a source of infection for the rest of society, he was offering a biologized version of long-standing religious and cultural distrust. When he named "Jewish finance" and "Jewish Bolshevism" as spearheads of a Jewish plot to destroy society and seize world power, he was elaborating on the old image of the Jew as doubter or enemy of the eternal verities.

Modern theologians, such as Paul Tillich and Romano Guardini, have explored the incompatible yet intimate relationship between faith and doubt. The presence of doubters and dissenters tangibly expresses this relationship: the dissenter serves as an objective surrogate for conflicts in the believer's soul, a target for hostile projection. Historians have often pointed to this element in religious fanaticism and intolerance. As we have seen, Christian Europe habitually assigned the subverter's role to the Jew, the supposed challenger of Christian faith. The anti-Semitic nativists of modern times, up to and including Hitler, were doing essentially the same, though in secular terms: They saw the "liberal," "revolutionary," or "racially inferior" Jew as a destroyer of basic values.

The Present Outlook

It has often been said that anti-Semitism is the classic form of religious and ethnic antagonism. But this is true only if a "classic" case is taken to mean one carried to the ultimate extreme, not one that is typical or average. Anti-Semitism possesses a stock of images more deep-seated and protean than does any other form of intergroup hostility known to Western man, because it is the summation of self-confirming experience extending over two millenniums. In century after century, hostile sentiments arose from the unhappy relations between gentiles and Jews, fed back into these relationships, and thus constantly perpetuated and deepened themselves. The question today is whether this vicious circle is at last being broken.

As we noted at the outset, Stember has shown that expressed anti-Semitism markedly declined in the United States during the last two decades, even though there was no dearth of occasions structurally analogous to those which have given rise to anti-Semitic reactions in the past. Specifically, he has demonstrated that certain unfavorable and pseudo-favorable traits traditionally ascribed to Jews are less widely believed in than formerly, or at least less freely referred to. Now, the traits thus noted by Stember are part of the more variegated image whose history we have sketched, and the question thus arises as to what is happening to this broader image today. Its various aspects probably were never equally accepted or salient among all population groups. Dare we conclude, on the basis of poll findings since 1944, that it is dwindling away altogether?

"It is either impossible, or a task of no mean difficulty, to alter by words what has been of old taken into men's very dispositions," wrote the philosopher, jurist, and churchman Guillaume du Vair (1556-1621). We have assumed that the baneful psychological heritage of anti-Semitic imagery cannot be dissipated unless there is a change in the Jewish-gentile relationships in which it originated and found continual reinforcement; but we have also found reasons to believe that some such alteration has, in fact, taken place in America. We have seen how the ideology of secularism, the imagery of sectarian Protestantism, and the conditions of assimilation to American life combined to make the Catholic (particularly the Irish Catholic) a more salient target of hostility than the Jew. We have observed that, with the progressive secularization of the culture after the Civil War, the Jew became still less salient, gradually losing the characteristic "otherness" that made him a target in the old country. In addition, we note that America's belief in equality, together with her more or less conscious repudiation of certain aspects of European social and political conservatism, subtly helped to make Jewish-gentile relations in this country different from those in Europe. And, finally, we are mindful that assimilation has been the telling, significant long-term process in the history of all ethnic and religious groups in America, notwithstanding nativist (often militantly nativist) episodes.

In short, America has not let ethnic and religious differences remain a solid base for long-term hostility, as has been the case in more homogeneous nations. Today, thanks to structural changes in our society, Jews and gentiles are coming together in a variety of occupational and educational contexts quite unlike traditional forms of confrontation; their relationship does appear to be undergoing a genuine change. We thus might think ourselves safe in accepting the polls at their hopeful face value.

Yet a note of caution is indicated. We have seen how among American Protestants of the 1840's anti-Catholic stereotypes that had been inactive for some time turned quickly into focuses of sentiment and action when immigration brought large numbers of Catholics to these shores. And we know that in later years many one-time Protestants who had become liberal agnostics nevertheless retained the deep-seated anti-Catholic feelings of their sectarian backgrounds, now rationalizing and expressing them in liberal philosophical terms. The same subterranean psychological transfer of energy, the same coalescing of old and new imagery, has so often occurred in the history of anti-Semitism that we dare not jump to overoptimistic conclusions.

Thus our explorations must of necessity close on a tentative note. We do not regard the attitude changes reported in the polls as assured gains in a unitary favorable trend. Rather, they seem to us to stem from two distinct, though related, social processes— the one perhaps ephemeral, the other probably permanent.

From centuries of European history, we know that anti-Semitism may go through periods of quiescence without any diminution in the underlying hostile imagery. In our opinion, part of the reported drop in anti-Jewish feeling during recent decades may well reflect merely such a temporary lull among part of the public. Thus, for all we know, the possibility of renewed anti-Semitism still lurks underground.

But we have also seen that under the particular conditions of American life the basic structure of gentile-Jewish relations has altered to the point where the old hostile imagery evidently is fading at last. Beyond doubt, part of the spectacular opinion change revealed by the polls mirrors this decline of ancient, deep-seated hostility. Obviously, the accumulated hatreds of two thousand years could not have been dissipated altogether in a few decades. Yet, over and above the momentary fluctuations of public opinion, we appear to be witnessing a historic change—a change which opens up new opportunities for studying the deeper sociopsychological reality of intergroup hostility and for effectively combating the age-old evil of anti-Semitism.

N O T E S

1. Ray Allen Billington, *The Protestant Crusade, 1800-1860* (New York: 1952).

2. Franklin H. Littell, *From State Church to Pluralism* (Garden City, N.Y.: 1962).

3. Will Herberg, *Protestant, Catholic, Jew* (New York: 1955), pp. 270-289.

4. *Ibid.*, pp. 85-104.

5. Seymour M. Lipset, "Religion in America: What Religious Revival?" *Columbia University Forum*, II, No. 1 (Winter, 1959), 17-21.

6. Herberg, *op cit.*

7. Earl Raab, "The Nature of the Conflict: An Introduction," in Earl Raab, *Religious Conflict in America* (Garden City, N.Y.: 1964), pp. 1-28.

8. For a brief presentation of the classical period, see Ralph Marcus, "Antisemitism in the Hellenistic-Roman World," in Koppel S. Pinson, ed., *Essays on Antisemitism* (New York: 1964), pp. 61-78.

9. James Parkes, *Antisemitism* (Chicago: 1964), p. 62.

10. *Ibid.*, p. 64.

11. Malcolm Hay, *The Foot of Pride* (Boston: 1950), p. 69.

12. Charles Journet, *The Church of the Word Incarnate* (New York: 1955), I, 229.

13. Quoted in Hay, *loc. cit.*

14. See *Summa Theologica*, II-II, q. 10, a. 12; III, q. 68, a. 10. "Jews are bondsmen of the princes by civil bondage which does not exclude the order of natural and divine law" (*Summa*, II-II, q. 10, a. 12, ad. 3). Scotus agrees with the tradition that people cannot generally be baptized against their will, nor children without the consent of their parents; but in the latter case he makes an exception of princes, who can legitimately baptize the children of unbelievers and Jews.

15. Hay, *op. cit.*, p. 68.

16. Joshua Trachtenberg, *The Devil and the Jews: The Medieval Conception of the Jew and Its Relation to Modern Anti-Semitism* (New Haven: 1943), pp. 188-189.

17. *Ibid.*, pp. 190-194.

18. See Hannah Arendt, *The Origins of Totalitarianism* (Cleveland: 1958), p. 24.

T E N : Anomie and the "Quest for Community": The Formation of Sects among the Puerto Ricans of New York

With Renato Poblete, S.J.

Immigration and assimilation of immigrants are sociological processes that have long been part of the American scene and have received their share of attention from sociologists. For some years after 1924, legislation restricting entrance to this country resulted in substantially lessening the importance of these phenomena in our midst. However, in recent years such problems have again come to the fore as a result of political conditions in Europe and the attraction of large numbers of migrants from the Commonwealth of Puerto Rico to continental United States.

The migration of the Puerto Ricans introduces important new elements into the picture of cultural assimilation. First of all, these arrivals are citizens of the United States. Second, they arrive at a time when most other groups whose American origin goes back to a similar immigration experience have advanced far along the path of assimilation to general American culture patterns. Third, despite their American citizenship, the Puerto Rican migrants come from a culture that is quite different from that of the people of the mainland. Thus to the discrimination that such arrivals usually meet is added the note of irony that they are in fact legally citizens of the Republic.

From *American Catholic Sociological Review*, XXI (Spring, 1960) 18–36.

A fourth point is of considerable importance. Earlier immigrants clustered together in communities where adaptation to the new situation was eased by the preservation of important elements of the older culture. As time went on, more extreme ideas of rapid acculturation were replaced by the recognition of the vital role of the immigrant community in avoiding the worst effects of social and personal disorganization in the acculturation process.

> In view of this the concept of *cultural pluralism* became widely accepted. This helped scholars to recognize the importance of the culture of the immigrant, and to recognize that his loyalties and values and customs should be able to exist in America together with the other culture that we have come to call American.[1]

The Puerto Ricans, however, have been attracted chiefly to the eastern part of the country and in large numbers to New York. In New York City, which is our concern here, the Puerto Ricans have found themselves dispersed into almost every section of the city.

> There are noticeably large concentrations of them in East Harlem, in the South Bronx, on the Lower East Side and in downtown Brooklyn. But in considerable numbers they are scattering into almost every section of the city. This is reflected in the large number of public schools that have Puerto Ricans in attendance in large numbers, and in the parishes, so many of which require the assistance of a Spanish-speaking priest.[2]

There are many factors which are responsible for this dispersal. The city is built up and crowded. Public housing projects often replace older decaying tenements and disperse forming immigrant communities, and the criteria of admission to such projects when completed make impossible the development of a Puerto Rican immigrant community in them.

> In this situation, it is doubtful whether the Puerto Ricans will be able to form the type of community which earlier immigrants formed. If they do, they will have done it in circumstances much more difficult than those faced by earlier immigrant groups.[3]

The new arrivals come from a culture that may in certain respects be called "Catholic," and their reception by coreligionists here on the mainland is therefore of great significance. The official policy of the Archdiocese of New York has paralleled the conditions we have described. There has been no attempt to set up national parishes, but rather to integrate the Puerto Ricans into the already existing parish structure. Yet in these circumstances "it is clearly acknowledged that an intermediate process must take place, that special services must be provided in Spanish, and opportunity given for the practice of traditional customs and devotions by the new parishioners."[4]

In this situation, then, the new arrivals experience cultural assimilation, a process that is already begun at home in the Commonwealth, for the island has been a United States possession for over half a century and the people have enjoyed citizenship for four decades. English was for a time the standard language of instruction, and although that is no longer the case, it is a compulsory subject at all levels of the educational system. Moreover, the political and also the business integration of the Commonwealth into the American community has opened other avenues of acculturation.

This chapter is concerned with one element in that acculturation process: a response to conditions of social and cultural uncertainty in terms of religion. Any visitor to a densely populated Puerto Rican section of New York City will see a large number of what are often referred to as "store-front churches." These are religious groups that use as a place of meeting or worship stores formerly occupied by retail merchants. In one section in East Harlem in 24 blocks (between First and Third Avenues, and between 100th and 105th Streets) there are 30 of these store-front churches. These sects will be our concern here; more specifically, the Pentecostal Sects or the *Asambleas de Dios*.

Protestantism in Puerto Rico

First of all, however, let us look for a moment at the situation of Protestantism in Puerto Rico. Protestantism began its activities in that island about fifty years ago. The *World Christian Handbook* for 1952 mentioned 522 areas where Protestant activity was being carried on. Another publication, *Midcentury Pioneers and Protestants,* gives the number of Protestant church members who are active communicants as 46,433, and the total size of the Protestant group seems to be about 160,000. The study states that at least 10 per cent of the population could be characterized as Protestant and "probably eighty per cent of the island population would say they were Catholics if pressed with the question of religious orientation."[5] According to a study done at Columbia University in 1948, 53 per cent of the 5,000 persons who answered the question claimed that they were "religious in my own fashion."

Such, then, insofar as we know it, is the religious complexion of the Puerto Rican people before migration: largely nominally Catholic, with a strong Catholic group and minority of Protestants.

Protestantism among Puerto Ricans in New York

The only information we have of a detailed kind on Protestantism among Puerto Ricans in New York City is found in a report made by the Church Planning and Research group of the Protestant Council of Churches of New York City in November, 1953. The survey covers 146 non-Roman Catholic churches in the seven areas of heavy Puerto Rican concentration. Fifty-four Negro churches responded, saying that they had almost complete lack of contact with the Puerto Ricans. Fifteen other nondenominational churches said that Puerto Ricans were attending their groups and listed a total of 134 active members and 217 who only attend services. Fifteen of the 43 denominational churches have no contact at all with the Puerto Ricans in their neighborhoods. The survey revealed that the Protestant churches in the communities where Puerto Ricans reside were doing little to welcome them or to evangelize the "unchurched." The director of the survey has stated that the non-Spanish-speaking Protestant churches had only an infinitesimal contact with the Puerto Ricans.[6] The situation in these respects has changed because of the efforts made in an intense campaign to contact and attract Puerto Ricans, but no statistics are available. In a study of three Bronx communities[7] completed in November, 1956, we find 15 per cent of the Puerto Rican population attending Protestant churches. The figure underestimates the actual state of affairs, since many of the small store-front churches do not turn in any reports of this kind.

What is the situation of the Spanish-speaking Protestant churches? It is, in fact, quite different.

The 1953 survey quoted above admits that it is almost impossible to arrive at an exact figure of the number of such churches and of their membership. It has been possible, the survey states, to draw up a list containing the names of 204 non-Catholic Spanish-speaking churches in New York City. Of these, however, only 169 provided sufficient data to permit meaningful study. Yet this figure was three times as large as the number located in 1947 by the Pathfinder Service. Despite the inadequacy of statistics, the fact of growth seems indisputable.

Of these churches reported by the Protestant Council, 55 per cent are classified as Pentecostal, but those listed under the category of "Independent" appear to be very similar and could without serious distortion of the situation be added to the total of the Pentecostal Movement. That would mean that probably 70 per cent of the Spanish-speaking churches can be classified in the Pentecostal category. This figure is impressive at first sight, and a closer examination of what it involves reveals it to be particularly significant. For it is readily seen that

> these two groups—Pentecostals and Independents—are largely a real indigenous expression of Protestant convictions. They receive no aid from denominational agencies . . . they have a strong evangelical spirit and are willing to work with other Protestant Churches toward a limited number of specific short term goals. Generally they are reluctant to identify themselves with institutionalized efforts for Protestant cooperation.[8]

This striking phenomenon of vitality of the Pentecostal groups among people of a Latin culture is not something confined to New York Puerto Ricans. In Italy such groups had 120 places of worship in 1944. Ten years later they had 380 places of worship and comprised 60 per cent of all Protestant churches in the country.[9] In Chile the Pentecostals had around 182,000 adherents in 1955.[10] In fact, the Pentecostals are the most numerous and active of all Protestant groups throughout Latin America.

In New York the Pentecostal churches have an average membership of 85 persons, while the Independents have an average membership of 67 in each church group. The store-front churches have very little resemblance to the typical denominational church. The physical layout consists of a small store which is rented and transformed into a single large room with seats similar to those in a theater. These seats face what had originally been the rear of the store, but is now the front of the church. Here facing the congregation is a pulpit from which the Bible is read. Behind this, separated from the church by a curtain, is a small room in which members can go and pray in solitude and in silence. This is called the *cuarto alto,* the upper room.

The Pentecostal groups are self-starting and self-sustaining. They are evangelical and missionary-minded. They stress a way of life rather than a creed: the emphasis is on intensity rather than universality, and they tend to maintain uncompromisingly radical religious attitudes, demanding from their members the maximum in their relationships to God, to the world, and to men. The moral standards are very high, and there is a genuine austerity about their attitudes and patterns of living. This rigorism often expresses itself in external details: no smoking, no consumption of alcoholic drink, no use of cosmetics for women. Membership is available only after a probationary period of from six months to one year and upon public confession of a personal religious experience. There is a high ratio of lay leadership and responsibility. Tithing is a common practice. One or two collections at one service are common. A community with 80 to 100 members supports a full-time minister. One survey found that "of 96 churches reporting, 45 have full-time pastors, that is to say, serving only one church and having no other employment. Thirty-six have pastors who work at other jobs during the week and 15 share a pastor with another church."[11]

Theory on Sect and Church

It is interesting to recall here the classic definitions of sect and church deriving from the work of Ernst Troeltsch and Max Weber. Troeltsch declares, in his conclusion to his monumental study of church and sect in Christian history, that "the history of the Christian Ethos becomes the story of a constantly renewed search for . . . compromise, and of fresh opposition to this spirit of compromise."[12] Park and Burgess, Simmel, von Wiese, Becker, H. Richard Niebuhr, and Liston Pope[13] have elaborated this basic idea. For these writers a

> church or *ecclesia* is characterized by the following: (1) membership on the basis of birth; (2) administration of the means of grace and its sociological and theological concomitants—hierarchy and dogma; (3) inclusiveness of social structure, often coinciding with ethnic or geographical boundaries; (4) orientation to conversion of all; and (5)

a tendency to compromise with the world. The sect, on the contrary, is characterized by (1) separatism and defiance of or withdrawal from the demands of the secular sphere, preferring isolation to compromise; (2) exclusiveness, expressed in attitude and social structure; (3) emphasis upon conversion prior to membership; and (4) voluntary election or joining.[14]

Moreover, the sect is always ascetic and usually attempts to implement the "priesthood of believers" in an egalitarian social structure. From these definitions it is quite clear that the church is usually associated with settled cultural and social conditions, while the sect is a response of groups that do not for one reason or another fit into the going institutionalized religious bodies of the larger society. H. Richard Niebuhr has shown the social sources of denominationalism to be related to the position of deprived social classes in the total society, and Liston Pope has studied the role of the sect in the adaptation of rural workers to industrial conditions.

In short, it may be said that the sect represents a response of the restructuralization of religious attitudes and orientations in a condition of what Durkheim has called anomie. For Durkheim, anomie was characterized by two interrelated elements. First of all there is a breakdown of those social structures in which the individual found the psychological support and nurture requisite to personal and psychological security. Second, there is a loss of consensus or general agreement on the standards and norms that previously provided the normative orientations and existential definitions in terms of which individual and group life were meaningful. Talcott Parsons has shown that the prevalence of anomie was positively related to rapid social change which brought about social differentiation and the upsetting of old standards and relationships in a changing situation, which prevents the crystallization of new attitudinal and social structures.

It is quite clear that the Pentecostal groups we have described meet most of the criteria of a sect put forward by the classical definitions. While the theological aspects of sectarianism are interesting and important, the sociological level of analysis seems to offer a more fruitful area of research for a fuller understanding of what these developments really signify. Over two decades ago Christopher Dawson suggested something similar with respect to the history of the church. Said Dawson, "Most of the great schisms and heresies in the history of the Christian church have their roots in social and national antipathies, and if this had been clearly recognized by the theologians, the history of Christianity would have been a very different one."[15]

The Anomie Hypothesis

On the basis of the information which this preliminary and exploratory study has provided us so far we can safely conclude that the rise and development of the Pentecostal movement among the Puerto Rican migrants in New York represents a typical example of sectarian formation and development. That it is a serious religious phenomenon is clear to any informed observer. Moreover, historically such a development has been found to be associated with anomie and to be a form of the recrystallization of attitudes and the re-formation of solidarity in the face of such anomie. Since we are dealing here with people who all the available objective evidence would suggest are suffering the concomitant anxieties of social and cultural change incumbent upon migration and assimilation to a new culture, it seems a fruitful hypothesis to suggest that such movements represent precisely such a reaction to the anomie involved in migration.

It is necessary to recall that one important aspect of anomie for Durkheim was the disruption of existing social structures. Certainly removal to a new city under the conditions of dispersal would suggest that element in the present case. Moreover, Parsons, following Max Weber, has suggested that the "process of rationalization" by introducing impersonal relationships in the place of the more personal relationships of the older cultures played an important part in undermining personal securities and contributing to the anomique condition of the people involved.[16]

Sectarianism: A Response to Anomie

The hypothesis to be explored in the remainder of this chapter may be stated as follows: The development of sectarianism among New York Puerto Ricans is a response to anomie. It is, furthermore, a response that represents a positive quest for community in the face of the loss of more traditional social structures and the impersonalization (universalism and functional specificity, in Parson's terms) of modern American urban society.

The larger frame of reference in which this problem must be considered is one that includes Western civilization as a whole. Modern man is haunted by the specter of insecurity in consequence of the many reasons which we have indicated above. "There is a decided weakening of faith in the inherent stability of the individual and in psychological and moral neutrality; individualism has become in recent decades a term to describe pathological conditions of society."[17] The release of the individual from the traditional ties of class, religion, and kinship has made him free, but on the testimony of innumerable works of our age, this freedom is accompanied, not by the sense of creative release, but by the experience of disenchantment and alienation. Erich Fromm has shown that it may be accompanied by intense psychological anxiety.[18] In fact, the theme of uprooted man seeking fellowship is as frequent in our time as was the theme of the individual's emancipation from tribal or communal conformity in the past. Riesman speaks of a new need for "other directedness" among Americans, and popular magazines exploit the theme of "togetherness."[19] The loss of what Durkheim called consensus is what Nesbit has called a loss of moral certitudes and is followed by a sense of alienation from one's fellow man.[20] Industrial sociology has shown the importance of the work community for the morale of the individual workman. Drucker has commented on the "end of the economic man." Since the larger framework of human orientation includes what Paul Tillich has called "the ultimate," that such a loss of solidarity and consensus has religious significance and that the response to it may take the form of a religious quest are not difficult to see.

Today there is visible a reaction against the heritage of the immediate past. Men seem to be seeking integration, status, membership; there is a desire for recognition, for the formation of small groups, for personal relationships. This is a reaction against the impersonalization of a technological society characterized by urbanism. Toennies saw the history of the West as the transformation of *Gemeinschaft* into *Gesellschaft,* what in Redfield's terms may be called the transition from a folk to an urban society. Today, American society seems to be reacting in an opposite direction. The much heralded and quite ambiguous revival of religion seems to be an associated phenomenon.[21]

If religion appears to offer a way out of this situation—especially to a people whose cultural background is characterized by important religious elements—the reverse is also true. Religious life requires the support and underpinning of social solidarity. André Brien emphasizes the need of small communities in order that Catholic people may be able to live the faith.[22] He refers to the proliferation of sects in the popular milieu as a sign of the importance of the formation of small communities in the urban world of today. These groups, characterized by enthusiasm in the eighteenth-century meaning of that term, and sometimes to the point of fanaticism, are capable of evoking from the impersonalized man of our age a spirit of unity and sacrifice. The intense life of the group exalts the personality; the person caught up in the current of irresistible enthusiasm discovers in himself a force of life which previously had lain dormant. This gives the individual a feeling of participation and consequently of strength and worth.

The Quest for Community

What we have reviewed so far would suggest that anomie is a fairly general problem in modern urban society and that reaction against it—attempts to escape it—are far from uncommon. We are suggesting that a similar condition is characteristic of the Puerto Rican migrants in response to the concrete conditions of their migration. At this point, in view of our general characterization of this phenomenon as a quest for community, it will be helpful to consider recent theoretical discussions of the meaning of that term among sociologists.

George A. Hillery, in his study of areas of agreement in the definitions of community used in sociological literature, states that "a majority of the definitions include as important elements . . . an area, common ties and social interaction."[23] For MacIver a community is a social unity whose members recognize as common sufficient interest to permit the common activities and interactions of common life.[24] In his book *Society,* the same author states that we have community when the members live their lives wholly within the general group. He stresses community sentiment as the most important ingredient of community, since modern transport has made a territorial base relatively unimportant. For MacIver this community sentiment has three elements: "we-feeling," that is, a sense of collective participation in an indivisible unity, a sense of belonging to the group which can use the term "we" with the same referent; "role-feeling," a sense of status which consists in the fact that each person feels he has a part to perform, a function to fulfill in the reciprocal exchange, involving a subordination of the individual to the whole; and "dependency-feeling," closely associated with role-feeling, involving the individual's feeling of dependency on the community as a necessary condition for his own life. It involves either physical or psychological dependency since the community is the greater home which sustains him. It is the refuge from solitude and the fears that accompany the individual isolation so characteristic of modern life.[25]

Toennies found the supreme form of community in what he called the "*Gemeinschaft* of mind" implying "cooperation and coordinated action for a common goal."[26] August B. Hollingshead concluded that the term "community" was defined in at least three different ways in current literature: *(a)* as a form of group solidarity, cohesion, and action around common and diverse interests; *(b)* as a geographic area with spatial limits; or *(c)* as a sociogeographical structure which combines the first two definitions.[27]

The elements of these classical and contemporary definitions of most concern to us would appear to be those stressed in Toennies' *Gemeinschaft* of mind and MacIver's community sentiment and represented in other terms in the other definitions.

A Test of the Anomie Hypothesis

Let us restate our hypothesis more fully at this point: *The formation of sects is one of the known ways out of anomie, and the facts of Puerto Rican life in New York suggest the presence of such a condition among these new arrivals. The sect represents a search for a way out of that condition and is therefore an attempt to redevelop the community in the new urban situation.*

In attempting to explore this hypothesis and to prepare for

some kind of observational testing of it, a small area in the Southern Bronx was studied. This area coincides with St. Athanasius Roman Catholic Parish. In this area we were able to locate ten store-front churches and two larger churches of the same type, the Christian Church of Juan 3:16, at Westchester Avenue, and the Independent Church, Iglesia del Señor, with characteristics quite like those of the Pentecostals.

These store-front churches did not have more than sixty members each. They have almost daily meetings with an attendance of half to two thirds of the membership present. It is quite difficult to get reliable figures on the exact membership since there are always some visitors at the services who either come from other store-front churches or may be just curious outsiders. Each evening's services are organized by a different subgroup: the men's group, the women's group, or the youth group. The service begins around eight o'clock in the evening and lasts until around ten. When a stranger attends he is greeted immediately, given a songbook, and offered a seat. The amount of cordiality shown to the visitor is remarkable to the field worker. The minister or some person from the congregation reads the Bible and explains what has been read. Accompanying the words of the speaker there gradually develops a kind of spontaneous participation by the congregation. This takes the form of spontaneous ejaculations such as *Amen, Alleluia, Gloria à Dios, Gloria à Jesus, Dios todopoderoso,* and *Alabado Dios.* In this way the group actively participates even in that part of the service in which a leader has the structured ascendancy and initiative.

After the sermon, which is punctuated by such exclamations from the congregation, the whole community sings. Some of the melodies are old American folk songs with special religious Spanish text or are translated Protestant hymns. Frequently somebody volunteers to sing a solo or to play an instrument. The minister during this period invites people to speak a few words or relate their own religious experience or the history of their conversion. Some members of the congregation express gratitude for favors received, or ask for prayers for some need. This is followed by more singing.

Then plans for evangelical work are proposed or reports of current activities are heard. At the end everybody prays in a loud voice and spontaneously. One can feel the enthusiasm and desire for the *Spirit* in the group. At times an individual manifests the reception of the Holy Spirit by "speaking with tongues." When that happens the members begin to shout incoherently or just to utter words. The speech of the person who has the gift of tongues may be "interpreted" by another member. Then the members of the community thank God and pray that all may receive these gifts.

On Sunday, service lasts for two hours. Here the minister, either the regular minister or a guest, will have a more important role. He will give instruction to the people on the Bible or on moral precepts.

In addition to using what sociologists call "participant observation" of these groups, ministers and members were interviewed. We were able to interview 28 persons. The interviews were conducted in Spanish by the field worker, for whom Spanish is his native language. All but 3 of the 28 were baptized Catholics. Yet these 25 did not have any real knowledge of the Catholic Church. There appeared to be no ground to assume that their conversion was in any intellectual sense a protest against the Catholic Church. The element of protest was not important in what they reported about themselves. Moreover, the interviews revealed that their knowledge of the ideology of the sect was rudimentary. The Bible is held to be the only norm of life, a point of view that involves a very fundamentalistic interpretation of the "Word." They all hold that we have been redeemed by Christ's death. They hold the importance of two baptisms, one of water and one of the spirit. There is much emphasis on a total way of life involving brotherly love and the rejection of sin. There is no systematic doctrinal body of beliefs.

The people interviewed talked very frankly about their conversion. They consider the frank revelation of the history of their conversion as a "testimony," bearing of witness to the Holy Spirit. The form of such testimonies shows that despite the spontaneity of communal religiosity there is a degree of stereotyping. It would appear that each convert has heard many testimonies and makes the attempt to interpret and fit in his own experience into a normatively desired pattern. They usually go in this way. "I used to drink. . . I was a drug addict . . . I used to run around with women. . . I was on the wrong path. . .but one day I received the Spirit, I got to know the 'Word.' " They always attribute a great sinfulness to their previous life. The form of the testimony emphasizes a great experience of sinfulness and the religious experience of being possessed by the Spirit. And the latter appears to give them a certitude of regeneration.

The formal "design" of the testimony reveals consciousness of sinfulness—conversion—regeneration. While this is not a spontaneous product of subjective personal disposition unaffected by social conformation to an expected pattern, there is reason to suspect that subjective experience lent itself readily to such conformation. That is to say, while these testimonies may be elicited in an interview situation without any direction suggested by the interviewer, the sectarian expectations do, in fact, act to standardize them. Yet they also seem to reflect something important of the experience of conversion which seems in itself (as well as in its retelling) to have been shaped for subjective awareness by the sectarian stereotype. Moreover, the original need dispositions of the subjects appear to have lent themselves to precisely this kind of standardization. Although it would be very difficult to separate the elements analytically and perhaps impossible to observe them empirically, there appears a measure of congruence between the "primitive" experience and the content of the sectarian stereotype. This bears obvious resemblance to the general sectarian conviction of regeneration and to that aspect of the world religions that Max Weber referred to in his treatment of "salvation religions." These people feel saved from something and incorporated into something new and clean and good.

Conversion—the classical phenomenon of religious psychology—is something that follows upon some months of attending services as spectators. When the interviewees were asked why they started coming to meetings, why they first became interested in the sect, their answers also revealed a degree of uniformity, and possibly one less affected by a cultural stereotype. "The first time I went there, I was impressed by the way everyone shook hands with me and the way everybody said 'hello' to me." "I was sick; they came to my home to say a prayer for me." "I used to go to the Catholic Church, there nobody knew me . . . now in my church they call me sister." A very typical answer was "Me senti como en mi casa." (I felt at home.) "I was lost here in New York; a friend invited me and I liked the way they sang and that we all could sing." "I like to read the Bible." "The first time I went, when the service was over, someone came to me and asked my name and invited me to come again." Participant observation at the meetings confirms the interpretation of warmth, welcome, and participation related by the converted.

The interviews strongly suggest that isolation is one of the things from which such people are saved by the salvation experience of conversion. Isolation appears to be associated with a loss of orientation in life. Thus the material offered by those interviewed would tend to support the contention that conversion offered a way out of anomie, in terms of both providing social relationships and giving meaningful orientations to the converted.

That the sect is a real community according to elements stressed in the sociological literature is confirmed by both the content of the interviews and participant observation. For example, the three elements of community sentiment stressed by MacIver are present to a high degree in the Pentecostal sect.

The presence of we-feeling is clearly evident in the way members talk about the sect. The church to which they belong is not something foreign or removed from them. The service is a common enterprise; the members support the group with great financial generosity; there is a real conviction of membership in a brotherhood. They all know each other by name: "hermano Juan," "hermana Maria," and so on.

Role-feeling is also quite evident. Each member has a role in the community, and so marked is such participation that one report concluded that "it is hard to know to what degree we can call these churches a lay association."[28] The individual member has opportunities to direct the service, to tell his troubles, to recount his religious experiences, to ask for prayers and to give thanks for prayers said, or to ask for help. The members not only participate in religious services in this way but also take part in such work as visiting the sick. The minister of the East Harlem Protestant Parish, a parish divided into five small communities following the example of Abbé Michoneau in France, stated to us that the activity of the layman was in his opinion the clue to the success of these Protestant sects.

Moreover, MacIver's feeling of dependency is also present. Each person knows that he is a part of the group, that he needs the group in order to sustain his regeneration. He feels this dependency at the service when the minister asks the names of those who are sick, or the names of those whose birthdays fall in the coming week. If a person gives his name, the whole community prays for him.

It is important to note that the group solidarity appears to the converted, not as a loss of individuality, but rather as a chance to develop his own personality—to experience a worthwhile fulfillment.

One indication of what has been said concerns the question of size. It would seem that such close in-group sentiment would require small groups and that a larger membership would inevitably introduce secondary relationships with concomitant impersonalization. In this respect it was interesting to find in the area of our study a large Pentecostal church with a membership of 800. This church had been founded in 1935 and began, as all such groups begin, as a small one with a small meeting place. By 1954, it had grown to 500 members and was able to purchase for $70,000 a reconditioned theatre with a seating capacity of 1,800. Now two full-time ministers care for the community. At their weekly meetings they have between 200 and 300 persons. Though this figure in comparison with that of the total membership suggests a lower degree of participation, it is nevertheless remarkable to find there all the characteristics we found in the smaller bodies. H. Richard Niebuhr has developed the Troeltschian theory to show that sects in time also have to make some kind of compromise with the world in which they live and become routinized. Such a routinized sect he calls a denomination. This larger group in our area does not, in the opinion of the observer, show any impressive signs of such routinization, but our research has not proceeded far enough to answer the important questions in this respect.

While we do not consider our hypothesis unambiguously confirmed at this stage of the game, we do feel entirely justified in stating that a hypothesis based on such a firm body of sociological theory as this one is provides a very helpful device for understanding the phenomenon with which we are dealing. Moreover, the evidence to date does bear a striking congruence with the hypothesis itself. Since the hypothesis is based on a body of theory that has considerable congruence with religious life as it has been studied in a multitude of different concrete settings, the congruity of our preliminary material with it gives us greater confidence than would be the case were our hypothesis merely an *ad hoc* construction unrelated to a larger body of theory and empirical generalization.

Theoretical Suggestions

Following this provisory and tentative confirmation of our hypothesis, several questions of importance arise in addition to the need for more data on the points discussed above. Many of them cannot be answered definitively by this study even when it is completed, but what we have uncovered so far makes their formulation possible and worthwhile.

1. *Why do some people form specifically religious groups as a way out of anomie?*

Some suggestions might be made here in relation to the general religious culture from which these people come. The Pentecostals bear a strong resemblance, and possibly an obscure historical relationship, to the Joachimite enthusiasm of the Middle Ages. First of all, there is the emphasis on the Holy Spirit. Second, while the Joachimites expected the "rule of monks" in a third age of the world, the Pentecostals are in a certain sense monks in the world. Moreover, during the ages when religion was a dominant element in the culture of the West in a sense that has long ceased to be the case, many movements of social and even political significance found expression in religious forms and with a religious ideology; the followers of Thomas Münzer in the German Peasant War, for example. With secularization, such movements found socialistic or syndicalistic forms for expression. Certainly, the communist parties in their period of revolutionary opposition offer an analogue to the sect in the sphere of political life, while their becoming a ruling core of functionaries after they take power shows structural and functional equivalents to the transformation of a sectarian movement into a church. The Social Democratic parties appear in many ways similar to denominations, with sectarian traditions accommodated to the present in a practical way. The Puerto Ricans, despite the remoteness of institutional Catholicism from many of their needs, would appear to come from a cultural situation more like that of Europe before secularization had proceeded very far than like the culture of urban workers in Europe today. Hence their needs for orientation and personal security take on a religious form of expression and become a religious need.

2. *If anomie is a result of migration, how do we explain the success of Pentecostal groups in Puerto Rico and in other Latin countries as well?*

One might suggest that the relation of the institutional church to the needs of people in certain conditions of life in these countries is worth a good deal of study. It appears that institutional Catholicism fails to meet these needs, and hence people turn elsewhere. The gap between them and the church would appear to leave a void that involves some aspects of anomie. Yet the church has kept them sufficiently Christian in their outlook so that they seek the answer in a Christian idiom.

3. *How long does regeneration last? What about backsliding?*

We have no real information on this important point. Backsliding has been an important and ubiquitous phenomenon in American Protestant revivalism, from which the term derives.

4. *What are the sociological concomitants of the need for salvation, or, as our interviewees express it, the sense of sinfulness?*

Certainly isolation and the concomitant loss of meaningful orientation are important in this respect. But much more needs to be known. Certain conditions of life predispose people to certain needs and attitudes. Which of these are found associated with the sense of sin?

5. *Do social mobility, status, and class play a role in these sectarian movements? Does the frugal life of the sectary lead to worldly success, as has so often happened with such groups? Does regeneration withstand worldly success?*

We have as yet no information on these questions.

6. *What about the suggested congruence between the stereotype of sinfulness—conversion—regeneration and the "primitive" experience of needing to be saved from something?*

This question is largely a problem for religious psychology, but it is also important to the sociology of religion, for such experiences bear a relationship to socially structured and shared conditions. For, they are in part at least, a response to anomie.

NOTES

1. Joseph P. Fitzpatrick, "The Integration of Puerto Ricans," *Thought*, XXX, No. 118 (Autumn, 1955), 406.

2. *Ibid.*, p. 413.

3. *Ibid.*, p. 415.

4. *Ibid.,* pp. 415–416.

5. Meryl Ruoss, *Midcentury Pioneers and Protestants.* A survey Report of the Puerto Rican migration to the U.S. mainland and in particular a Study of Protestant Expression among Puerto Ricans in New York City, 2d ed. (New York: 1954), p. 2.

6. *Ibid.,* p. 14.

7. *Morrisania, Melrose, Mott Haven, Three Bronx Communities* (New York: 1956), p. 3.

8. Ruoss, *op. cit.,* p. 16.

9. *Revista el Clero Italiano,* Rome (February, 1950).

10. Ignacio Vergara, "Los Evangelicos in Chile," *Revista Mensaje,* Santiago, Chile (August, 1955).

11. Ruoss, *op. cit.,* p. 22.

12. Ernst Troeltsch, *The Social Teachings of the Christian Churches,* Olive Wyon, tr. (London and New York: 1931), II, 999–1000.

13. Cf. Robert E. Park and Ernest W. Burgess, *Introductory to the Science of Sociology* (Chicago: 1921), pp. 50, 202–203, 611–612, 657, 870–874; Howard Becker, *Systematic Sociology: On the Basis of the "Beziehungslehre und Gebildelehre" of Leopold von Wiese: Adapted and Amplified* (New York: 1932), pp. 624–628. H. Richard Niebuhr, *The Social Sources of Denominationalism* (New York: 1929), pp. 17 ff.; and Liston Pope, *Millhands and Preachers: A Study of Gastonia* (New Haven: 1942).

14. See "Mormonism and the Avoidance of Sectarian Stagnation: A Study of Church, Sect, and Incipient Nationality," Chapter 6 in the present volume.

15. Christopher Dawson, "Sociology as a Science," quoted from the republication in *Cross Currents,* IV, No. 2 (Winter, 1954), 136.

16. Talcott Parsons, *Essays in Sociological Theory* (Glencoe: 1949), especially "Democracy and Social Structure in Pre-Nazi Germany," pp. 104–123, and "Some Sociological Aspects of Fascist Movements," pp. 124–141.

17. Robert A. Nesbit, *The Quest for Community* (New York: 1953), p. 7.

18. Erich Fromm, *Escape from Freedom* (New York: 1941).

19. David Riesman, *The Lonely Crowd* (New Haven: 1950).

20. Nesbit, *op. cit.,* p. 11.

21. Will Herberg, *Protestant, Catholic, Jew* (Garden City, N.Y.: 1955).

22. André Brien, "Les Petits communautés soustenance de la Foi," *Etudes,* Paris, CCLXXIX (November, 1953), 168–186.

23. George A. Hillery, "Definitions of Community: Areas of Agreement," *Rural Sociology,* XX (June, 1955), 111–123.

24. R. M. MacIver, *Community* (New York: 1936), pp. 110–131.

25. R. M. MacIver and Charles H. Page, *Society* (New York: 1939), p. 293.

26. Ferdinand Toennies, *Fundamental Concepts of Sociology,* Charles Loomis, tr. (New York: 1940), p. 40.

27. A. B. Hollingshead, "Community Research: Development and Present Condition," *American Sociological Review,* XIII (April, 1948), 136–146.

28. Ruoss, *op. cit.,* p. 20.

SOCIOLOGY OF RELIGION: SOCIOLOGICAL THEORY

ELEVEN: Sociology and the Study of Religion

Sociology as a social science is based on the recognition that uniformities reveal themselves in human behavior, which are not to be completely understood in terms of either the psychology of the individual actors or the ideas and values of a given cultural tradition. This recognition points to the existence of social structures and social processes which are neither reducible to individual psychology nor to be explained as the effects of ideas. That relatively autonomous level of social phenomena provides the context of relationships within which human action takes place and as such exercises independent causal influence on such action. Sociology is the disciplined and systematic study of this level of social structure and social process both in itself and in relation to individual motivation and the ideas and values of the culture.[1] Hence sociology is closely related to psychology and to the study of culture, but it is also related to history, with which it shares important common interests. It is not true to say that sociology studies historical phenomena "from the outside." Sociology is concerned both with the inner content of ideas and values and with the previous course of historical development of the phenomena it studies, but that interest is restricted by its concentration on analysis, understanding, and prediction in terms of social structure and social process.[2] Hence sociology is one discipline among many requisite to the study of religion, but it is one whose contribution is of considerable importance.

The sociology of religion is the study of religion in relation to social structure and process, both those involved in the relation

From an Invitational Conference on the Study of Religion, October 23–25, 1964 (New Haven: 1965) by permission of The Society for Religion in Higher Education.

201

between religion and the general society and those internal to the religious organization and institution. There has developed in the present century a sizable and respectable body of ideas which provide a conceptual frame of reference and a vocabulary of analysis useful to sociologists in the study of religion. Although neither the theoretical implications nor the research potentialities of these ideas have been developed fully,[3] such a body of theory in this sense does exist. In the years since World War II there has been a renewal of interest in the study of religion on the part of sociologists—an interest reflected in an increasing number of empirical studies, an increase in textbooks on the sociology of religion for the college level and to some extent in the composition of sociology faculties.

This body of ideas which comprise a theoretical structure for the sociology of religion, although still left in a relatively undeveloped state, is, in fact, quite impressive. It derives from a number of significant figures and traditions in the social sciences: Malinowski and the cultural anthropologists,[4] Durkheim and his successors,[5] Ernst Troeltsch,[6] Max Weber,[7] and later Joachim Wach[8] and Talcott Parsons, who has done much to make explicit the relation of the ideas of his predecessors to sociological theory generally.[9] There has also been some influence from Karl Marx and the Marxists[10] and from economic historians such as R. H. Tawney and Amintore Fanfani.[11] The contributions of these men and the scholarly and scientific traditions they represent do not permit lengthy presentation and criticism in the scope of this chapter. Instead we shall describe two common theoretical contexts in which religion is studied by contemporary sociologists—contexts constructed largely on the insights and contributions of these men.

Functional Theory: Traditional Religion and the Stable Society

We shall begin with functional theory, which rests primarily on the insights of Durkheim and the cultural anthropologists. Functional theory is based (in its concern with religion) primarily on studies made on small-scale nonliterate societies and may with some justice be accused of overemphasizing the traditional and conservative aspects of religion in its relationship to the general society. Nevertheless, it raises and provides useful answers to fundamental questions and thereby contributes to sociology an overall frame of reference and an approach to the study of religious phenomena. Functional theory conceives of societies as "social systems"; that is, as ongoing equilibriums of social institutions, which pattern human activity on the basis of a normative consensus—of shared norms held by the actors themselves to be legitimate and binding on them. The social system itself is composed of subsystems, of institutional complexes, which are interdependent with another and with the social system as a whole. Such a point of view rules out the search for simplified cause-and-effect relationships and introduces instead a concern with multiple causation and reverse "feedback" relationship of effects on causes in the systemic whole.[12] Changes anywhere in the system affect other institutional complexes and are affected by events in the other institutional complexes in reaction to the change.

Religion is looked upon as one kind, although in certain ways a unique kind, of institutional behavior existing in a state of interdependence with other institutions and the society as a whole. It is a postulate of functional theory that all forms of institutionalized behavior have a function in relation to the maintenance of the social system, although that function may be manifest or latent, obvious or subtle, intended and recognized or unintended and unrecognized by the actors involved.[13] Hence there arises the functional question with respect to religion: what is the contribution of religion to the maintenance of the social system?

Functional theory also views culture as a more or less systematic body of knowledge and lore, and values and beliefs, transmitted and developed from generation to generation, which provides orientation, in terms of both cognition and evaluation, to the participants in a society or social system. It is an ideational system whose elements may be implicit or explicit, possessing some kind of meaningful integration, though not necessarily on the model of Western rationality. It is integrated with the social system in that it enters into the definitions of means and ends, prescriptions and proscriptions, which define the roles in which society's members act out the events of their lives and insofar as it affects, through the training and education of the young, the motivations and aspirations of individuals. It is the creation of men, emerging together with stable social forms, from human activity under the conditions and demands of the environment. It presents a fabric of meaning to the members of the society and, once established, exhibits a partial autonomy and, by defining the meaning of events, affects future human action. Religion is seen as an important aspect of this cultural phenomenon. Functional theory would accept the definition of Wendell T. Bush that "religion is a very important part of the world of imagination that functions socially, and its verbal expressions represent only a small fraction of it."[14]

Contemporary sociology further recognizes that while men share ideas and values and act in socially structured contexts subject to the manifest and latent forces of social control, nevertheless it is the individual human being who acts, and feels, and thinks, and not some hypostatized entity such as a group mind or a cultural or historical tendency. Hence sociology accepts the contributions of dynamic psychology and thereby often considerably enriches the insights of its founders. For example, Max Weber's interest in religion as an independent causal factor in human history, particularly in connection with the origin and development of capitalism, when supplemented by a sophisticated concern with its psychological implications, leads to the study of the ways in which societies may or may not develop in their members attitudes toward work and achievement of far-reaching consequences.[15]

Culture, social system, and personality are seen as three aspects of a complex social phenomenon whose effects are observed in human behavior. The functional question is raised necessarily in relation to all three. What is the effect of religion and of religious institutions on the ongoing system of social relations, on the maintenance of the culture, and on the functioning of personality? This question expresses the basic frame of reference in which sociology studies the phenomenon of religion and its role in human life. It obviously does not exhaust the human significance of religion, but it does raise an important question concerning it. Within its broad context narrower, more specific questions can be asked as the basis of empirical research.

Functional theory distinguishes two types of needs and propensities to act as characterizing man in society. He must act in a practical manner so as to ensure his survival in a given environment, and a human society with its culture is seen as the unit of survival, sometimes requiring the nonsurvival of some of its members to assure its own. Human activity must to some degree be instrumental and adaptive in an active or passive sense, promoting mastery over or at least permitting adjustment to the environing conditions. Men also have expressive needs—needs to act out emotions and to enter relationships. In the course of their problem-solving activities they develop relationships and rituals which acquire value in their own right.[16] Here, too, the functional question arises: What is the significance of religion in terms of these adaptive and expressive needs and in terms of supporting the social contexts which render life orderly and meaningful?

In this general functional context, religion is seen as something that transcends empirical adaptive experience and allows and patterns the expression of important expressive needs. Human beings in all societies, including the technologically advanced societies of the West, confront problems and dilemmas which cannot be handled in terms of empirical knowledge alone. Moreover, the ways in which problems are solved by men—for example, the development of a system of economic or political institutions—involve a patterning of relationships which inflict deprivation and cause frustration to some and often to many of the participants. Institutional patterns involve consensually validated allocations of power, resources, functions, facilities, and rewards, both material and nonmaterial, and such patterned allocation inevitably involves both discipline and deprivation and, consequently, frustration. Since such frustration is involved in society's functioning, it usually presents individuals with situations beyond their capacities to change. Hence some way must be provided to ensure human acceptance of and adjustment to them.

Most important of these aleatory and frustrating elements in the human situations which transcend human control are those involved in what has been called the "uncertainty context" and the "impossibility context." The former refers to the unhappy fact that all human ventures, however well planned and executed, are liable to disappointment and that such ventures often involve an extremely high investment of human interest and human emotion. "The best laid schemes o' mice and men gang aft a-gley." The latter refers to the equally unhappy fact that not everything men desire can be realized here on earth in their lifetimes and that the aspirations men set their hearts upon are often beyond human capacities.

There is a strategic importance in the way in which the

uncertainty and impossibility contexts bring men beyond the everyday life of the workaday world. The problems and dilemmas involved bring men not simply *beyond* the skills and capacities of their cultural milieu but also *beyond* the established and defined situations of everyday social behavior and cultural definitions of goals and norms. The inherent element of contingency in the human situation brings men to a confrontation with situations in which human knowledge and social forms display a total insufficiency for providing either means of solution or "mechanisms" for adjustment and acceptance. They provide men with "breaking points" in the socially structured and culturally defined world of mundane existence. As "breaking beyond" the everyday, they raise questions which can find an answer only in some kind of "beyond" itself.

If these questions are not answered, the worth of everyday activity itself and the value of institutionalized goals and norms are called into question. It is at these breaking points that what Max Weber has called the "problem of meaning" arises in a sharp and poignant form. Suffering and death, disappointment and deprivation, frustration and oppression, what in theology is called the "problem of evil," arises as a fundamental existential problem in the lives of men and threatens the stability of human societies. These problems and dilemmas are inherently involved in man's attempt to handle his environment and in the social contexts he evolves as the framework for such activity. They must be made to make sense, and ways of adjusting to the tragic realities must be provided. Man must achieve a measure of security in a fundamentally inscrutable world which is characterized by a large measure of contingency and often condemns him to injury and pain. Unless this is provided, human morale for everyday activity founders, and the acceptance of the normative consensus on which society rests is undermined.

If man can go beyond the appearances and make a relationship with some ground of experience and existence, however variously conceived and given symbolic form in various cultures, and if a larger view can be formulated transcending the empirical experience of the "here and now"—a view in which the evil events and experiences can be seen as making sense—and further, if the norms of society which are a cause of frustration can be seen as justified in terms of such a larger view and in relation to such a ground, contingency can be borne and frustration and misfortune accepted. All is not in pieces, and all coherence is not gone, and the "here and now" becomes meaningful by being seen in the context of a larger *beyond*.

Moreover, functional theory sees that "beyond" not simply as transcending everyday existence in a cognitive sense but as possessing a specific quality radically differentiating it from the world of everydayness. It is perceived by men as "sacred" and therefore as eliciting from men an attitude and response of intense respect. Durkheim's treatment of the sacred, which paralleled in important respects that of Rudolph Otto, distinguishes it as radically heterogeneous from the profane sphere of experience and characterized as nonutilitarian, ambiguous, being both propitious and threatening, as involving forces and powers deeper than the appearances of things, as superior in power and seriousness, as evoking awe and respect, and as strength-giving and demanding to those who enter into relationship with it. Thus religion provides an answer to contingency by allowing the worshiper to make a relationship with a more powerful, sacred ground of experience and justifies norms that frustrate men by sacralizing them. Functional theory also calls attention to man's attempt not only to enter into a religious relation to the sacred but also to manipulate these forces and powers through magic. In discussing ritual and rite involved in these two forms of human commerce with the sacred, Malinowski points out that the religious rite is an acting out of attitudes for their own sake, while magic is an attempt to manipulate the sacred forces for empirical ends. Both are, however, characterized by the qualities of the sacred suggested above.[17] Durkheim has emphasized the way in which the performance of the religious rite reasserts the sanctity of the norms and reestablishes the solidarity of the group;[18] Malinowski, the way the performance of magic supplements the limitations of empirical skills in situations of danger and threat and thereby supports human morale in situations in which it might otherwise fail.

Thus functional theory sees religion as meeting the problem of meaning at the breaking points of human experience where a transcendental referent becomes necessary. It sanctifies the norms of society and thereby makes an important contribution to the maintenance of social control and of order in society. Kingsley Davis has summarized this functionalist point of view with brevity and succinctness:

> Religion, then, does four things that help to maintain the dominance of sentiment over organic desire, of group ends over private interest.

First, it offers, through its system of supernatural belief, an explanation of group ends and a justification of their primacy. Second, it provides, through its collective ritual, a means for the constant renewal of the common sentiments. Third, it furnishes, through its sacred objects, a concrete reference for the values and rallying point for all persons who share the same values. Fourth, it provides an unlimited and insuperable source of rewards and punishments—rewards for good conduct, punishment for bad. In these ways religion makes a unique and indispensable contribution to social integration.[19]

Religion contributes not only to the integration of society and culture but to human personality as well. It provides the necessary answer to the ultimate question of meaning; it integrates the individual into a meaningful realm by placing him in relation to the sacred and into his group by its ritual reassertion of its values and norms. It thereby enlarges his significance for himself. It provides him with mechanisms for adjustment to loss and frustration and reconciles him to the difficulties and tragedies involved in the uncertainty and impossibility contexts. Davis summarizes this aspect of religion's function as well. Religion, by providing

> goals beyond this world serves to compensate people for the frustrations they invariably experience in striving to reach socially valuable ends. It replaces a possibly dangerous aggression with a benevolent faith in the unseen. . . . Religion thus gives release from sorrow and fear. . . . Ritual means are freely provided for wiping away guilt, so that one can count on divine grace.[20]

I have presented functional theory in some detail because it represents the theoretical basis of most sociological approaches to the study of religion. Moreover, it is the conceptual framework in which college textbooks in sociology and anthropology typically present religion as a social phenomenon. Most important, it contains certain important insights for the study of religion. Its posing of the functional question in the context of society, culture, and personality actually opens up a vast area for empirical research. It represents a great advance on those theories in the social sciences at the turn of the century which tended to view religion as a survival of superstition or as the ignorance and error of backward people and treated all human activity not based on technological or economic rationality as of negative significance for the progress of human societies.[21] Yet functional theory as formulated in our texts and even in theoretical works exhibits a number of serious shortcomings. Commenting on Davis' summary of functional theory, Charles Y. Glock has justly stated:

> These propositions are drawn primarily from studies of religion in nonliterate societies and, in large part, from studies of a generation or more ago. Since these studies were made, there have been frequent attacks on their inability to account fully for the place of religion in modern, complex, and changing societies. The task of elaborating them to increase their applicability to modern society, however, has been almost wholly neglected.[22]

Moreover, based on observation of traditional societies, functional theory tends to focus attention on the conservative function of religion and neglects the role of religion in innovation and even in revolution. Also, while its general propositions on the function of religion are useful and suggestive, there has been insufficient attention to delineating the degree of contribution to integration of a particular religion or of particular types of religion and an almost total neglect of the importance of religion surrogates (functional equivalents of religion) which in the secularized societies of the West today perform many of the functions of religion in the past. These present a most varied array, from political ideology to medical psychiatry. The rate of secularization in our day, not only in the West but in the developing countries, makes this a most significant oversight.[23]

Moreover, an overemphasis on function has tended to keep some sociologists from paying sufficient attention to the effect on the development of religious institutions of the doctrines implicit in the original religious experience of the founders. Such a tendency tends to keep the sociological perspective removed from internal problems of religious organization and to militate against the development of an internal functionalism of religious institutions themselves.[24]

The Developmental Point of View

Functional theory in the form stated above, however, does not exhaust the theoretical resources of the sociology of religion. Turning to the works of Ernst Troeltsch and Max Weber, we find a body of ideas of considerable utility to empirical study in the religious field. Max Weber, in his treatment of charisma, introduces a way of looking at religious movements which enables us to follow their direction of development sensitized to its strategic crises and moments. Charisma is for Weber a characteristic of spontaneous leaders which exhibits unusualness, spontaneity, and creativity and often a character bearing marked resemblance to the sacred and the holy as discussed by Durkheim and Otto. Religious movements (and other movements as well, many of which may be functional equivalents of religious movements) are seen beginning with a charismatic leader, who stands to some degree outside tradition and the established social structures of the time and whose message in some way offers innovation and novelty, and the circle of disciples which he succeeds in drawing about him. While Weber has stressed that charisma is specifically foreign to routinized life, to rational economic activity, and to tradition, he has not been much concerned with attempting to specify the kinds of conditions which give rise to various types of charisma or account for its success with masses of people. Nor have sociological research and theory since his time done much to further our knowledge on this important topic. Weber does show the instability of charisma and its need to become transformed into established social forms if the charismatic movement is to survive and possess any future. He calls especial attention to the first succession crisis when the charismatic leader is no longer present and to the importance for the future of the movement of the kind of leadership which emerges in those circumstances. From this charismatic moment of origin there develops a routinization of charisma in which the charisma of institution and office replaces the older originating form. This transformation is at the same time a diminution and a containment of charisma within structured roles, rites, and procedures. This process of routinization may develop in either a rational or a traditional direction, or in some mixture of the two, as was the case with Christianity.[25]

What Weber has worked out in generalized categories of analysis, Troeltsch has done historically in his monumental *Social Teaching of the Christian Churches*. In this work Troeltsch traces the transformations in the inner structure of the church together with its changing relationship to the larger society in which it exists. He pays careful attention to the effects on Christian developments of both the content of the Christian Gospel and the social conditions under which the new church finds itself. He also points up the inner demands of the process of development itself as presenting problems to be solved by the developing church. The compromise of the church with classical society is the result of Christian ideas and values, of the orientations and needs of social classes to whom Christianity appealed, and of the needs of the developing organization. Here we see a sociological study which involves both an "external" and an "internal" view of the multiplicity of factors involved.[26]

Much of Weber's work concerned the sociological study of religion on a grand scale. Weber was concerned to show that religious ideas and institutions exerted a causal influence on human action and history and to oppose to a one-sided interpretation of Marxism a view in which both so-called "material" and "ideal" factors would be given their specific value as causal forces. This aspect of his work is best known from his essay on *The Protestant Ethic and the Spirit of Capitalism,* which Parsons translated in 1930.[27] But in recent years other portions of his study of the world religions have appeared in English. Weber's concern with ascetic Protestantism as a causal element affecting economic life, and with Christianity in general as one important cultural element influencing the rise of modern capitalism in Europe in contrast with the religions of Asia which presented the masses with no road to economic rationality, has influenced much sociological study on the relationship of religion to economic life.[28] In a part of his work translated into English and published under the title *The Sociology of Religion,*[29] Weber explores the relation between religious phenomena and a great variety of social factors. For example, he shows that religious messages have differential appeal to different social strata and that socially generated needs may coalesce with and affect religious needs. Thus lower classes show a tendency to embrace religions which preach a doctrine of salvation, while ruling classes display an elective affinity for religions which legitimate their position and function. Moreover, he shows the tendency for lower-middle class groups, especially the artisan class, to embrace and develop rational ethical religion, while peasants and warriors show a much greater predilection for magical phenomena. Furthermore, he points out the significance of the kind of internal differentiation that develops in a religious movement for its course of development. Thus the development of a rational theology must await as its necessary, though not necessarily its sufficient, condition the development of a priesthood enjoying a special status apart from the common run of membership. Weber also deals with religious surrogates and sees in nineteenth-century socialism such a functional equivalent of religion for the working classes of western Europe. Like Troeltsch, Weber shows a concern with the content of religious doctrines, with the social setting of religious groups and its effects on their development, and with internal structure in religious bodies. He is specially concerned with the effects of religion on economic developments.

In his work on the Christian churches, Troeltsch has provided a model for the study of social movements and institutions which base themselves in some part on situationally transcendent ideals. For such movements and institutions, as for historic Christianity, practical adjustment to the world as it faces the religious body from without and as it penetrates that body in its own members comes into conflict with important aspects of its transcendent goals and ethic. Troeltsch proposed two sociological forms which embody the approach of compromise and the reaction against compromise in the development of such movements. The church represents the tendency to compromise with the world, to embrace universalism, and to come to peace with secular culture. In his study Troeltsch traces out this development in the spheres of family life, economic life, politics, and intellectual endeavor. He presents the sect as the embodiment of revolt against the whole spirit of compromise. A number of sociological studies have utilized this conceptualization in contemporary American sociology. These concepts have found further refinement in the works of J. Milton Yinger, H. Richard Niebuhr, and the present writer.[30] Troeltsch also deals with another alternative to the church-sect dichotomy: the more individualized and subjective reaction against highly institutionalized religion, mysticism. Unfortunately, sociologists have not paid much attention to this aspect of Troeltsch's conceptualization and have generally reduced his trichotomy of church-sect-mysticism to a church-sect dichotomy. This is more the pity because of the great importance of mystical reactions against the institutionalized church for long periods preceding and following the Reformation and also because of the importance of a sociological study of functionally equivalent phenomena in the secularized society of the West in our own day (for example, some aspects of existentialism, nationalism, the beatnik phenomenon, and some forms of secular quietism in the face of baffling social developments).

Thus the substantive and theoretical work of Troeltsch and Weber has enriched the sociology of religion with conceptualizations more adequate for the study of religion in complex modern societies and of religious movements and institutions in terms of their internal functional problems as well as their adjustment problems in the modern world. Glock has remarked that more case studies are needed in contemporary American sociology dealing with the conditions leading to the establishment and affecting the development of "several score of major and minor religions indigenous to America."[31]

Joachim Wach has reduced some of this rich complexity to order, especially with respect to the internal structure and development of founded religions.[32] Starting with Rudolph Otto's treatment of the religious experience,[33] which in its basic outline presents a remarkable parallel to important aspects of Durkheim's treatment of the sacred, Wach presents a scheme of analysis which shows the religious movement proceeding from its original form of a charismatic leader and his circle of disciples, through an intermediate state of a loose and charismatic brotherhood, to become a fully institutionalized ecclesiastical organization. This course of development parallels in important ways Weber's treatment of the routinization of charisma and Troeltsch's analysis of the developments in early Christianity. A comparison of the three men offers a rich and many-sided view of what is involved in the institutionalization of religion and offers the sociologist a set of concepts for the formulation of problems and of hypothesis and the development of analysis. Moreover, Wach sees the institutionalization of religion proceeding on three levels, each separably identifiable with its own problems involved in the process.

He agrees with Troeltsch and the best insights of Durkheim concerning the sacred and of Weber with respect to charisma, in making the strategic level or aspect that of worship. Worship is central to the religious institution and continues in altered and symbolic form the original religious experience of the founding generation under new and changing conditions. The performance of cult, moreover, contains by implication much that is later developed as explicit doctrine and much that becomes institutionalized in the role structure of the religious organization. Thus the development of the Lord's Supper into the Mass contains the germs of both Trinitarian doctrine and the later defined idea of

Christ's dual nature, and role of mediatorship, and the strategically significant inner differentiation of the church into two distinct orders, clergy and laity.

The second level or aspect is the intellectual expression of religion in myth and doctrine. Comparable to Weber's idea of two directions of the routinization of charisma, one traditital, the other rational, is Wach's notion of two possibilities in the intellectual development from the religious experience, one in the direction of myth, the other toward rational theologies. Like Weber, Wach sees also a long-term trend toward rationality.

The third level is that of organization, the development of the ecclesiastical body. These three aspects are seen as interpenetrating and affecting one another in the course of development. Wach, of course, sees this whole religious development taking place in specific social and cultural settings with which it is in reciprocal relationship. Such developments of religious bodies proceed from the immanent implications of the original religious experience of the founding generation and are strongly affected by the structural necessities of development itself and by the social and cultural conditions of their milieu. For example, gnosticism and its attendant threat of misinterpreting Christian ideas, together with the existence of Greek philosophy, as elements in the world of early Christianity intensified the normal tendency toward an intellectual expression of religious belief in a rational theology.

Wach introduces the important category of "protest," a universal category of analysis for the understanding of religious developments. New adjustments to the world, new specifications of points of doctrine, new changes in liturgy or in church organization, affect sections of the membership differently. There are groups unable to go along with the new developments, who have become alienated from the changing ecclesiastical organization, and who revolt. Such revolts either may become secessionist or may be reintegrated into the larger church structure. Wach's thinking here follows closely that of Troeltsch on the sectarian response and its nonsecessionist variation, monasticism, though Wach proposes a more generic universal category, since protest may take other than sectarian forms, as may be seen in schism and the larger churches of the Reformation.

Wach's paradigm of religious development actually opens up the possibility of integrating into the sociological point of view the work of many students of religion, mythology, and symbolism. For example, the development of cult in the context of the developing religious body and developing myth and doctrine opens up to sociology the perspectives to be seen in the work of people like Susanne Langer,[34] Mircea Eliade, Van der Leeuw, and many others.[35]

The Study of Religion and Other Sociological Specializations

Other disciplines of sociology have also developed analytic concepts of help in the sociological study of religion. The institutionalization of religion in its ecclesiastical form results in a hierarchically organized church, whose functional problems resemble closely those characteristic of hierarchical bureaucracies generally. A body of theory, which owes much to Max Weber but has been considerably refined by American researchers, is available for an analysis of religious organizations.[36] The study of social disorganization has long been a concern of sociologists, as have the social forms developed by men in response to disorganization and anomie. For example, a study in which the present writer participated has shown that the formation of store-front churches among Puerto Rican migrants to New York represented an attempt to rebuild community in response to the personally and socially disorganizing impact of the metropolis on the newcomers.[37] The study of the assimilation and conflict involved in the integration of immigrants into American culture has opened up further areas of interest to sociological study. In this country, as well as in some other parts of the world, there is a tendency for religious identity to become synonymous with ethnic identity. A conflict, for example, between Catholics and Orthodox in Yugoslavia is at the same time a conflict between Croatians and Serbs, with their different cultural values and traditions and rivalry for power. This merger of religious with ethnic identity in social conflict has also been studied by sociologists, with results highly suggestive for future research.[38] For to fail to recognize in what Billington has called the Protestant crusade of the first half of the nineteenth century a nativist reaction against the Irish on the part of American Anglo-Saxons is to be insensitive to a large element involved. Moreover, a new religious identity can lead to the development in time and under propitious historical circumstances of a new ethnicity, as may be seen in the effects of the millet system under Turkish rule in the Middle East, or the quasi ethnicity of the Mormons whose development traversed a course from "near sect" to "near nation."[39]

American sociological research has been much interested in voting behavior, and it has been gradually recognized that religious identification is among one of the most important variables affecting voting.[40] Even when others, such as social stratification, income, and education, are held constant, religious identity among Catholics and Protestants permits reliable prediction. The findings on voting behavior suggest the significance of the religious tradition for personal identification and perception of interests in this country.

Finally, the sociology of knowledge which is concerned with studying the relationship between cognition and social conditions stands in close relationship to the sociology of religion, a fact to be seen in Durkheim's treatment of it in his *Elementary Forms of the Religious Life*. The present writer has attempted to combine the two in a study of the problems involved in the intellectual life as it has developed in American Catholicism.[41]

Thus there exists in sociology a body of concepts useful in the analysis of the human situation in terms of its component of social structure and social process, and one specifically derived from and of utility in the study of religious behavior and religious institutions. This body of concepts and ideas comprises "theory" in the scientific sense of that word. It is "theory," not theories in the sense of empirical hypotheses about future or regular behavior, since it is a frame of reference and a system of analytical categories. In its context, problems may be defined and hypotheses stated as the basis of empirical research. Such a body of theory is continually corrected, made more adequate, and expanded in terms of empirical study itself. What actually exists for the study of religion represents a rich heritage of sociological work and thought.

This body of theory is not, however, without serious lacunae, and much work remains to be done in the theoretical as well as the empirical field. There is needed, first of all, more empirical research in which this body of theory is used. This is required in order both to enrich our knowledge of religion from the sociological perspective and to refine and develop the conceptual scheme itself. There is also a need for a clearer working through and systematization of the implications of the theory as it now stands. It may be safely declared that in neither the theoretical nor the empirical spheres has the sociology of religion realized its potentialities as these already exist.

Second, there is needed a greater cooperation and cross-fertilization between the sociology of religion and psychology, especially depth psychology of the psychoanalytic and related schools. Although some work has been done in this area, there is still much to do.[42] Third, the sociology of religion must strengthen its relationship to history, since in modern complex societies a knowledge of past developments is often crucial to any adequate comprehension of the contemporary situations with which the sociologist deals. Finally, the sociology of religion must develop some degree of dialogue with theology and the philosophy of religion. Since the content of the particular religious view enters into the structuration of the religious institution and the norms which pattern behavior in it, the sociologist must develop a degree of competence in his understanding of this content. The sociology of religion is not simply the study of religion in relation to society, as some sociologists seem to assume, but rather the study of religion in relation to social structure and social process, not only as these are to be observed between the religious organization and ideology and the general society but also as these enter into the development and functioning of the religious organization and its ideology.

This implies that sociology enters into the study of religion in three ways. First of all, as the sociology of religion it is concerned with the relation of religion to social structure and social process, including the function of religions in particular societies. Second, in the study of given societies or of separate institutions in any society, the sociologist is concerned with the functional relationships between religious institutions and the particular area of his concentration. Thus a study of social structure and motivation for achievement will have to take into account the effects of various religious identifications and backgrounds on its subject matter. Third, the study of particular religious groups or of particular religious problems must pay attention to the effects of social structure and social processes on the religious group and its ideas. Christopher Dawson once declared, "Most of the great schisms and heresies in the history of the Christian church have their roots in social and national antipathies, and if this had been clearly recognized by the theologians, the history of Christianity would have been a very different one."[43] To ignore the sociological level of study and analysis in the study of religion is to leave out of account important factors influencing the developments and adaptations, and the problems and crises, of religious groups and religious ideas.

What has been said points up the importance of sociology for adequate understanding of religious phenomena. It also defines its limitations. The sociology of religion is not the complete study of religion, but is rather one of a number of disciplines engaged in exploring the human meaning and significance of religion. To the student of religion it is an ancillary and complementary approach to his own central concerns, but one of considerable importance for him. To the sociologist studying religion, the work of the specialists in religious study offers also an ancillary and complementary approach to his own, and one with which he must have some acquaintance if he is to make the optimum use of his own theory and techniques.

NOTES

1. A detailed theoretical presentation of what is implied here may be seen in Talcott Parsons, *The Social System* (Glencoe: 1951).

2. See Werner J. Cahnman and Alvin Boskoff, eds., *Sociology and History* (London: 1964). Also Talcott Parsons, *The Structure of Social Action* (Glencoe: 1949).

3. Cf. Charles Y. Glock, "The Sociology of Religion," in Robert K. Merton, Leonard Broom, and Leonard S. Cottrell, Jr., eds., *Sociology Today: Problems and Prospects* (New York: 1959), pp. 154 ff.

4. See Bronislaw Malinowski, *Magic, Science, and Religion and Other Essays* (Glencoe: 1948), and William J. Goode, *Religion among the Primitives* (Glencoe: 1951), Chapter 1.

5. The chief reference is Emile Durkheim, *The Elementary Forms of the Religious Life*, Joseph Ward Swain, tr. (Glencoe: 1954). Also particularly his French successors such as Marcel Mauss, *The Gift* (Glencoe: 1954). Interesting is the work of Francis M. Cornford, influenced by Durkheim, *From Religion to Philosophy* (New York: 1957).

6. Ernst Troeltsch, *The Social Teaching of the Christian Churches*, Olive Wyon, tr., Vols. I and II (London and New York: 1931).

7. See especially Max Weber, *The Theory of Social and Economic Organization*, A. M. Henderson and Talcott Parsons, trs. (New York: 1947); *The Protestant Ethic and the Spirit of Capitalism*, Talcott Parsons, tr. (New York and London: 1930); and *The Sociology of Religion*, Ephraim Fischoff, tr. (Boston: 1963).

8. Joachim Wach, *The Sociology of Religion* (Chicago: 1944).

9. See especially Talcott Parsons, "The Theoretical Development of the Sociology of Religion," in *Essays in Sociological Theory*, rev. ed. (Glencoe: 1954), pp. 197–211.

10. For a good overall view of the Marxist position, see Karl Marx and Friedrich

Engels, *On Religion* (New York: 1964—Schocken paperback reprinted from the edition of 1957, published by The Foreign Languages Publishing House, Moscow, USSR); and Friedrich Engels, *The Peasant War in Germany* (New York: 1924).

11. R. H. Tawney, *Religion and the Rise of Capitalism* (New York: 1947), and Amintore Fanfani, *Catholicism, Protestantism and Capitalism* (New York: 1955).

12. For a sophisticated attempt to show this by mathematical method using factor analysis, see Alvin W. Gouldner and Richard A. Peterson, *Technology and the Moral Order* (Indianapolis and New York: 1962).

13. See the discussion of Robert K. Merton, "Manifest and Latent Functions: Toward the Codification of Functional Analysis in Sociology," in *Social Theory and Social Structure* (Glencoe: 1957), Chapter 1, pp. 19–84; and Goode, *op. cit.*, pp. 33 ff.

14. Quoted from Horace L. Friess, "Growth of Study of Religion at Columbia University, 1924–1954," *Review of Religion*, XIX, Nos. 1–2 (November, 1954), 15.

15. For example, see David C. McClelland, *The Achieving Society* (Princeton: 1961).

16. The classic work on the topic of this paragraph is Ferdinand Toennies, *Community and Society—Gemeinschaft und Gesellschaft*, Charles P. Loomis, tr. and ed. (East Lansing, Mich.: 1957).

17. See the first essay in Malinowski, *op. cit.*

18. Durkheim, *op. cit.* See also the discussion in Talcott Parsons, *The Structure of Social Action* (Glencoe: 1949), pp. 435 ff.

19. Kingsley Davis, *Human Society* (New York: 1948), p. 529.

20. *Ibid.*, p. 531.

21. The entire background of this statement is explored thoroughly in terms of its significance for sociology in Parsons, *The Structure of Social Action*.

22. Glock, *op. cit.*, p. 155. See also Merton, *op. cit.*, pp. 30–32, 41–47; and Allan W. Eister, "Religious Institutions in Complex Societies: Difficulties in the Theoretic Specification of Function," *American Sociological Review*, XXII, No. 2 (1957), 387–391.

23. For example, see Daniel Lerner, with Lucille W. Pevsner, collaborator, "Modernizing the Middle East," in *The Passing of Traditional Society* (Glencoe: 1958). Also Jules Monnerot, *Sociology and Psychology of Communism*, Jane Degras and Richard Rees, trs. (Boston: 1960), especially "Psychology of Secular Religions," Chapter 10, and "Projections of the Sacred," Chapter 14.

24. See Chapter 13 in the present volume.

25. Weber, *The Theory of Social and Economic Organization*, pp. 358 ff.

26. See Troeltsch, *op. cit.*, Vol. I.

27. Weber, *The Protestant Ethic and the Spirit of Capitalism*, Talcott Parsons, tr. (New York and London: 1930).

28. In addition to the works of Weber listed above, this is discussed in the following translations of his works: *The Religion of China: Confucianism and Taoism*, Hans H. Gerth, tr. (Glencoe: 1952); *Ancient Judaism*, Hans H. Gerth and Don C. Martindale, trs. (Glencoe: 1951); *General Economic History*, Frank Knight, tr. (New York: 1927).

29. See footnote 7 above.

30. See J. Milton Yinger, *Religion and the Struggle for Power* (Durham: 1946); H. Richard Niebuhr, *The Social Sources of Denominationalism* (New York: 1929); Bryan R. Wilson, *Sects and Society* (Berkeley, Calif.: 1961), and "An Analysis of Sect Development," *American Sociological Review*, XXIV (February, 1959), 3–15. Also Chapter 6 in the present volume. For a further exploration of the problems opened up in Troeltsch's work in terms of theological alternatives, see H. Richard Niebuhr, *Christ and Culture* (New York: 1951).

31. Glock, *op. cit.*, pp. 159–160. The studies suggested as examples by Glock are: Marshall Sklare, *Conservative Judaism* (Glencoe: 1955); Thomas F. O'Dea, *The Mormons* (Chicago: 1957); H. H. Stroup, *Jehovah's Witnesses* (New York: 1945); and Hadley Cantril, "The Kingdom of Father Divine," in Cantril, ed., *The Psychology of Social Movements* (New York: 1941).

32. Wach, *op. cit.*

33. Rudolf Otto, *The Idea of the Holy,* J. W. Harvey, tr., 2d ed. (London: 1950).

34. Susanne K. Langer, *Philosophy in a New Key* (Cambridge: 1951).

35. See, for example, Mircea Eliade, *Patterns of Comparative Religions,* Rosemary Sheed, tr. (New York: 1958).

36. For example, see Peter M. Blau and W. Richard Scott, *Formal Organizations* (San Francisco: 1962), or Robert K. Merton, *et al., Reader in Bureaucracy* (Glencoe: 1952).

37. See Chapter 10 in the present volume.

38. See, for example, Kenneth W. Underwood, *Protestant and Catholic* (Boston: 1957), and John J. Kane, *Catholic-Protestant Conflicts in America* (Chicago: 1955).

39. See Werner J. Cahnman, "Religion and Nationality," in Cahnman and Boskoff, *op. cit.,* pp. 271–279, and Chapter 6 in the present volume.

40. For a good summary, see Seymour Martin Lipset, "How Big Is the Bloc Vote?" *New York Times Magazine,* October 25, 1964, pp. 32 ff.

41. Thomas F. O'Dea, *American Catholic Dilemma* (New York: 1958).

42. See, for example, W. Earl Biddle, *Integration of Religion and Psychiatry* (New York: 1962), and O. Hobart Mowrer, *The Crisis in Psychiatry and Religion* (Toronto, New York, and London: 1961).

43. Christopher Dawson, "Sociology as a Science," republished in *Cross Currents,* IV, No. 28 (Winter, 1965), 136.

T W E L V E : The Sociology
of Religion

In sociology, the conception of man held by the investigator will determine in large measure the direction of research. Sociology itself was the product of two main currents of thought. The first was the growing ability to see social relations as objective structures and social movements as objective trends: in short, to see the uniformities of social processes as an *objective* of investigation. The second was the positivism of the nineteenth century, which elevated the methodological rules of the natural sciences, then currently accepted, into an antimetaphysical metaphysic. From the first current much was gained. It is from the efforts of men like Machiavelli, Sir William Petty, and Montesquieu that economics and sociology were born. Moreover, the second current was not without value, for despite the narrowness of positivism, it has contributed a certain mental ascetic to distinguishing the level of empirical investigation from that of philosophical inquiry, a certain tough-mindedness in facing facts, and has militated against a misplaced teleology. Yet all these gains are equivocal, for they were purchased at a heavy price. The human person, neither a mere object of observation nor a conceptual or statistical abstraction, but a conscious agent capable of interiority and freedom—an open concentrate of existence—was somehow lost from sight.[1] So important was this loss that we now stand in danger of finding the great gains of social science speculatively impoverished and practically limited unless it is rectified.[2] This loss of a worthy and adequate conception of the person stands in the background of our present

From *The American Catholic Sociological Review*, XV (June, 1954), 73–92.

fractionization of research areas and in the way of their achieving even a moderately satisfactory synthesis. One wonders if a conception of man as other than person is any longer capable of guiding genuinely fruitful research or of integrating the results of past research.

These two currents met in Auguste Comte, the father of both sociology and nineteenth-century positivism. The influence of this unbalanced genius and of others whose views were similar, especially Herbert Spencer, was considerable in early American sociology.[3] One hears little of either Comte or Spencer in contemporary sociology. Yet in a very fundamental sense sociology has not gone beyond the conception of man implied in Comte's Law of Three Phases. This situation prevails despite valiant attempts to transcend the biases of the founding generations.

In order to present the implications of this situation for the sociology of religion as concisely as possible, it is, perhaps, best to concentrate on the work of one man. I have chosen Talcott Parsons[4] because, despite his differences in background and in conceptualization from many American sociologists, despite the peculiar Parsonian fascination with abstraction, deplored by some, his work in the sociology of religion (theoretical rather than empirical) is typical of the basic premises accepted by non-Catholics in the field in this country. The exceptions are mainly men with theological connections.[5] Parsons, moreover, has the good taste to avoid some of the more extreme fallacies.[6]

Parsons constructs his sociology of religion on the basis of the work of four men: Pareto, Malinowski, Durkheim, and Weber. None of these is an American; yet all of them have had a great influence on American social science. Parsons starts with what he calls the "rationalistic variation of positivism,"[7] "the tendency to treat the actor as if he were a rational scientific investigator acting 'reasonably' in the light of the knowledge available to him."[8] From this point of view religion is a matter of superstition and ignorance, a survival of a more primitive past. Parsons is fully aware of the painful inadequacy of this view and has drawn extensively on his European predecessors to broaden it.

Starting with an actor in a situation in which he must act, Parsons accepts Pareto's distinction between the "rational" and the "non-rational."[9] The former refers to positive knowledge, whether or not it is in a scientifically formulated state. The latter is divided by Pareto and Parsons into two categories. The first category of the nonrational is ignorance and error—logical or empirical error. "Failure to conform with logico-empirical standards was not, however, confined to this mode of deviance, but included another, 'the theories which surpass experience.' "[10] Parsons has argued cogently that Pareto has "left the question of the more ultimate nature of noncognitive factors open,"[11] as it seems safe to say does Parsons himself.[12] Pareto's notion of equilibrium influenced the functional aspects of later Parsonian theory. Together with Pareto, Parsons repudiates "the hypothesis that they [the sentiments and the theories that surpass experience] are biologically inherited drives alone."[13] Thus a new element is contributed to the positivist conception of action which is not reducible to the others or explained in terms of error.

Malinowski's basic position coincides in major particulars with that of Pareto outlined above, as does his contribution to Parsons' approach. In his study of gardening, canoe building, and fishing in the Trobriand Islands, he distinguished a sphere of action characterized by uncertainty and in which the prevailing level of technique was inadequate. The area of uncertainty was precisely where magical rites were found, and Malinowski defined magic as the manipulation of nonempirical means for empirical ends.[14] Magic is seen as a device to allay emotional stress involved in the experience of uncertainty—an experience encountered when empirical techniques will not work. It answers a psychological need and by preserving morale serves a personal and social function. Parsons accepts this view and feels that it clearly refutes both the view of Levy-Bruhl[15] that "primitive man confuses the realm of the supernatural and the sacred with the utilitarian and the rational [possibly an oversimplification of the significance of Levy-Bruhl's work], and also the view which has been classically put forward by Frazer[16] that magic was essentially primitive science, serving the same fundamental functions."[17] Uncertainty is not confined to matters of technical inadequacy, however. The relationship between personal interest and emotional stress is important in death, where no empirical goal is sought. Both Malinowski and Parsons make much of death in this respect. Here the rites are religious, and religion is defined as the manipulation of nonempirical means for nonempirical ends.[18]

The views of both Pareto and Malinowski deserve note, for they contain implications never brought to conscious and explicit fruition in the academic sociology of religion. By his theory of the "residues," Pareto in effect affirmed that man does not live by manipulation and self-interested control alone but by sentiments rooted deeply in the human heart. Behind the concretely derived statements of these may be found the irreducible "residues," inescapably inherent in the structure of man and his condition. Indeed, we have here an approach to what in another idiom is called natural law—a negative approach somewhat analogous to the approach and attitude of negative theology. Malinowski, on the other hand, says nothing to contradict this insight. On the contrary, his repeated emphasis on the element of reverence in primitive religion, his stress on the meaning of the religious act to the individual as well as on its social function, his several declarations that the religious act is its own end, his lively sense of a premonition of providence in savage faith, his brilliant statement that "the roots of sacrificial offering are to be found in the psychology of the gift," and his recognition that the ontological significance of these empirically found facts of sociological investigation transcends the task of sociology—all point to a sociology aware of the deeper springs of human action and the deeper roots of human religiosity.

There is no doubt that it was this very metaphysical depth that attracted Parsons to the works of these authors. While *The Structure of Social Action* both formulates and attacks a problem in a different intellectual idiom from that which most Christian sociologists would choose, it shows a great sensitiveness to the deeper aspects of the problem and nowhere more than in the section on Pareto, unquestionably the best criticism in the English language. Yet this promise is not genuinely realized in the Parsonian formulation of elements of the sociology of religion. For despite the strong desire—always evident in the works of Parsons' early and middle period—to escape the limitations of positivism and behaviorism, these latter-day manifestations of the Comtean mentality are not transcended. Those elements of human action which find no place in positivistic and behavioristic schemata remain ever residual in his approach. The positivistic starting place remains the center of the circle, and other elements, despite the author's undoubted recognition that they are important, remain on or near the periphery. Moreover, some of Parsons' students and many of his imitators remain unaware of his struggle to transcend these limitations without violating his commitment to rationality as he conceives it.

Indeed, earlier metaphysical anxieties appear to impinge with less evidence on his later work.

By the introduction of these elements from Pareto and Malinowski, however, the positivistic conception of human action has been seriously altered, although its basic notion of the "actor-situation" or subject-object relation remains. Parsons is aware of the central importance of worship and ethics, although his work shows a far livelier sense of the latter than of the former. At this point he introduces Durkheim's distinction between the sacred and profane.[19] He sees "one fundamental feature of the sacred to be its radical dissociation from any utilitarian context"[20] and its evocation of a "certain specific attitude of respect, which Durkheim identified with the appropriate attitude toward moral obligation and authority."[21] This was as close as Durkheim came to understanding transcendence. How close and yet how far! His positivist bias prevented his grasping any adequate idea of the holy. Durkheim recognized that sacred objects used in primitive rites were symbols, but he concluded that they must symbolize the group and particularly the moral norms of the group. God became from this point of view the hypostatization of society.[22] Parsons shares this "pre-phenomenological" position. For him the important thing here is "Durkheim's view that religious ritual was of primary significance as a mechanism of expressing and reinforcing the sentiments most essential to the institutional integration of society."[23]

It is in his work as a student and continuator of Max Weber that Parsons has lifted this entire scheme to a new level, relating it on one hand to what Weber called the problem of meaning and on the other to the variability of social structures, and possibly of personality types, in various societies. Earlier in his career Parsons wrote a long, closely reasoned work to convince the positivistically inclined of the independent role of normative ideas in social action.[24] Now, in his approach to the sociology of religion, he relates the problem of meaning both to situations of uncertainty and to morality. He says that "correlative with the functional need for emotional adjustment to such experiences as death is a cognitive need for understanding, for trying to have it 'make sense.' "[25] Moreover, "if we can speak of a need to understand ultimate frustrations in order for them to 'make sense,' it is equally urgent that the values and goals of everyday life should also make sense."[26] He holds that in religious doctrine we have the integration of these two attempts after meaning.

The different institutional structures of various societies are seen by Weber and Parsons as corresponding in important respects to differences in religious doctrine. Thus religion not only plays an integrative role for individuals and for societies but also enters into the shaping of social institutions and through them into the formation of human personality or character. It is here that Parsons' work is, perhaps, most interesting. Moreover, Parsons is not unaware of the serious effect which religious doctrine may have on the general apperception of so-called "rational-empirical" cognition.

Of this scheme, Parsons said in 1942:

> It is of course never safe to say a scientific conceptual scheme has reached a definitive completion of its development. Continual change is in the nature of science. There are, however, relative degrees of conceptual integration, and it seems safe to say that the cumulative results of the work just reviewed constitute in broad outline a relatively well-integrated analytical scheme which covers most of the more important broader aspects of the role of religion in social systems. It is unlikely that in the near future this analytical scheme will give way to a radical structural change, though notable refinement and revision is to be expected. It is perhaps safe to say that it places the sociology of religion for the first time on a footing where it is possible to combine empirical study and theoretical analysis on a large scale on a level in conformity with the best current standards of social science and psychology.[27]

The later work of Parsons has, indeed, been a matter of "refinement and revision." Refinement has meant a more abstract statement of the basic view given here, especially in terms of the Parsonian "pattern variables."[28] Revision has been chiefly along the lines of the relation between what Parsons now calls "cultural systems," "social systems," and "personality systems."[29] In the latter effort a genuine addition has been made. I refer to his attempt to use psychoanalytic concepts in constructing a systematic theory of personality in the context of the larger whole of "Action Theory." One suspects that the extreme abstraction of the effort will militate against fruitfulness, while at the same time one fears that the demand for systematic closure in terms of a Paretian-Freudian frame of reference will inhibit new insights not already implicitly present. On the whole, Riesman's work on personality and social structure is more interesting. Its concreteness shows far greater understanding of both living people and the social situations in which they act.

The Parsonian sociology of religion, which is taken here as typical of the field, sees man as an actor in the context of a situation. This situation is known to the actor by means of positive knowledge alone; that is, in terms of phenomenal and instrumental knowledge. Such knowledge, however, leaves a vast personally relevant area outside its scope. This area includes moral and social norms, goals of action, orientation to "uncertainty," and, of course, their sources. Yet this area must be defined somehow, for it is necessary for man to achieve what is vaguely called "adjustment to the total situation" for which "rational knowledge and technique could not provide adequate mechanisms."[30] Attempts after meaning in this area are nonrational; they "surpass experience"—experience meaning instrumental adaptation or control and the kind of knowledge on which it is based and which results from it. The significance of this sort of "meaning" is residual to "logico-experimental" knowledge (Pareto), or to "rational-empirical" knowledge (Parsons). Although both Pareto and Parsons left open the problem of the source of this second-rate "knowledge" (one wonders if many other sociologists really do), its chief significance lies in its function for personal and social adjustment. It is relegated in practice to a purely psychological and adjustive role in human life. In his later efforts Parsons draws on psychoanalysis to enable the sociologist to postulate mechanisms which will "explain" this adjustive process.

Religious doctrines are developed to provide orientation in this area—to answer the problem of meaning in areas where life "surpasses" instrumental experience. Once developed, such doctrines, through their informing role in the development of social institutions and their shaping effects on personalities, become historical causes.[31] The normative aspects of such doctrines give human action its teleological character and make social control possible. Thus on the basis of a primary adjustive significance for individuals and a functional importance for human association or society, religion, by providing definitions of the situations of action, by informing social institutions, and by shaping character, comes to exercise social causation. The earlier "rationalist positivist" view of man has been seriously amended. Yet man is still conceived "as if he were a rational, scientific investigator," that is, in terms of the positivistic caricature of the existing scientist—a hypostatization of positivist methodology—now qualified by the necessity of adjustive "mechanisms" for personal stability and social order.

One cannot deny that important research can be done in terms of such a scheme; yet obvious biases will inhibit understanding at a certain point: to wit, at the point where the basic positivist premises can no longer "explain" religious phenomena. In other words, where religion is not understandable in terms of psychological and sociological function, it is not to be understood. Everything involved in religion, since it is "nonrational," must be explained on the psychological and sociological levels alone; that is, in terms of function, rather than content, since genuine noetic content is excluded. It is this view which has militated against academic psychology and sociology of religion developing a profound theory of symbol and mythos, and important works on these problems reach the corner drugstore in cheap editions before they are given serious attention by many in sociology. A genuine subject-object relation is confined to "practical situations" involving "rational knowledge and technique."

This amendment of the older positivist view of religion as ignorance and error makes it possible for the sociologist to consider religion *sui generis,* rather than something to be reduced to "real factors." But the gain is more apparent than real. Religion has been promoted from the status of an illusion appropriate to certain stages in human development to that of a perpetual and necessary aberration.[32] It is basically an adjustive mechanism, and everything except "rational-empirical" knowledge is finally consigned to epiphenomenal status. The most important contribution of this approach is its recognition of the functional role of religion, both formative and integrative, in social life. Yet here the contribution is hardly original.[33] In short, the entire scheme, despite all the laborious amendment, is based on the positivistic theory of cognition. Rational-empirical knowledge so-called, so central to the whole conception, is instrumental knowledge, and all else is illusion, albeit necessary to personal and social stability and therefore a "social fact" to the sociological observer. In this most fundamental sense the sociology of religion has failed to transcend the Comtean Law of Three Phases.[34]

Behind the positivist conception of knowledge on which this scheme is erected is the positivistic definition of man. What is this definition of man? It is that of a being whose only effective way of relating himself to the world in which he lives is by manipulating it. Talk of rationality and knowledge must be understood in this context. Instrumentally tested knowledge elaborated by discursive reason is what is to be understood by these terms. Reason is a matter of tautology, after the fashion of Logical Positivism. In other words, this man is a *Homo faber,* whose only significant intellectual operations are constructive or manipulative. All other human acts and attitudes are to be explained as adjustment or adaptation. The possibility of what Buber has called an I-Thou relationship either is nonexistent or is psychologized away. What we have here is an example of what Whitehead called "misplaced concreteness." The dimensions of scientific method, narrowly construed and dogmatically asserted, are concretized into the image of a man. It is comparable to the concretization of the dimensions of economic theory into the figure of the "economic man" which was so popular in the recent past.

Obviously, worship, mythos, symbol and sacramental, and even theology (or is it especially theology?) can have no real (read "instrumental") significance for such a man. They help him to adjust to the "dark mystery" which "surrounds the slight circle of human knowledge." His response to this mystery is one of frustration: he cannot successfully manipulate it. Hence all the items above can be explained psychologically; they are significant in terms of mechanisms for inner calm and have no more than an arbitrary and projective connection with the extrinsic world. Such a man, of course, does not exist; he is merely the positivistic theory of cognition writ small. The processes of social life and of the inner life of man, having been first *objectized*—seen simply as objects to a scientific investigator—are then attributed to reference points in an analytic scheme. Observed men are arbitrarily and naively identified with such reference points. To the extent that this "methodologic-chopping" is forgotten in empirical work, to that extent the poverty of human reference inherent in the scheme is overcome. To this effort to substitute the concretization of positive method for the human person, we can say to the sociologist what Ernst Cassirer said to the philosopher: "The philosopher is not permitted to construct an artificial man; he must describe a real one."[35] Certainly this applies in a discipline where observation has been given such an important status.

The development of social science has been based on the

growing ability to see social relations and social movements as objective structures—in Durkheim's words, as "social things." Yet this too often results in a loss of the conception of the concrete man as an acting agent. For the human person and his concrete existence, which are largely part of the "mystery which in all ages surrounds the slight circle of human knowledge" (that is, of instrumental knowledge), there is substituted a hypostatized particle understood in terms of a set of conceptualizations based on the *objectized* knowledge of "social things." In the study of religion, where this concrete person is seen confronting this mystery in other than a manipulative way, such a procedure can only obscure our understanding. It can only help to explain away what in its own terms cannot be understood.

I have indicated that the most important and most typical aspect of the present scheme is its making us aware of the functional role of religion in social action and the influence of religious doctrines and institutions on society and character as well as the influence of the latter on religious institutions and doctrines. Yet these are all items of secondary importance with regard to religion itself. It may be said that from the point of view of sociology these secondary aspects of religion are of primary interest. Such an argument is not untenable, but it demands some comprehension of both religion and the point of view of sociology. The question is raised in this context of the possibility of a nonnormative study of religion which is other than mere description. An affirmative answer to this question demands agreement from persons with the most varied points of view on a minimal recognition of what constitutes religious experience and religious attitudes. This in turn demands recognition of certain minimal characteristics of the human person. First of all, it must be granted that there are nonmanipulative ways of relating oneself to the world and that they are not merely residual to manipulation. The implications of Pareto and Malinowski pointed out above and so far left dormant by the American academic sociology of religion must be recognized. This recognition can be cast in several forms: in scientific terms as in Angyal's "trend toward homonomy,"[36] in philosophical terms as in the Platonic Eros which is born of man's metaphysical yearning after wholeness,[37] "the spontaneous feeling, that our existence has its center not in itself,"[38] "our relation to what concerns us ultimately,"[39] an experience of the Holy, *"mysterium tremendum et fascinosum,"*[40] or the I-Thou relation.[41] To comprehend what these "pointers" point toward in terms of human experience may be difficult for the young sociologist trained in an atmosphere of positivistic thought. That is altogether understandable; yet one for whom none of these terms suggests a human reference would do well to eschew the sociology of religion as a field of endeavor. He will never know what he is looking at.

A second requirement would be some recognition that religion is not simply a "response without a stimulus."[42] As religion is an expression of something intrinsic to the person, it is at the same time a response to something extrinsic. This much must be granted, for any a priori assumption of Feuerbach's position or its contemporary variants will make any comprehension of the religious phenomena studied impossible. The extrinsic reality which evokes the response must be admitted, no matter how much the investigator may disagree with the believer's conception of it. This reality is not an object of sense perception. A human subject confronting the mystery of existence in an attitude of reverence and using reason and imagination to comprehend as best he can what ultimately comprehends himself—this minimal definition must be granted. To see mythos and ritual in any other context is to betray a certain metaphysical naïveté which will militate against understanding even the sociological expressions of religion. It betrays as well a historically specific ideology which is incapable of understanding that only a particular variant of the modern Western consciousness apprehends the world

> Viewing all objects, unremittingly
> In disconnection dead and spiritless.

Such a view is provincial and culture-bound: it is encysted within the narrow confines of the Comtean mentality. Only in terms which grant these minimal requirements can worship and belief and all their symbolic, cultic, and sociological manifestations be understood, as well as their relation to man's normative and evaluative capacities and their products.

In terms of this genuine subject-object relationship, the expressions of religious beliefs and of religious attitudes must be studied for their content. This will permit the development of a sophisticated understanding of symbolism and the utilization of much philosophical inquiry both abroad and at home. The psychological problems of projection can be discussed with intelligence only in such a context. When sociologists of religion learn to understand what mythos, doctrine, and their cultic and aesthetic expression are about, the problem of projection and its significance will be greatly refined. In other words, when the investigator stops seeing everything as projection, it will be possible to discern the phenomenon itself.

Such are the bare minimum requisites for a nonnormative study of religion.[43] It is not the task of the sociology of religion or of the psychology and history of religion to pass judgment on the ultimate truth of religious doctrines. Yet certain criteria of genuineness may and do emerge in such studies. One might, for example, ask whether the Parsonian hypothesis that magic is the manipulation of nonempirical means for empirical ends is an adequate definition. Must one not also consider Jaspers' definition of magic as an ever-present perversion in which "the reality of the symbol becomes a purposive and instrumental technique"?[44] As a result, one might be able to talk of perversions and of levels of adequacy and the like. Above all, here one would attempt to comprehend his data and not merely classify it in terms of the shallow concepts of a functional scheme.

What is the task of the sociology of religion in terms of this approach? The sociology of religion is the empirical study of the expression of religious experience, religious conceptions, and religious attitudes in the formation and emergence of social relationships, both in terms of the particular forms of religious groups, and beyond their confines, in more secular social institutions and relations, including the reverse influence of social forms, religious and secular, on religious expression, attitude, and belief.[45] Hence the sociologist of religion studies the same data as the psychologist and historian of religion. Nothing less than a constant dialogue between these disciplines can prevent a narrow one-sidedness which leads to a subtle usurpation of the field by each. Moreover, the necessity of understanding the realities of religion requires a dialogue between these nonnormative students of religion and theologians.

What is the purpose of this study pursued by the sociology of religion? There are two possible answers. First, it is to deliver to men a knowledge of social existence. Such knowledge enables them to know themselves better and to understand those matrices of human association and conflict which condition them, in order to resist those formative influences which distort them—a knowledge which enhances human liberty by aiding men to avoid what one might call the analogues of the "occasions of sin." Second, as an applied science, it may aid religious institutions to understand more thoroughly the milieu in which they must deliver their message and the consequent problems to be faced.

A recognition of the human person, the subject who lives in the bosom of human association, and a refusal to hypostatize society will make possible the integration of the knowledge of the social sciences in the service of man. But it means giving up all attempts to erect sociology as a generalizing science of man.[46] Sociological analysis does not touch the center of human interiority. In making an object of man, it succeeds only in making objects of successive aspects of man. The living person is a whole, a unity in his interior self. It is here that all relations are grounded. To fit the human person and his religious interests into a closed conceptual construct, concerned especially with social structure and function, is to commit on the grandest possible scale the old logical error of including the whole in a part. Both the person and the object of his religious concern transcend conceptualization. Both transcend social structure and its functional uniformities. When such an attempt involves a subtle hypostatization of *objectized* aspects of human life and thereby obliterates the human person, it fails to relate the genuine knowledge gained by sociological research to human life in any but an externalistic manipulative way. Here too it remains basically Comtean.[47] The sociology of religion in America today, to the extent that it achieves an explicit conceptualization as a closed system, commits these errors. To the extent that it undertakes research and the presentation of its findings in terms of the basic assumptions of such schematization, it approaches them. In fact, the work in the field shows all forms of this influence from implicit traces to conscious interpretation of the material.

Of course, one will not argue against limited frames of reference in sociological research. To interpret this criticism in that manner would be to miss the point. But the knowledge which social science possesses must be related to human existence in the interest of the dignity and freedom of man, and not remain merely *objectized* aspects of social processes perceived from a particular disciplinary perspective. This is of special relevance to the sociology of religion, which, in Tillich's terms, studies man as he is related to what ultimately concerns him.

Our frames of reference, then, must be modest—recognizing the partial quality of our approach—and open at the center where dwells this mysterious being, man, who resides in his personal interiority—I would say his *subjectness,* to avoid a purely psychological connotation. Such modesty is not at all incompatible with the spirit of scientific research. It requires a discipline of mind and attitude which would make the word more than a conventional label for a branch of academic activity. Sociology is justified in concentrating on its own problems, social structure and function, growth, development, disintegration, and change. But it must see them within a genuinely human vision which cannot be encapsulated in any conceptualization. It must engage in a dialogue with other scientific and humanistic disciplines if it is to prevent the hardening of a narrow disciplinary perspective. It must be conducted as part of a dialogue with larger views of human existence and human destiny.

In brief, the critical appraisal of Parsons' approach reveals the chief obstacles in the way of an adequate understanding of religion by academic sociologists. These are:

1. Reliance on a narrow positivistic definition of cognition.
2. The positivistic conception of man and its derivatives.
3. The hypostatization of society or social system.
4. The "residual" conception of religion.
5. The "psychologizing" of religious content.
6. Isolation from history and philosophy, including theology.

These basic errors, in which Parsons is typical of the field, constitute the Comtean complex of the contemporary sociology of religion. I have suggested a minimal proposition for a more adequate approach.

To conceive sociology otherwise is to conceive it theoretically as alienated from personal existence and practically as merely the construction of manipulative devices by the expert for the administrator. Sociology must be a study of the existential context of human life, its conditions and its conditionings. It is a study of one aspect of existential man with his freedom and his conditioning, his formation and his deformation, his achievements and his failures. The task of sociology is to aid men in achieving a better concrete understanding of the human situation. The sociology of religion is the study of the way in which man's religious concern enters into all these problems. Social circumstances and societal structures enter into the expressions of this concern, as does this concern enter into the formation of social structures and institutions. A most thorough empirical study of all the conditioning circumstances, situations, social relations, historical and cultural conditions, their interrelations, transitions, and metamorphoses—all these are the legitimate concern of the field. Yet these can be understood only in terms of an approach that at least suspects what an adequate conception of man and his situation involves. Obviously I do not put this forward as a "Catholic definition" of the sociology of religion. I suggest it as a *minimum* consideration for any definition, whether by Catholic or non-Catholic, believer or unbeliever. It is nothing less than the reintroduction of the human person into the center of the sciences of man—sciences so materially enriched by the developments of the last four centuries.

NOTES

1. "The first sociologists, particularly Auguste Comte and Saint-Simon, constructed a philosophy which declared that Society was to be real and the Individual hypostatized." Albert Salomon, "Sociology and the Total State," *Cross Currents*, II, No. 4 (Summer, 1952), 42.

2. For example, see Ernst Cassirer, "The Crisis in Man's Knowledge of Himself," in his *An Essay on Man* (New Haven: 1944), Chapter 1.

3. Albion W. Small, in his *Origins of Sociology* (Chicago: 1924), stated: "We must specify that Lester F. Ward, whose influence was for a long time the most evident factor of American sociology, avowedly represented the Comtean succession while Sumner and Giddings developed more immediately, though not exclusively, the initiatives of Herbert Spencer" (p. 239). There were also important German roots of American sociology. *Ibid.,* pp. 326 ff. For an important critical study of the role of the "Comtean" mentality in early American sociology, see William T. O'Connor, *Naturalism and the Pioneers of American Sociology* (Washington, D.C.: 1942). For an interesting discussion by an Anglican theologian who is also a sociologist, see Julian Victor Langmead Casserley, *Morals and Man in the Social Sciences* (London, New York, Toronto: 1951), especially Chapter 7, "The Origins and Axioms of Modern Sociology."

4. Talcott Parsons, Chairman of the Department of Social Relations at Harvard University, is well known in American sociology, and the influence of his work is growing. His main concerns are theoretical rather than empirical, and he has recently finished an ambitious effort to present a closed conceptual system for the guidance of sociological research and the synthesis of its findings (*The Social System* [Glencoe: 1951]). He has been criticized, notably by Ellsworth Faris (*American Sociological Review*, XVIII, No. 1 [February, 1953], 103-106) for an apparent unfamiliarity with the background of American sociology. His own background and training, to be sure, lie elsewhere. Yet, in a profound sense his work may be considered representative of the general American approach to the sociology of religion. His explicitness, which derives from his self-conscious attempts at theory building, has made it possible for him to state openly what

others have tacitly assumed. Some see his theorizing as an escape into a conceptual empyrean, but that is not our concern here.

5. Their work is very important; for example, Liston Pope, *Millhands and Preachers: A Study of Gastonia* (New Haven: 1942); H. Richard Niebuhr, *The Social Sources of Denominationalism* (New York: 1929); and Joachim Wach, *The Sociology of Religion* (Chicago: 1944). When I speak of the sociology of religion in this chapter I refer, unless explicitly stated otherwise, to the work in this field by academic sociologists. I am aware that, in the words of Wach, "Contributions to the sociology of religion from the side of sociologists are not so weighty as might be expected" (*op. cit.,* p. 8, n. 33), and I hope the present analysis will cast some light on that situation.

6. For example, we find this statement in Dr. Kinsey's report. "The mores, whether they concern food, clothing, sex, or religious rituals, originate neither in accumulated experience nor in scientific examinations of objectively gathered data. The sociologist and anthropologist find the origin of such customs in ignorance and superstition, and in the attempt of each group to set itself apart from its neighbors." This is extreme, but is it extreme in content or only in crudity of expression?

7. See Talcott Parsons, *The Structure of Social Action* (Glencoe: 1949), Chapters II and III. Hereafter referred to as *The Structure*.

8. "The Sociology of Religion," in *Essays in Sociological Theory: Pure and Applied* (Glencoe: 1949), p. 54. Hereafter referred to as *Essays*.

9. Vilfredo Pareto, *Traite de sociologie generale,* translated into English under the title, *The Mind and Society,* by A. Livingston and A. Bongiorno, 4 vols. (New York: 1935). See also A. Bongiorno, "A Study of Pareto's Treatise on General Sociology," *American Journal of Sociology,* XXXVI (1930–1931), 349–370; George C. Homans and Charles C. Curtis, *An Introduction to Pareto: His Sociology* (New York: 1934); P. A. Sorokin, *Contemporary Sociological Theories* (New York: 1928), Chapter I, pp. 37–62; Talcott Parsons, "Pareto's Central Analytical Scheme," *Journal of Social Philosophy,* I (1935–1936), 244–262; *The Structure,* Chapters V–VII; Ellsworth Faris, *The Nature of Human Nature* (New York: 1937), Chapter XVI; and L. J. Henderson, *Pareto's General Sociology: A Physiologist's Interpretation* (Cambridge, Mass.: 1935).

10. *Essays,* p. 55.

11. *Ibid.,* p. 56.

12. See *The Structure,* pp. 200 ff. and 241 ff.

13. *Essays,* p. 56.

14. Bronislaw Malinowski, *Magic, Science, and Religion and Other Essays* (Glencoe: 1948), *Foundations of Faith and Morals* (London: 1936), *Coral Gardens and Their Magic* (London: 1935). For A. R. Radcliffe-Brown's criticism, see his *Taboo, Frazer Lecture,* 1939. Also see Homans' discussion on the controversy in George C. Homans, *The Human Group* (New York: 1950), Chapter 12. Also see George C. Homans, "Anxiety and Ritual," *American Anthropologist,* XLIII (1941), 164–172.

15. L. Levy-Bruhl, *How Natives Think* (London and New York: 1926), *Primitive Mentality* (New York: 1923), *The "Soul" of the Primitive* (New York: 1928).

16. James G. Frazer, "The Magic Art and the Evolution of Kings," in *The Golden Bough,* 3d ed. (New York: 1935), I, 220 ff.

17. *Essays,* pp. 57–58.

18. Compare William G. Sumner in W. G. Sumner and Keller, eds., *The Science of Society,* (New Haven: 1927), II, 1466, where religion is seen as a development to handle the "aleatory element." It is "the sole means of adjustment to the dark mystery which in all ages surrounds the slight circle of human knowledge."

19. See Emile Durkheim, *The Elementary Forms of the Religious Life,* J. W. Swain, tr. (London: 1915). Also see Parsons' discussion of Durkheim in *The Structure,* Chapters VIII–XII, and the criticism of Durkheim by C. C. J. Webb in his *Group Theories of Religion and the Individual* (London: 1916). For other criticisms, see H. R. Lowie, *Primitive Religion* (New York: 1924), Chapter VII, and Georges Gurvitch, *La Vocation*

actuelle de la sociologie (Paris: 1950), Chapter VIII. For a Catholic criticism of Durkheim, see Simon Deploige, *The Conflict between Ethics and Sociology,* C. C. Miltner, tr. (St. Louis: 1938).

20. *Essays,* p. 59.

21. *Ibid.*

22. Parsons says (*ibid.,* p. 60), "In this form the proposition is certainly unacceptable." Yet this is one variation of an attitude of mind widely held in sociological circles. For example, see T. H. Grafton, "Religious Origins and Sociological Theory," *American Sociological Review,* X, No. 6 (December, 1945), 726–739, where the author basing himself on Mead, Cooley, and Dewey makes the "supernatural" the "Other" which is created by man in order to respond to it. The most famous statement of this point of view is that of Ludwig Feuerbach, in *The Essence of Christianity,* M. Evans, tr. (London: 1881): "Man— this is the mystery of religion—projects his being into objectivity and then again makes himself an object to this projected image of himself, thus converted into a subject, into a person" (p. 29). Of this book Frederick Engels said: "Then came Feuerbach's 'Wessen des Christenthums.' With one blow it cut the contradiction, in that it placed materialism on the throne again without any circumlocution. Nature exists independently of all philosophies. It is the foundation upon which we, ourselves products of nature, are built. Outside man and nature nothing exists, and the higher beings which our religious phantasies have created are only the fantastic reflections of our individuality. The cord was broken, the system was scattered and destroyed and the contradiction, since it only existed in the imagination, was solved. One must himself have experienced the delivering power of this book to get a clear idea of it." Engels, *Feuerbach: The Roots of Socialist Philosophy,* A. Lewis, tr. (Chicago: 1903), p. 53. Engels refers to his liberation, not from Theism as generally understood, but from Hegel's system. There were other ways of "stepping out of the Hegelian system", for example, that of Kierkegaard, who was in Berlin these very years. While Durkheim seems to approve of this projective act as a social act, Feuerbach saw it as the source of man's alienation from himself.

23. *Essays,* p. 61.

24. *The Structure.*

25. *Essays,* pp. 62–63. See *The Structure,* Chapters XIV XVII; Max Weber, *The Protestant Ethic and the Spirit of Capitalism,* Talcott Parsons, tr. (New York and London: 1930); Max Weber, *The Religion of China: Confucianism and Taoism,* Hans H. Gerth, tr. (Glencoe: 1951). For criticism, see Amintore Fanfani, *Catholicism, Protestantism and Capitalism* (London: 1955), pp. 3 ff. and Chapters II, VII; H. M. Robertson, *Aspects of the Rise of Economic Individualism: A Criticism of Max Weber and His School* (Cambridge: 1933); and Albert Hyma, *Christianity, Capitalism and Communism* (Ann Arbor: 1937). See also R. H. Tawney, *Religion and the Rise of Capitalism* (London: 1926).

26. *Essays,* p. 63.

27. *Ibid.,* p. 64.

28. See Talcott Parsons and Edward A. Shils, eds., *Toward a General Theory of Action* (Cambridge: 1951); and Parsons, *The Social System.*

29. *Ibid.,*.

30. *Essays,* p. 57.

31. "The manner in which ideas become effective forces in history," Weber, *The Protestant Ethic and the Spirit of Capitalism,* pp. 90 ff. Ernst Troeltsch generally follows Weber in his work *The Social Teaching of the Christian Churches,* Olive Wyon, tr. (New York: 1931). See note 25 above.

32. For the mass of mankind, of course, but not for the sociologists, who constitute in this regard a kind of elite. This reveals another aspect of the Comtean mentality.

33. Cf. Charles A. Ellwood. "The Social Function of Religion," *American Journal of Sociology,* XIX (1913–1914), 289–307.

34. The view of man, of which the Parsonian theory is one specific manifestation, is widely accepted as "scientific tradition" by sociologists. It is what some humanists call

"scientism." As tradition, for which one would think there was no place in such a conception, it is not questioned. It is frequently accompanied by an awkward and simple-minded imitation of natural science, especially of theoretical physics as understood by the sociologist. Parsons has constructed the most complex of such schemes. Moreover, following Weber, he tries to incorporate Dilthey's notion of *Verstehen*. But the relation of meaningful communication between men and phenomenal knowledge is seen in this over-all scheme, based on the premises of positivism. This part of Parsons' work is derived from the German conflict between the *Geisteswissenschaften and Naturwissenschaften*. This aspect of the problem cannot be handled here. Suffice it to say that the solution is unsatisfactory and that the significance of Weber's own personal distinction between objective knowledge and his action as an agent and his freedom as such is all but lost. The significance of *Verstehen* for Parsons amounts to little more than avoidance of the stricter positivistic characterization of an "operational definition" as one in terms of measurable physical operations, an acceptance of which would make social science impossible.

35. Cassirer, *An Essay on Man,* p. 11. Cassirer is here summarizing Pascal. Cassirer would study the symbol as a "clue to the nature of man." In the approach we are analyzing here, the nature of man is postulated in terms of positivistic assumptions and the symbol is then explained in terms of the resulting conception.

36. "The integration of the individual into superindividual units is not restricted to membership in a phylogenetic succession, in a family, a society, and a culture. Man in his religious attitude experiences himself as a member of a meaningful cosmic order.... The direction and range of sharing may vary greatly. One person may turn toward religion, another toward some social unit, but one has to have some object for one's homonomous tendency.... The objective existence of supernatural wholes is a problem for philosophy and as students of personality we need not be concerned with such problems.... For the study of personality it is important only to recognize that man's attitudes are to a large extent oriented toward superindividual units. Since such attitudes represent a powerful source of human motivation, they are vitally important factors in personality organiza-tion." (The term "superindividual" here means transcending the individual person.) Andras Angyal, *Foundations for a Science of Personality* (New York: 1941), pp. 170-171. Compare Etienne de Greeff, *Instincts de defense and de sympathie* (Paris: n.d.), and *Aux Sources de l'humain* (Paris: 1949).

37. *The Symposium.* See Werner Jaeger, *Paideia,* Gilbert Highet, tr. (New York: 1945), II, Chapter 8.

38. Erich Frank, *Philosophical Understanding and Religious Truth* (London, New York, Toronto: 1945), p. 16.

39. Paul Tillich, "Trends in Religious Thought That Affect Social Outlook," in F. Ernest Johnson, ed., *Religion and World Order* (New York: 1944), pp. 17-28.

40. Rudolf Otto, *The Idea of the Holy* (London: 1950). See also Joachim Wach, "Rudolf Otto and the Idea of the Holy," in his *Types of Religious Experience* (Chicago: 1951), Chapter 10.

41. Martin Buber, *I and Thou,* Ronald Gregor Smith, tr. (Edinburgh: 1937).

42. I borrow the expression from John MacMurray, *The Structure of Religious Experience* (New Haven: 1936), pp. 4, 23 ff., whose recognition of stimulus in this regard is inadequate.

43. For an important discussion of these problems, see Wach, *Types of Religious Experience,* especially Chapters I, II, III, and X. However, Ellsworth Faris found this book having "only marginal contact with the questions which sociologists discuss." See his inadequate review in *American Sociological Review,* XVII, No. 2 (April, 1952), 253-254.

44. Karl Jaspers, "Freedom and Authority," *Diogenes,* I, No. 1, 33. Such an explora-tion would reveal to sociologists what historians know well: that there is a relationship not only between magic and religion but also between magic and science. After all, the great period of magic in Western civilization was the sixteenth and seventeenth centuries.

45. For the best discussion of these problems in English, see Wach, *The Sociology of Religion*. This book, as the late Professor Edgar Sheffield Brightman said, is one that "no serious student of religion should neglect to own and study."

46. Parsons explicitly repudiates the view that sociology is a generalizing science of man. But he substitutes instead "Action Theory," a conceptual scheme for the analysis of human life built on the basis of the positivistic conception of man discussed in this chapter. In *The Social System* he distinguishes personality systems, social systems, and cultural systems and tries to show their interpenetration. This is an *objectized* construction based on the objectionable assumptions we have already discussed. It does not avoid a subtle hypostatization of objectized structures in place of a comprehension of existence and the human person. Significantly, its basic component is called "social action." In many sociological texts the notion that sociology is a generalizing science of man is the unvoiced premise of the presentation. In other sociological works the idea is explicitly espoused.

47. "The innovators of sociology changed these standards completely [the ideals of Western civilization]. They limited the historical process to the progress of the technological and industrial development of mankind. By doing so they made Society or the Collective Being the very reality of history. They declared the individual an abstraction, and recognized him merely as an agent or functionary of society. For this reason they did not attach any significance to the evaluation of human freedom and human dignity. Man's life was held meaningful to the extent that he fulfilled his functions as a member of society. *These sociologists turned the social process into the very universe of human existence.*" Albert Salomon, *op. cit.*, p. 37 (my emphasis).

THIRTEEN: Five Dilemmas in the Institutionalization of Religion

I

Although much fruitful research has been done in the sociology of religion, the explicit formulation of an adequate conceptual scheme for observation and interpretation of data still leaves much work to be done. American thinking in this field in recent years has largely been in terms of what may be called a "functional" frame of reference. While helpful in the study of many aspects of religious life, the functional approach does not focus attention squarely on the problems of the sociology of religion as such. Rather it raises two questions, important in their own right. First of all it concerns itself with what religion does for and to society, seeing religious institutions as one set of institutions among others and interesting itself in the contribution of religious institutions and religious ideas to the maintenance of the ongoing equilibrium of the social system. In a more psychological, but still basically functional, frame of reference, it also asks what is the contribution of religion to the preservation and achievement of adequate adaptation and stability for the individual personality.

The first question is not, of course, the sociology of religion in any but a peripheral sense. It is rather the sociology of total social systems, particularly concerned with the contribution of one institutional complex, in this case the religious, to the

From *Journal for the Scientific Study of Religion,* Vol. 1 (October, 1961).

functioning of society. The second, while directing our understanding to important problems involving religion and stratification, religion and social disorganization, religion and social
change, and the general area of problems involved in selfhood
and identity, does not aim its sights squarely on religious
phenomena in their own right.[1]

The functional approach sees the importance of religion in
that religion gives answers to questions that arise at the point of
ultimacy, at those points in human experience that go beyond
the everyday attitude toward life with its penultimate norms and
goals. The study of religion is an important part of the study of
human society because men are cognitively capable of going to
the "limit-situation," of proceeding through and transcending the
conventional answers to the problem of meaning and of raising
fundamental existential questions in terms of their human
relevance. Such "breaking points" of routine experience often
appear in the context of experienced uncertainty, of adversity
and suffering, and in the frustrating but inevitable experience of
the limitations of human finitude.[2]

Moreover, the ultimate tends to be apprehended in a special
modality all its own. In terms of Durkheim and Otto, man
experiences the "sacred" or "holy" as an irreducible category of
existence that is drastically other than the ordinary prosaic
workaday world.[3] From a functional point of view, religion is
important because it sustains life precisely at these breaking
points. From the religious point of view, however, these breaking
points are important precisely because they are the occasions of
the experience out of which religion arises. Talcott Parsons years
ago emphasized the importance in sociological study of taking
the point of view of the participators in the social action studied.[4]
Since religious institutions arise out of this experience of ultimacy
and the sacred, the sociology of religion must begin with
considerable empathy precisely at this point.

From the unusual religious experiences of unusual people the
founded religions emerge, translating and transforming the
insights of founders into institutional structures. Thus there arise
the formed and formulated entities of belief systems, systems of
ritual and liturgy, and organization.[5] It is important, therefore,
especially in the study of the founded religions to begin with a
phenomenological analysis of the religious experience as such, for
out of it emerge the chief dimensions of religious institutions as
well as their chief functional problems. Here man is seen in terms

neither of the Cartesian "I think, therefore I am," which was the model of seventeenth-century thinking, nor of the "I do, therefore I am," of nineteenth-century thought. Rather he is recognized as a being who is not a dichotomous compartmentalization of "adaptive" and "expressive" needs, but one capable of and exhibiting holistic response and commitment to what he experiences as impinging on his consciousness.[6] It is, indeed, because man is primarily a responding animal, and because his responses in interaction with those of his fellows become crystallized into stabilized expectations and allegiances, that contemporary sociology has proved its greater adequacy for the study of human action over the rationalistic conceptions of the past century. Yet modern sociological theory often reads as though it had not, in fact, superseded those older partial views of man.

Religion is first of all a response, and a response is to something experienced. The religious response is a response to the ultimate and the sacred which are grasped as relevant to human life and its fundamental significance. While the religious response is, indeed, peripheral and residual to the day-to-day life of men and the penultimate ends of that life and related to them only as their ultimate ontological underpinning, it is central to the religious life. It is its constitutive element, and out of it proceeds the process of the elaboration and standardization of religious institutions. Since such institutionalization involves the symbolic and organizational embodiment of the experience of the ultimate in less-than-ultimate forms and the concomitant embodiment of the sacred in profane structures, it involves in its very core a basic antinomy that gives rise to severe functional problems for the religious institution. In fact, this profound heterogeneity at the center of religious institutionalization constitutes a severe and unavoidable dilemma from which problems arise for religious movements and institutions that recur again and again and can never be finally solved. Moreover, since the religious experience is spontaneous and creative and since institutionalization means precisely reducing these unpredictable elements to established and routine forms, the dilemma is one of great significance for the religious movement.

This view, which concentrates on religious phenomena, makes possible an "internal functionalism" of religious institutions themselves since it concentrates attention on the peculiarly religious problems or more precisely the specific problems of religious institutions qua *religious* institutions.

II

An institutional complex may be viewed as the concrete embodiment of a cultural theme in the ongoing life of a society, as the "reduction" of a set of attitudes and orientations to the expected and regularized behavior of men. These institutionalized expectations include definitions of statuses and roles, goals, and prescribed and permitted means, and they articulate with the culture of the society and with the personality structures that the socialization processes have produced in a given society.[7]

It is the great virtue of social institutions from the point of view of the functioning of social systems that they provide stability in a world of inconstancy. The unusual and creative performance of the hero, sage, or saint, though of great exemplary and genetic importance, is too unpredictable to become the basis of everyday life. The human world would be an unsteady and incalculable affair, indeed, were it chiefly dependent on such phenomena. Yet the achievement of the necessary stability involves a price. It involves a certain loss of spontaneity and creativity, although these are often found operating in some measure within the expectations of institutional patterns.

The founded religions display this fundamental antinomy in their histories. They begin in "charismatic moments" and proceed in a direction of relative "routinization." This development, necessary to give objective form to the religious movement and ensure its continuity, may in Weber's terms proceed in either a traditional or a rational-legal direction.[8] Such routinization is an unavoidable social process and as such represents for religious institutions a many-sided and complex paradox.

The charismatic moment is the period of the original religious experience and its corresponding vitality and enthusiasm. Since, as we have seen, this experience involves the deep engagement of the person involved with a "beyond" which is sacred, it is unusual in a special sense. It would remain a fleeting and impermanent element in human life without its embodiment in institutional structures to render it continuously present and available. Yet in bringing together two radically heterogeneous elements, ultimacy and concrete social institutions, the sacred and the profane, this necessary institutionalization involves a fundamental tension in which five functional dilemmas take their origin.

In other words, religion both needs most and suffers most from institutionalization. The subtle, the unusual, the charismatic, the supraempirical, must be given expression in tangible, ordinary, and empirical social forms. Let us now examine the five dilemmas which express this fundamental antinomy inherent in the relation of religion to normal social processes.

THE DILEMMA OF MIXED MOTIVATION

In the preinstitutionalized stage of a religious movement, the classical type of which is the circle of disciples gathered about a charismatic leader, the motivation of the followers is characterized by single-mindedness. The religious movement does satisfy complex needs for its adherents, but it focuses their satisfaction on its values and their embodiment in the charismatic leader. The charismatic call receives a wholehearted response. With the emergence of a stable institutional matrix, there arises a structure of offices—of statuses and roles—capable of eliciting another kind of motivation, involving needs for prestige, expression of teaching and leadership abilities, drives for power, aesthetic needs, and the quite prosaic wish for the security of a respectable position in the professional structure of the society.

The contrast we have drawn between the earlier and later stages is not absolute, as we can see in the Gospel where we read of the disciples of Jesus concerning themselves with who shall be highest in the kingdom (Mat. 18:1, Mark 10:37). Yet such self-interested motivation is in the charismatic period easily dominated by the disinterested motivation of the charismatic response.[9] Moreover, while the charismatic movement offers security to its adherents, it does so quite differently than do the statuses of well-institutionalized organizations.

It is precisely because of its ability to mobilize self-interested as well as disinterested motivation behind institutionalized patterns that institutionalization contributes stability to human life. Yet if this mobilization of diverse motives is its great strength, it is paradoxically also its great weakness. It may, in fact, become the Achilles' heel of social institutions. The criteria of selection and promotion in the institutional structure must of necessity reflect the functional needs of the social organization and emphasize performance and therefore will not distinguish very finely between the two types of motivation involved. Thus it may develop that the self-interested motivation will come to prevail. There will then result a slow transformation of the original institutional aims, in many cases amounting to their corruption. When the institution so transformed is suddenly confronted by threat or crisis, the transformed motivation and outlook may reveal themselves as impotence. Careerism that is only formally concerned with institutional goals, bureaucratic rigorism of a type that sacrifices institutional goals to the defense or pursuit of vested interests,[10] and official timidity and lethargy are some evidences of the transformation.

Such developments give rise to movements of protest and reform, ever-recurring phenomena in the history of the founded religions. The Cluniac reform of the Middle Ages offers a striking example, as does the Protestant Reformation of the sixteenth century.

This dilemma of mixed motivation is found not only among those who occupy important positions in the religious organization. It is also characteristic of changes in the composition of the membership with the passing of the charismatic movement and the founding generation. The passing of the founding generation means that the religious body now contains people who have not had the original conversion experience. Many are born members, and their proportion increases with the years. The selection process which voluntary conversion represented often kept out of the organization precisely the kinds of persons who are now brought up in it. Already in the year 150 A.D., Hermas in *The Shepherd* draws a most unflattering picture of some of the lukewarm "born Christians" in the church.

THE SYMBOLIC DILEMMA:
OBJECTIFICATION VERSUS ALIENATION

Man's response to the holy finds expression not only in community but also in acts of worship.[11] Worship is the fundamental religious response, but in order to survive its charismatic moment worship must become stabilized in established forms and procedures.[12] Thus ritual develops, presenting to the participant an objectified symbolic order of attitude and response to which he is to conform his own interior disposition. Worship becomes something not immediately derivative of individual needs, but rather an objective reality imposing its own patterns on the participants.

Such objectification is an obvious prerequisite for common and continuous worship, for without it prayer would be individual and ephemeral. The symbolic elements of worship are not simply expressions of individual response, but have an autonomy enabling them to pattern individual response. Yet here too the element of dilemma appears. The process of objectification, which makes it possible for cult to be a genuine social and communal activity, can proceed so far that symbolic and ritual elements become cut off from the subjective experience of the participants. A system of religious liturgy may come to lose its resonance with the interior dispositions of the members of the religious body. In such a case the forms of worship become alienated from personal religiosity, and whereas previously cult had evoked and patterned response and molded personal religiosity after its own image,[13] now such an overextension of objectification leads to routinization. Liturgy then becomes a set of counters without symbolic impact on the worshipers. It may, of course, retain its element of sacredness through the very fact of its obscurity and mystery, a situation conducive to the development of a semimagical or magical attitude.

This process may be seen in the Christian history of the Middle Ages when it became necessary for churchmen to replace the lost correspondence between external act and gesture and interior psychological disposition in the Mass with an elaborate secondary allegorization such as that of Durandus which appears so ridiculous in the light of modern liturgical research. One result of such alienation of symbolic systems is to weaken the social character of worship, with a consequent weakening of the solidarity of the religious community. Individual prayer as a concomitant of public rites replaces communal worship.

What we have indicated with respect to cult could also be traced out with respect to graphical and musical expression as well. Here, too, overextension of the objectification of symbols can turn them into counters, themes can degenerate into clichés, and at times symbols may become simply objectively manipulatable "things" to be used for achieving ends. In the last case religion becomes semimagic. Parallels can be made with verbal symbolism where the statements of important religious insights in words suffer routinization and a consequent alienation from interior religiosity and deep understanding occurs. Profound statements then become merely facile formulas.

The alienation of symbolism is one of the most important religious developments, and its possibility and likelihood derive from the fact that the religious symbol is in itself an antinomy— an expression par excellence of the dilemma of institutionalizing religion.[14] To symbolize the transcendent is to take the inevitable risk of losing the contact with it. To embody the sacred in a vehicle is to run the risk of its secularization. Yet if religious life is to be shared and transmitted down the generations, the attempt must be made.

Historians have too often failed to see the importance of this dilemma, although the history of religious protest movements is full of evidence of just how central it is. The symbol—word, gesture, act, or painting, music, and sculpture—provides the medium of genuine communication and sharing and thereby the basis for socializing the religious response. When it is is lost, a central element in the religious life disappears. Moreover, when the resonance between the external and internal is lost, the symbol often becomes a barrier, where previously it had been a structured pathway. It then becomes the object of aggression. Hence it is that the English Reformation concentrated so much of its fire on the Mass and the priest as the celebrant of the Mass, leading to destruction of altars, stained glass, statues, and the like. The radical antisymbolism of the Puritans derives from the same experience of lost resonance with the established liturgy. This is one kind of protest that can arise as a response to this dilemma. In the Catholic and Protestant movements for liturgical renascence to be seen in our own day, we see another kind of response to these developments.

THE DILEMMA OF
ADMINISTRATIVE ORDER:
ELABORATION VERSUS EFFECTIVENESS

Max Weber showed that charismatic leadership soon undergoes a process of routinization into a traditional or rational-legal structure made up of a chief and an administrative staff. There are an elaboration and standardization of procedures and the emergence of statuses and roles in a complex of offices. One important aspect is the development in many cases of a distinction between the office and its incumbent, which has become characteristic of the bureaucratic structures of the modern world. The Catholic Church has been the chief prototype in this evolution of the concept of office in European society.

It is characteristic of bureaucratic structure to elaborate new offices and new networks of communication and command in the face of new problems. Precedents are established which lead to the precipitation of new rules and procedures. One result may be, indeed, that the structure tends to complicate itself. This state of affairs evolves in order to cope with new situations and new problems effectively. Yet such self-complication can overextend itself and produce an unwieldy organization with blocks and breakdowns in communication, overlapping of spheres of competence, and ambiguous definitions of authority and related functions. In short, developments to meet functional needs can become dysfunctional in later situations. Weber noted that bureaucracy of the rational-legal type was the most effective means for rational purposeful management of affairs. Yet the word "bureaucracy" has not become a pejorative epithet in the folklore of modern Western societies for nothing. The tendency of organization to complicate itself to meet new situations often transforms it into an awkward and confusing mechanism in whose context it is difficult to accomplish anything.

This dilemma of the necessity of developing a system of administrative order versus the danger of its overelaboration must be seen in relation to the first dilemma—that of mixed motivation. For the involvement of secondary motivation in bureaucratic vested interests complicates this third dilemma considerably. Genuine organizational reform becomes threatening to the status, security, and self-validation of the incumbents of office. The failure of many attempts at religious and ecclesiastical reform in the fourteenth and fifteenth centuries is significantly related to this third dilemma and its combination with the first. The Tridentine insistence on organizational reform in the Catholic Counter Reformation as well as the great concern of the Protestant Reformation with the forms of ecclesiastical organization indicate that contemporaries were not unaware of this aspect of their problems.

Certainly such self-complication of procedures and offices is one of the elements involved in Arnold J. Toynbee's observation that an elite seldom solves two major problems challenging its leadership, for successful solution of the first transforms and incapacitates it for meeting the second.

THE DILEMMA OF DELIMITATION: CONCRETE DEFINITION VERSUS SUBSTITUTION OF LETTER FOR SPIRIT

In order to affect the lives of men, the import of a religious message must be translated into terms that have relevance with respect to the prosaic course of everyday life. This translation is first of all a process of concretization. It involves the application of the religious insight to the small and prosaic events of ordinary life as lived by quite ordinary people. In that process the religious ideas and ideals themselves may come to appear to be of limited prosaic significance. Concretization may result in finitizing the religious message itself. For example, ethical insights are translated into a set of rules. Since rules, however elaborate, cannot make explicit all that is implied in the original ethical epiphany, the process of evolving a set of rules becomes a process of delimiting the import of the original message. Translation becomes a betraying transformation. Moreover, the more elaborate the rules become in the attempt to meet real complexities and render a profound and many-sided ethic tangible and concrete, the greater the chance of transforming the original insight into a complicated set of legalistic formulas and the development of legalistic rigorism. Then, as St. Paul put it, the letter killeth, but the spirit giveth life.

Yet the fact is that the ethical insight must be given some institutionalized concretization or it will remain forever beyond the grasp of the ordinary man. The high call of the ethical message may well, however, be reduced to petty conformity to rules in the process. Brahmanic developments of ritual piety, Pharisaic rituals in late classical Judaism, and legalism in Catholicism offer three examples. This fourth dilemma may be compounded with the third, and the overelaboration of administrative machinery be accompanied by a deadening legalism. It may also become compounded with the second, and the delimitation of the religious and ethical message may contribute to and be affected by the loss of interior resonance of the verbal and other symbols involved.

THE DILEMMA OF POWER: CONVERSION VERSUS COERCION

The religious experience exercises a call. In Otto's words, its content "shows itself as something uniquely attractive and *fascinating.*"[15] Moreover, the propagation of the religious message in Christianity has involved an invitation to interior change. This interior "turning" or "conversion" is the classical beginning of the religious life for the individual. With institutionalization of the religious movement, such a conversion may be replaced by the socialization of the young so that a slow process of education and training substitutes for the more dramatic conversion experience. Yet even in this case, the slower socialization in many instances serves as a propaedeutic for conversion. Christians, both Catholic and Protestant, agree that the act of acceptance must be voluntary, involving such interior turning.

However, as religion becomes institutionalized it becomes a repository of many of the values from which much of the life of the society derives its legitimation. Thus the preservation of religious beliefs and even the maintenance of the religious organization can come to be intertwined with societal problems of public order and political loyalty. This tends to become the case, whether or not there is a legal separation of church and state.

In addition, since religion is dependent on interior disposition and since that disposition is subject to numerous unexpected shocks and is always weak among those merely nominally religious, there is always the subtle temptation for religious leaders to avail themselves of the close relation between religion and cultural values in order to reinforce the position of religion itself. A society may find itself unable to tolerate religious dissent, since such dissent is seen as threatening the consensus on which social solidarity rests. Religious leaders may be tempted to utilize the agencies of a society so disposed to reinforce the position of their own organization.

While such an interpenetration of religious adherence and political loyalty may strengthen the position of religion in the society, it may also weaken it in important respects. It may antagonize members of the religious body who are political oppositionists, and it may antagonize political oppositionists who otherwise might have remained religiously neutral. Second, it may produce an apparent religiosity beneath which lurks a devastating cynicism. History offers many examples of such a coalescing of religious and political interests. Punitive use of the secular arm, the later confessional states in both Catholic and Protestant countries with their "union of throne and altar," and the real though unofficial identification of Protestantism with

American nationalism and even nationality in the nineteenth century offer some cases.

A genuine dilemma is involved. Religion cannot but relate itself to the other institutions of society since religious values must be worked out to have some relation to the other values of a particular cultural complex. Since religion is concerned with ultimate values which legitimate other values and institutions, a relation with established authority and power structures is unavoidable. Such partial identification of basic values in religion and culture tends to strengthen both religious conformity and political loyalty. Yet with the progressive differentiation of society, the confusion of the two soon tends to be detrimental to both. It weakens the bonds of the religious community by weakening voluntary adherence and thereby diluting the religious ethos and substituting external pressures for interior conviction. It weakens the general society by narrowing the possibility of consensus among the population by insisting on a far greater area of value agreement than would, in fact, be necessary to the continued life of society. Yet some relation between the functionally essential values in a society and the ultimate sanction of religion is requisite, and it necessarily involves a relation between religious institutions and power and authority structures.

Anyone acquainted with the religious wars of the sixteenth century will readily recognize this dilemma as one important element involved. The long and painful travail of the development of religious freedom was made more difficult by such a confusion of religious and societal interests. Moreover, this confusion caused many men to welcome secularization since it brought a measure of liberation from the fanatical conflicts of the preceeding period.

III

These five dilemmas represent five sides of the central dilemma involved in the institutionalization of religion—a dilemma which involves transforming the religious experience to render it continuously available to the mass of men and to provide for it a stable institutionalized context. The nature of the religious experience tends to be in conflict with the requisites and characteristics of the institutionalization process and the resultant social institutions. From this incompatibility there derive the special problems of the functioning of religious institutions delineated in this chapter. Some of these antinomies have their analogues in other social institutions. Yet there is reason to suspect that because of the unique character of the religious experience, its elements of incompatibility with institutionalization are more exaggerated than is the case with other areas of human activity. Yet, *mutatis mutandis,* these dilemmas are applicable to other institutions as well. Indeed, the present theoretical formulation represents one way of apprehending general instabilities inherent in social processes, or more precisely in the relation between institutionalization and spontaneous creativity.

Such instabilities have been studied—in some cases for a very long time—in terms of other categories of analysis. The first and fifth dilemmas are related to the problem of restraining force and fraud which besets all societies and which has been a concern of European political philosophy since the Middle Ages. Yet our treatment reveals important new elements. It gets away from an ethical treatment to an analysis of inevitable tendencies in the development of social organizations and their changing relation to their participants. The second, third, and fourth dilemmas are really special forms of that general social process that Weber called "the routinization of charisma." Our formulation has, however, indicated facets of the problem which Weber did not pursue. Actually the fifth dilemma is discussed, in substantially the form presented here, by Talcott Parsons in his book *The Social System.* He was the first to use the term "dilemma of institutionalization," which he applied to this fifth dilemma.[16]

The present formulation obviously bears a close resemblance to Troeltsch's treatment of the perennial tension between the transcendent call of the New Testament and the world, giving rise to the ecclesiastical tendency to compromise and the sectarian rejection of compromise with the world. The present treatment, however, calls attention to other and more subtle aspects of the "world" which need considerable empirical investigation. For example, nowhere is the social and psychological problem of the alienation and "wearing out" of symbolism given the kind of investigation it deserves. Nor are the functionally unavoidable elements involved in the dilemma of mixed motivation the object of the kind of research which is needed if we are to understand on both sociological and psychological levels what actually is involved in the day-to-day functional problems of religious institutions.

The present statement does attempt to indicate how we can go beyond all these previous formulations and tries to gather their insights into a consistent scheme dealing with one important dynamic set of factors internal to the functioning of religious movements and bodies. It is a conceptual scheme derived chiefly from the history of Christianity, and particularly of Catholicism. In no way does it pretend to be an over-all framework for the sociology of religion, but rather to be what Merton called theory of the middle range dealing with one side or aspect of the complex phenomenon of institutionalized religion. A further examination of the meaning of ultimacy in the religious experience, for example, would throw meaningful light on the element of authoritarianism in much of the history of institutionalized religion in the West. For it is precisely this recognition of and response to the ultimate which, when objectified in institutionalized forms, has in the past led to ecclesiastical imperialism and authoritarian rigor.

In the present chapter we have simply attempted to indicate the importance of an internal functional analysis of religious institutions based on their own peculiar inner structure which derives from the particular religious experience on which they happen to have arisen. Then we turned to follow out such an analysis with respect to one aspect of the founded religions, that derived from the basic antinomy involved in an institutionalization of religion. The present statement has the advantage of articulating with other theoretical developments in sociology today. It is consistent with theory in the field of the analysis of social systems and with much theory and research on bureaucratic structure. Its emphasis on emergence relates it to work done by both sociologists and social psychologists on small groups. Moreover, it introduces the historical dimension into the heart of sociological analysis. The understanding of behavior in old established religious bodies requires some knowledge of the transformations which the group has undergone in its past history. Finally, it indicates the relation of certain of these historical processes to human motivation and its transformation and expression in institutional forms.

While specific to the field of the study of religious institutions, the present analytical scheme points to a fundamental dilemma involved in all institutionalization. It may be stated with stark economy as follows: what problems are involved for social systems in their attempt to evolve workable compromises between spontaneity and creativity on the one hand and a defined and stable institutionalized context for human activity on the other? Spontaneity and creativity are the very stuff of human vitality and the source of necessary innovation. Yet social institutions are necessary as the context for action, for without them life would dissolve into chaos. Moreover, men inevitably evolve stable institutionalized forms. The present emphasis provides some element of corrective to the kind of "sociologism" which sees the ready-made, the emerged, the products of past interaction as so important that the importance of the new, the emergent, the coming to be, is missed.

NOTES

1. For example, see Kingsley Davis, *Human Society* (New York: 1950), p. 529; Bronislaw Malinowski, *Magic, Science, and Religion and Other Essays* (Glencoe: 1948), among other works. For a worth-while discussion see Charles Y. Glock, "The Sociology of Religion," in Robert K. Merton, Leonard Broom, and Leonard S. Cottrell, Jr., eds., *Sociology Today* (New York: 1959).

2. See Talcott Parsons, "The Theoretical Development of the Sociology of Religion," *Essays in Sociological Theory* (Glencoe: 1959), pp. 194–211.

3. Emile Durkheim, *The Elementary Forms of the Religious Life,* J. W. Swain, tr. (Glencoe: 1954), and Rudolf Otto, *The Idea of the Holy,* J. W. Harvey, tr. (London: 1950).

4. Talcott Parsons, *The Structure of Social Action* (Glencoe: 1949), *passim.*

5. Joachim Wach, *The Sociology of Religion* (Chicago: 1944), Chapter II, pp. 17–34.

6. For a good discussion, see the final chapter, "Respondeo, ergo sum," in F. H. Heinemann, *Existentialism and the Modern Predicament* (New York: 1958), pp. 190–204.

7. See Talcott Parsons, *The Social System* (Glencoe: 1951).

8. Max Weber, *The Theory of Social and Economic Organization,* Talcott Parsons and A. M. Henderson, trs. (New York: 1947), pp. 363 ff. Also *From Max Weber, Essays in Sociology,* Hans Gerth and C. Wright Mills, trs. (New York: 1946), pp. 53, 54, 262 ff., 297, 420.

9. Talcott Parsons has most clearly shown how social structure is a balance of motivation. See his *The Social System* and *Essays in Sociological Theory.*

10. Robert K. Merton, *Social Theory and Social Structure* (Glencoe: 1957). See especially "Social Structure and Anomie," pp. 131–160.

11. An important book on this subject is Evelyn Underhill, *Worship* (New York: 1957). There is much modern liturgical research; for example, see Louis Bouyer, *Liturgical Piety* (Notre Dame, Ind.: 1955). See also Oscar Cullmann, *Early Christian Worship,* A. Stewart Todd and James B. Torrence, trs. (London: 1953).

12. Louis Duchesne, *Christian Worship: Its Origin and Evolution,* M. L. McClure, tr. (New York: 1904).

13. See Dietrich von Hildebrand, *Liturgy and Personality* (New York, London, Toronto: 1943).

14. See Mircea Eliade, *Comparative Patterns of Religion,* Rosemary Sheed, tr. (New York: 1958).

15. Otto, *op. cit.,* p. 31.

16. Parsons, *The Social System,* pp. 165–166.

17. Ernst Troeltsch, *The Social Teachings of the Christian Churches,* Olive Wyon, tr., Vols. I and II (London and New York: 1931).

FOURTEEN: The Adequacy of Contemporary Religious Forms: an Area of Needed Research

"Are contemporary religious forms adequate?" An exploration of what is involved in trying to answer this simple question reveals how great is our dearth of empirical information in important areas of knowledge concerning religious organization and practice. We shall attempt here to examine this question from the perspective of the sociology of religion. Perhaps we should first offer a brief definition of this discipline. The sociology of religion is the empirical study of the relationship between religion on the one hand and social structures and social processes on the other. It includes the examination of the emergence, development, and decline of religious institutions. It is the study of both the relation between religion and society and the functional problems, dilemmas, and crises of religious organizations and movements themselves. As such, it has developed a theoretical framework, which is both impressive and useful, and a considerable amount of empirical research in some areas of its concern.

In the United States, important contributions have been made to the field by academic sociologists and by men in religion, often in Protestant seminaries, who have made use of sociology to enable them to deal more adequately with religious problems in a number of spheres. Also a number of Roman Catholics, priests, religious, and laymen, often academic sociologists themselves, have like those in Protestant seminaries sought to utilize the sociological approach in deepening their understanding of religious problems. In Europe an attempt has been made to

From *Review of Religious Research*, VII, (Winter, 1966), 85–92.

distinguish a "religious sociology" as an empirical study conducted for the practical help it offers to the pastoral work of the
church from the "sociology of religion" as the scholarly and
scientific study of religious phenomena not viewed in terms of
the commitment of any one faith perspective, a distinction which
has not gained acceptance here.

The present question, however, suggests two things. It suggests
the need for a considerable increase in empirical research
conducted in a theoretical frame of reference of sufficient sophistication to aid our understanding of the real problems facing
religious institutions in American society in our day. It suggests
also the need for an applied sociology of religion which would
utilize the findings and theoretical equipment of the larger field
in the study of practical problems of religious organizations and
institutions. Such an applied discipline would function in the
field of religious behavior as industrial sociology does in the field
of industry. Like industrial sociology, an applied sociology of
religion, while profiting from the parent field, would also provide
it with enrichment as a consequence of its practical studies and
observations.

Religious Institutionalization

Let us turn, then, to an exploration of our question: "How
adequate are contemporary religious forms?" By the term "religious forms," the sociology of religion understands evolved and
stable patterns of thought and feeling, of response, and of
relationship, which have emerged and become institutionalized
in the history of religious groups. Joachim Wach has shown that
it is useful to distinguish three levels on which such religious
institutionalization takes place.

On the Symbolic Level

First, there is the symbolic level, the level of symbolic response,
which we call worship. Churches, to be sure, differ in terms of
the centrality, degree of elaboration, fixedness, and significance

which characterize their worship. In the development of a religious group, however, cultic behavior often plays a central and strategic role. The early church developed around the cult of the Risen Lord; and, as Troeltsch has observed, without this cult no church would have emerged at all. The question arises in our present examination: How adequate are contemporary forms of worship? The movements for liturgical reform and renewal in Roman Catholicism and also in Protestant groups indicate that this is a real problem in religious bodies. But to ask the question is to raise at the same time the problem of defining adequacy. Adequate to what? Adequate in terms of what? Worship and liturgy offer a vast area for research, and little has been done in that area. First of all, much research of a psychological kind on the meaning and function of symbolism in worship is needed. The psychological role of religious symbolism and its resonance with the deeper layers of human personalities is not well understood. Some symbols appear to have been derived *historically* by association and juxtaposition with meaningful entities and events; others appear to have a kind of universal structural affinity with significant human experiences and forms of consciousness. But much more needs to be known about these characteristics of religious symbols. Are there primordial symbols—archetypical symbols—fundamental to religious worship? If there are, how are they affected by unique historical elements in the religious experiences of groups and individuals?

Only on the basis of considerable research on questions of that kind can we approach the problem of the adequacy of forms of worship. Present-day worship involves symbolic complexes that arose in previous periods of history. These symbolic complexes reflect in some degree social and psychological conditions which no longer exist. They arose in response to needs that were to some extent specific to the culture and society of the time. How adequate are such symbolic complexes to the expressive needs of people in modern Western societies and in societies undergoing modernization in other parts of the world? Furthermore, there is reason to believe that much symbolism loses its resonance, that it "wears out" and becomes alienated from the interior religious dispositions of people. Can it be revived, or must new symbolic vehicles be discovered? There is obviously much research needed in this sphere of worship and cultic behavior. The symbolic acting out of the religious relationship in worship is a strategic area for the understanding of religion. It is an area of palpable significance to both psychoanalysis and sociology. But it has been neglected as an area for research.

On the Ideational Level

Religious institutionalization involves the emergence of stable forms in the realm of ideas as well. Here articles of faith, creeds, and doctrine are developed which work out explicitly the implication of the religious relationship in a particular religious group. Wach has called this the ideational level. The question has, indeed, arisen for modern Western man: How adequate is theology and the basic Judeo-Christian conceptualization of the human condition and of human destiny to the meaningful orientation of men in our age? Is the thought developed on the basis of biblical religion adequate to express the modern predicament (or predicaments) and to orient men in relation to it? Does institutionalized religion still answer what Max Weber called the "problem of meaning" for large groups of people? This is an area in which we all have opinions. It is one in which some survey research has been done, but it has not been explored to any degree commensurate with its importance in understanding contemporary religion and society.

On the Organizational Level

Both worship and belief develop in the context of community, of fellowship; and out of fellowship develops the religious organization. The organizational level constitutes the third level of the institutionalization of religion. This level has been the one most studied by sociologists. Beginning with the work of Troeltsch, sociologists have been concerned with the adjustment made by religious bodies to the demands of the secular society and with the implications of such adjustment for social structure. Troeltsch distinguished two major responses: one of compromise with and adjustment to the world and another involving rejection of the world and of the whole spirit of compromise with secular culture. The larger group which compromises he called the *church;* the more militant minority group opposed to the world and to compromise with it he called the *sect*. H. Richard Niebuhr, Pope, Johnson, Wilson, and the present writer and others have done a considerable amount of research in this area. Two typical trajectories of sectarian development have been formulated. Many sects go through a process of routinization, of adjustment and compromise, and end up as institutionalized bodies much like churches. These routinized sects Niebuhr has called denominations. Bryan Wilson has shown that other sects succeed in institutionalizing a continuing opposition to the general society and its values. Some of these withdraw in geographical isolation; others utilize methods of social isolation while remaining in urban centers. Benton Johnson and others have shown how sects, while remaining in militant opposition to secular values, often prepare their members to take part successfully in the secular middle-class world. The present writer has shown another alternative in the development of religious movements. The Mormon Church became neither church nor sect in the strict Troeltschian definition of the terms. Rather it developed into a highly organized semiecclesiastical organization which became and remains the organized core of a quasi-ethnic entity—the Mormon people.

Also on the organizational level of the institutionalization of religion arise all those problems derived from the internal differentiation of the church early in its history into two distinct strata, clergy and laity. This distinction developed on the basis of different functions in worship, in teaching, and in exercising authority; that is, on the three levels we have been discussing. With such a development, many changes were introduced into church life which later became a source of difficulties. The laity were long in a state of tutelage, a situation which caused (and continues to cause) protest and revolt. While such problems are quite obvious in the Roman Catholic Church, they are not insignificant in Protestantism, although Protestantism itself was in major respects a lay revolt against the older established ecclesiastical order. Closely related to problems of inner differentiation are those derived from the transformation of religious communities into formal organizations. A part of this transformation is the development of ecclesiastical bureaucracies characterized by all the functional strains and dilemmas of bureaucracy in general.

A closely related but widely ramifying set of problems derives from the fact that the layman is also a participant of another world—the secular world—the world which the layman has built over many centuries and which has now become the most significant arena of human activity. The secularization of culture has tended to make religion peripheral to the chief concerns of men, and strategic movements and significant decisions are found taking place in the secular sphere. It is true that today churchmen are found in the forefront of important social movements. An example of this fact may be seen in the movement for civil rights for the Negro in America. But it is equally true that churches and churchmen were by and large joiners and not initiators of such movements. The impulse for reform, while remotely deriving from prophetic and evangelical biblical influences in our culture, tends to come from secular sources. Similar observations could be made with respect to the development of the labor movement. Whatever one may think of the adequacy of the encyclical *Rerum Novarum* of Pope Leo XIII, the fact that it was issued nearly fifty years after Marx and Engels wrote *The Communist Manifesto* suggests the time lag characteristic of the response of religious leaders and organizations to social issues in Western society.

It may be suggested that religious organizations do offer community and fellowship in an urban world characterized by impersonality and anonymity. But actually how much community do religious organizations offer? How well do they, in fact, meet the modern quest for community on the part of secularized urban man? How adequate are the old forms of church organization, such as the parish built on the territorial principle, for meeting such needs? Have not the churches tended to become peripheral to many important modern concerns, ranging from the proper education of middle-class children to maintenance of living standards in the local community? Indeed, have not the churches tended to become obsolete with respect to their concrete forms of local organization in urban areas? These are some of the questions which can be raised on this level.

The Function of Religion

While it is clear that we do not have anywhere nearly sufficient empirical information to answer most of these questions adequately, it will help us to consider them more precisely if we review briefly what sociology has had to say concerning the function of religion and religious institutions. In raising the question of function, the sociology of religion asks the following questions: What do religion and religious institutions do for and to the individual and for and to the society? What is the contribution of religion and religious institutions to the continued existence of society? What is the contribution of religion to change in society? Sociology distinguishes two kinds of such functions. There are manifest functions which are obvious and recognized by the human actors involved, and there are latent functions which are not intended and not recognized by the actors. Sociology further distinguishes such functions from purpose. Purpose is what the religious body and its members intend; it is their definition of the aim and significance of their action. The purpose of worship is to express the religious relationship—to act out the relation of men to God. One of its functions is to enhance the group's consensus on beliefs and values and to reinforce the solidarity of the religious group. Sociology has been chiefly interested in the study of latent functions.

If we examine the sociological literature, it is possible to discover six significant functions which religion performs in modern secular societies, some of which it has long performed in traditional societies as well. Here we shall set down these six functions briefly.

The Supportive Function

Sociology has shown that from the point of view of its contribution to the development and stability of societies, religion is particularly significant because it answers the problem of meaning for men at those important points where human experience raises questions which go beyond man's empirical knowledge. Human life is essentially characterized by contingency; men face both anxiety-provoking uncertainty and frustrating impossibility. At these limit situations man's cognitive ability fails, as does his capacity for control. It is here that religion provides both a cognitive and an emotional answer and enables men to carry on with the business of life. Through its belief system, religion provides an answer to the "problem of meaning." Through its cultic rites and ceremonies it enables men to relate themselves to a ground of being which lies beyond the realm of mundane empirical experience. This fundamental function of religion reinforces men's engagement in and commitment to the goals and aims of life established in their society. From this basic function may be derived four functions found in the sociological literature.

One important historic function of religion is that of providing consolation, emotional support, and reconciliation to those who suffer oppression, frustration, and deprivation. Societies are patterned allocations of functions, facilities, and reward. All such allocations differentiate and discriminate in the distribution of opportunities, scarce values, and scarce goods. Thus there are always those who are deprived, at least relatively. Moreover, not everyone is able to realize the goals and aims set before him by his culture. To the limits imposed by scarcity must be added those derived from differential ability. Religion offers consolation to the deprived and to the frustrated. It offers emotional support in situations made difficult by deprivation. It serves to reconcile dissident or potentially dissident elements to existing conditions and to reintegrate possible subversive elements into society. An overemphasis on this function tends to place religion on the side of those desirous of maintaining the status quo and may indeed amount to an alliance, however consciously or unconsciously arrived at, between ruling and favored groups in society and leaders in religion. It was this function of religion which prompted Karl Marx to characterize religion as the opium of the people. This function of religion is concerned chiefly with what has been called "peace of mind" and "peace of soul."

The Priestly Function

Second, one may observe the priestly function. The priest is the leader in worship, and through worship the religious group is related to God—to the realm of the sacred or holy. Obviously this is a fundamental purpose of religious organizations and is basic to a number of the other functions of religion. The priestly function also involves teaching of explicit religious doctrine and ruling in the religious community. The priest is a sacramental technician, a specialist in creedal problems, and an authority in the church. This priestly function is obviously important in providing support for the individual and underlies many other functions.

Normative and Legitimation Function

Third, religion performs a normative and legitimating function in all societies. The patterned allocation of functions and, hence, of facilities and rewards must be given a normative expression and must be made to appear as right and proper. It must be made to seem justified by both the favored and the deprived. Better and worse, favored and deprived, upper classes and lower classes, rulers and ruled—such social distinctions must come to be accepted not as the product of fortune, strength, or guile, but as deserved and resting on right, or social stability cannot be established. The rules and reciprocal expectations which characterize the basic institutions of society, such as those which define the rights of access, use, and disposal of material possessions in the institution of property, must be seen as normative for their legitimation. Similarly the rules and reciprocal expectations defining the role of law and of duly constituted authority must be seen as normative. Religion contributes to this normative and legitimating process by its sacralization of the norms and values on which they are based. Religion relates functionally strategic norms to a transcendent reference which is at once ultimate and sacred.

The Prophetic Function

Fourth, we may distinguish a function of religion which may not contribute to the stability of social order, but may, rather, be a source of instability and even of revolution. Religion may play a prophetic role, perform a prophetic function. Biblical religion has often performed this function. By holding up an ethical ideal or command which transcends the contemporary social forms and disregards established partisan interests, either religion may contribute to a more stable society by righting potentially disruptive wrongs, or it may become the supporter and initiator of revolution.

What is the real status of these four functions? What is the relative importance of each in the contemporary religious situation? What is their relation to contemporary forms of religious life on the three levels we have discussed above? What is their relation to the various differentiations which characterize church organizations: rural as against urban communities, clergy as compared to lay groups, various age groups, male as against female needs and interests? Obviously we cannot answer these questions. Partial answers may be found in the literature, but much more research is needed. We cannot even be sure of how accurately or helpfully we have characterized these functions, nor have we any idea of their relative empirical importance.

The Identity Function

We spoke earlier of six functions of religion, and so far we have discussed four. There are two additional ones which, while not exactly on the same level as the four discussed above, appear also to be derived from the fundamental role of religion in meeting ultimate needs of an emotional and cognitive kind for men at the limit situation. The first of these concerns role and identity. It would seem that by providing men with a definition of the ultimate meaning of life and by giving them a sense of belonging to the religious community, religion contributes significantly to self-definition. Durkheim, in stressing the social nature and role of religion in primitive society, has shown the importance of this function. Will Herberg has indicated the way this appears to operate in contemporary America. It is Herberg's contention that an older America was one in which ethnic group membership provided an important basis for self-definition and identity. With the present stage of assimilation and the current social mobility in the midst of general affluence, Herberg suggests that ethnicity is losing its former role. It is being replaced by membership in religious communions. He maintains that to be an American has come to mean being a member of one of the "three great religions of democracy," Protestantism, Catholicism, or Judaism. Moreover, he suggests that beneath the doctrinal divergences and cultic differences of these three there lies a consensus on those secular values which characterize the middle-class American way of life.

Yet it must be admitted that this function of religion is one in which religion has often failed. In both the provision of basic meaning and membership in significant solidary groups, other functionally equivalent groups may be observed in many societies. Secular movements and secular groups have become strategically significant in performing this identity function. In developing countries, nationalism would appear to be a successful religion surrogate in this respect, as was the socialist movement in nineteenth-century Europe. Moreover, among middle-class groups in America, it appears that occupation is becoming a highly significant reference point for the development of identity. What, in fact, is religion's effective role with respect to identity and self-definition in America at the present time? How does it differ for different religious bodies, for different social strata, and for different sections of the country? We do not have sufficient empirical information to answer these questions.

The Growth Function

Finally, as a sixth function we may point to the relation of religion to the individual process of psychological and intellectual maturation. Alfred North Whitehead once declared that religion ought to be an adventure of the spirit, and not a rule of safety. Is this, in fact, the case with institutionalized religion? We know that faith and doubt are intimately and intricately interrelated. We know that doubt arises at various stages of life and that these stages are by no means confined to childhood or adolescence. Growth is a matter of encounter and crisis. Does religion enable people to grow in such encounters and crises, or does it protect them from the challenge and maintain them in a stage of relative immaturity? Does religion contribute to growth, or does it offer fantasy escape? Does institutionalized religion play a role like Dostoevski's Grand Inquisitor? The affinity of some forms of religion with radicalism of the right, such as Birchism, suggests the seriousness of the question. Here is a whole area of vast importance waiting to be studied empirically.

Conclusion

Let us now recapitulate succinctly what we have been saying. We have surveyed briefly the three levels of the institutionalization of religion: the ideational level, the symbolic or cultic level, and the organizational level. We have indicated the kinds of problems existing on these levels and the kinds of questions pertinent to them on which empirical research would be useful. All religious organizations have inherited from the past stable forms on these three levels. We have asked the question of the current adequacy of these forms amidst contemporary societal changes—technological development, affluence, social mobility, and a vast communications revolution. In attempting further to refine and specify the significant areas for research, we distinguished six functions of religion treated in the sociological literature: (1) consolation, support, and reconciliation; (2) the priestly function; (3) the normative and legitimation function; (4) the prophetic function; (5) the identity function; and (6) the problematic function of religion in relation to personal intellectual and psychological growth and maturation. We asked what the empirical status and the functional effectiveness of these six functions might be in contemporary America. We also raised the same question with respect to the other countries, particularly the two-thirds of the world in transition to modernity. We were unable to answer these questions.

It is against these conditions and questions, against this background, that we must attempt to assess the significance of our original question: How adequate are contemporary religious forms? What impresses us immediately is the extent and profundity of our ignorance. The need for much more factual knowledge, the necessity for much more empirical research, before we can begin to discuss intelligently the questions we have raised—let alone answer them—is obvious, indeed, But the question of adequacy raises another problem. What does adequacy mean in this context? Does the judgment of adequacy involve a value commitment with respect to the function of particular religious bodies? Is the judgment of adequacy in part a judgment of value? Perhaps the most instructive analogy here would be with medicine. If we agree that medical practice is devoted to the restoration of health and alleviation of suffering (however we may define health, a common core is bound to emerge), then we may ask a sociological question: How adequate to the attainment of the ends of medicine are the institutional forms in the context of which medicine is practiced in America today? In that form the question, though complex and difficult, is a researchable one. Is our question concerning the adequacy of religious forms a researchable one?

Is adequacy of religious forms researchable? To answer this we may begin by asking, What are the functions of religion that are analogous to restoration of health and alleviation of pain in medicine? Is it the purpose of religious groups to maintain a relationship with a beyond, with the sacred? It would appear that such a relationship is supraempirical and therefore beyond the sphere of empirical observation. Yet certain aspects of religious behavior are clearly observable. Cultic behavior that has become formal to the point of alienation for the worshiper is clearly a matter that can be studied empirically through observation and interview. Is the function of religion one or more of the six functions we have distinguished in the sociological literature? We must remember that these six functions are largely latent—unintended by the actors involved. No religious movement sets out explicitly and primarily to solve the problems indicated by these functions. Rather, religious groups and movements define themselves in terms of religious purposes and seek the achievement of religious ends. We may take the Roman Catholic Church as an example. The Roman Catholic Church defines its function as institutional mediation between God and men. It is a function in which sacramental mediation and celebration of the Mass are of central significance. The church defines its own meaning in terms of this central function and sees in it the entire justification of its continuing existence. While the churches of the Reformation repudiated important aspects of institutional mediation as understood in the older church, yet they generally have seen their function related to the mediatorship of Christ. What is the relation of this explicit purpose and the activities based on it to the six functions we have considered? Obviously, it is the basis on which and the means through which the religious body provides the cognitive and emotional answer to the ultimate problem of meaning.

Sociology, which is an empirical discipline, probably cannot say anything directly about adequacy with respect to this central supraempirical function. But it can say something about how adequately the means used achieve the empirical aspects of the aims pursued. If symbolism wears out, research can tell us much about how and why it does. If community atrophies into formal membership without real solidarity, research can tell us much concerning how and why this process takes place. If religious doctrines appear irrelevant to many modern men, research can tell us much about how and why such irrelevancy develops and what it means to the alienated. In researching the problem of adequacy, we must define a partial aim—not the ultimate supraempirical one, but a partially empirical one. Then the adequacy of means—of forms of ideational, symbolic, and organizational patterns—can be researched. Such studies would seem to be one of the chief concerns of an applied sociology of religion analogous to industrial sociology which we suggested at the outset as appropriate here.

In a study of social change in the Middle East, the present writer found that if one took the needs of the community for economic and technological development as embodied in the aspirations of strategic elements of its population as the base line, then one could raise important questions of functional adequacy of religion that were researchable. One could ask, Does or does not Islam facilitate or does it obstruct the transformation of attitudes and aspirations necessary for the transition from a traditional society to modernity? One could ask, Is Islam rethinking its formulations in a way that is likely to be helpful to strata and classes in transition? One could ask important questions concerning the six functions we have outlined with respect to contemporary Islam. This example suggests another basis for answering the question of adequacy. If in contemporary America we cannot define adequacy of function in terms sufficiently empirical to enable us to do research—if we cannot define religious aims in terms comparable to medical aims—then, perhaps, we can propose general societal needs and needs for particular strata and groups of the society in terms of which adequacy can be empirically defined. Perhaps we can define for developed countries a need that will be functionally analogous to development for countries in transition.

In raising the "practical" question of the adequacy of religious forms, we have raised the fundamental theoretical question of the function of religion in society, its different functions in different kinds of societies, and its as yet unclear function in the dynamic and mobile society now emerging in the United States and the other advanced countries of the West. There is little doubt that religion has performed many of the functions we have indicated in the past. But we know too little about significant aspects of this past performance. In our period of transition, secularization, and rapid social transformation, we are in need of greater knowledge to enable us to understand the contemporary religious situation. Unfortunately, we actually know less.

Our exploration has indicated the great need for research. It also suggests the need for much rethinking on the part of religious leaders on the relation of religion to human needs, to social structures and processes, and to currently effective values. In the dialogue between researchers and religious leaders interested in such fundamental rethinking, there may evolve an applied sociology of religion of both scientific and practical significance.

FIFTEEN: "Acting Out"—
Man Makes Himself?

In 1936, V. Gordon Childe, concluding his survey of man's earliest efforts at civilization building, used these words to characterize human conduct:

> Actually, we have seen that this behavior is not innate. It is not even immutably fixed by the environment. It is conditioned by social tradition. But just because tradition is created by societies of men and transmitted in distinctively human and rational ways, it is not fixed and immutable: it is constantly changing as society deals with ever new circumstances. Tradition makes the man, by circumscribing his behavior within certain bounds; but it is equally true that man makes traditions. And so, we can repeat with deeper insight, "Man makes himself."[1]

Human behavior is seen here as fixed neither by biology nor by circumstances. It is highly influenced by tradition; but tradition itself is seen as constantly changing as men respond to a changing environment. Man makes tradition while responding to circumstances; traditions influence the making of men; tradition is itself changed by men in the course of their adaptive conduct. Man makes himself in the making of his traditions.

The Human Condition

It may be worth while at the start to delineate the elements of this process more sharply. There are first the environment and the tasks it requires for human survival and enhancement. (I add "enhancement" to the conventional "survival" because it is impossible to define that word in noncultural terms and because men do try to improve their condition.) There is the inherited biological and physical structure of man: his intellectual and manual potential; his lack of the kind of bodily specializations found in some other species limiting their scope for adaptation; his visual, auditory, and muscular capacities; and his life or growth cycle. Man displays needs, capacities, and propensities. One striking characteristic of man's capacities and equipment is that they make him flexible in his active potential for response and malleable in his receptive capacity for conditioning. One reason why man's responses are not fixed by the environment is the flexibility of his response capacities. Another, equally important, is that he is not related to his circumstances by narrow, fixed, biologically relevant sensitivities. He does not relate to the environment as a silkworm does to the chemical composition of the mulberry leaf. In fact, he does not respond to an "environment" at all; he responds to the circumstances about him as he defines and understands them, and his definition of the environment is highly influenced by his own mental set—by the ideas and values of his culture created by the experience of his society. Man responds to a culturally defined situation in which inescapable environmental elements play a significant part. Even the harshest environments admit of a range of successful human responses. Moreover, the culturally defined situation transcends the "environmental" elements; man's meaningful situation is a world, not a niche in the natural environment.[2] Finally, the response itself is not simply utilitarian—not simply adaptive; nor is it basically utilitarian and adaptive to which something more has been added. The separation out of sheer utility from a larger complex of expressive response has been a modern Western phenomenon. Man responds on many levels to many aspects of the environment. In this response he survives, develops a society and tradition, and makes himself; the society and tradition which he develops become the mold to shape the cultural formation of his offspring. Man responds—he acts, he does, he makes—and in this response he impresses himself in a variety of ways on his surroundings—on other men, on nonhuman material. He "objectifies" aspects of himself and thereby brings what is only potential in him to expression. Yet such "objectification" is not simply "projection," for the outside; the task, the material, and the other human beings all influence the shape and form in which the projection is realized.

Although it is not narrowly utilitarian nor shorn of any other characteristics than that of manipulation of the elements of his environment, man's response makes useful skills an important part of human activity—important in control of the circumstances of man's life and important in expressing human needs and propensities. Man is, indeed, a workman. Theodora Kroeber, writing about a Stone Age man who came to live in our civilization and to demonstrate his Stone Age skills to sympathetic anthropologists, says this: "Watching Ishi at work, the long road of history, lost in the darkness of remoteness, became illumined and its distances telescoped, for man is the world's craftsman, the maker of tools, and what one man fashions with his two hands is not strange to another man's appreciation and understanding."[3] Yet Ishi did not see the materials of his environment as objects of sheer use and consumption. Nowhere is this so conspicuously evident as in his behavior as hunter.

Ishi the hunter, and modern man the hunter, shared neither weapons, techniques, nor attitudes. Modern man hunts for sport, and he is wasteful of the game he takes, his need being not for the animal which he has killed, but to engage briefly and violently in the act of killing. Ishi hunted to live, used each hock and hair of the animal he killed, and lived in proximity to, and knowledge of, all animal life. American Indian mythology which has it that people were animals before they were people, recognizes in however literalistic a fashion, man's biological continuity with all animal life, a system of belief which precludes the taking of life except with respect for it in the taking.[4]

In work man gained control over his circumstances and, through disciplining himself in work, over himself as well. Making was self-making. In his expression of his larger relation to his world—his respect for life and his feeling of consanguinity with all life, for example—he crystallized his thinking and feeling and also made himself. Man makes himself in his activities, but he does so out of his own human material. "Human mental life has a structure of its own. It is difficult to describe it in terms of its connections with the land and the rain and the trees. The things that men think and feel are only partly connected with adaptation for survival. The land and the sky enter importantly into their thinking in ways that are not immediately adaptive."[5] As man acts in relation to his situation and makes himself, he creates a world of meaning. He puts into his actions deep, inchoate yearnings and aspirations which take form and shape only in their expression. "The world of men is made up in the first place of ideas and ideals."[6] As far back as we can follow the traces which men have left of their existence, we find the evidence of their craftsmanship and their efforts to relate themselves to the larger world in ritual and in symbol.

Man also, as far back as we can trace him, is a social animal. He lives in groups and responds as part of a group. Man's response to his situation gives rise to a division of function, which is at the same time a division of labor and of reward, of authority and of prestige. In time such division leads to a stratification of society and often to the emergence of classes with different functions, perspectives on the world, values, and ideals. Toynbee has formulated what is involved here by stating that civilizations arise in response to the stimulus of an environmental challenge. In their response a people make their society, their culture, and themselves. He suggests that in time internal problems become more important than environmental ones, and men come to achieve in relation to them an increasing capacity for self-determination.[7] Moreover, Toynbee suggests that not only does the response to the environmental challenge involve a division of function but the response is the achievement of a "creative minority." It is this creative minority who break the cake of custom and in a kind of psychological "take-off" start the process of self-direction. The creative minority becomes a leading elite eliciting the followership of the others. The working out of its response is at the same time the self-making of the creative minority. The elite minority develops its own ideas and values and its own character in the process and from then on is largely formed by this tradition which it has created. As a consequence, when a new challenge is to be met which is of a different sort than that to which the sensitivities, ideas, ideals, and values of the creative minority owe their origin, the creative minority is often incapacitated to handle it. There is here a kind of class "trained incapacity" similar to that which Veblen pointed out in the individual. The creative minority, unable to respond, appropriately loses its moral ascendancy over the rest of society; it ceases to lead and must now impose itself in increasingly coercive ways. It ceases to be a "creative" minority and degenerates into a "dominant" minority. Indeed, "the successful creator in one chapter finds his very success a severe handicap in endeavoring to resume the creative role in the next chapter."[8] The creative minority finds itself enmeshed in "the incubus of ineradicable and no longer profitable traditions and memories."[9] A new creative minority must arise, or the challenge will not be met successfully. "While the creative minority is certainly not predestined to undergo this change for the worse, the creator is decidedly predisposed in this direction *ex officio creativitatis*."[10]

Task and Gesture

The importance of work in this process in which man makes himself has been pointed out. In *The Phenomenology of Mind*, Hegel noted that while the division of function created master and slave, the slave's position was bound to improve, while that of the master deteriorated. Domination leads to a loss of substance, while labor impresses man's interiority on the outside world and gives substance to his activities. In work—in objectifying his consciousness in things made and done—the worker achieves self-consciousness.[11] Marx saw work as playing the basic role in the making of man. Moreover, he saw in the division of labor the fragmentation of man, the source of human exploitation, and the roots of human alienation. Man, he said, became subordinated to objectifications of himself in social structure and ceased to be meaningfully related to the product of his labor.

> History presupposes as its basic fact the existence of living human individuals, and these individuals, because of their physical being, are determined by their relation to nature. This might seem to place men on a par with animals. However, unlike animals, men actively transform nature in order *to produce* their means of subsistence. The basic requirements for subsistence are provisions for "eating and drinking, a habitation, clothing and many other things." But as soon as these fundamental needs are satisfied, other needs arise, which man with his newly acquired instruments, is equally able to satisfy. The creation of needs and their subsequent satisfaction constitute the first historical act of man. In the production of luxury he becomes a *human*, i.e., a civilized being. Because there is no limit to the needs he can create, or to the means of satisfying them, man continually transcends himself. Through this transcendence he becomes more and more human. This production process then is at once man's self

expression and his self-creation. "As individuals express their life, so they are." Man's essence depends upon his productive activity, and this activity is determined by nature.[12]

Marx's tracing out of the situational conditioning of man's self-making needs some reforming and some reformulation to take into account the nonutilitarian aspects of man's response and the less than determinative character of his relation to nature. But the centrality of man's relation to nature in a more flexible sense seems an important insight. More significant even is the notion of man's creation of expanding needs for himself in this process. Moreover, Marx sees that some strata get to participate positively in this process, while others are made rather than making, patient rather than agent.

> As long. . . as activity is not voluntarily but naturally divided, man's own deed becomes an alien power opposed to him, which enslaves him instead of being controlled by him. For as soon as labor is distributed, each man has a particular, exclusive sphere of activity, which is forced upon him and from which he cannot escape.[13]

Work is, indeed, important. It is central to man's relation to nature and is strategic to his own self-control and self-development. Yet the evidence of nonliterate societies suggests that man's work was originally part of a larger response to his world. And, indeed, men never simply do and make: they respond. "Man comes into being by an act of response; his evolution consists of interrelated and complicated acts of response."[14] If response seems more elusive to definition than do action and doing, it is because man's fundamental mode of awareness of and relation to his world does not function on the surface of his consciousness or confine itself to his more obvious forms of expression. Hence it is not amenable to easy definition or to easy circumscription in the abstract categories of conventional social science wisdom. It is out of response in situations that men form their identities, individual and communal; it is out of that relational matrix that there develop selfhood, community, and culture. These are many-faceted entities, and so, indeed, are the responses which objectify them and give them recurrent reality. "Human behavior is not only a food-getting strategy, but also a language; . . . every *move* is at the same time a *gesture*."[15] The roots of man's symbolic behavior "lie much deeper than any conscious purpose . . . in that substratum of the mind, the realm of fundamental ideas." Again it has been pointed out, "Whatever purpose magic may serve, its direct motivation is the desire to symbolize great conceptions—to symbolize a Presence, to aid in the formulation of a religious universe."[16]

Feuerbach long ago pointed out that in religion men came first to an obscure form of self-knowledge. Moreover, religion expressed men's aspirations and consequently was able to direct the human gaze above the here and now, making possible the expansion of man's vision, hopes, and, indeed, ambition. Yet too often established ideas and social structures, like creative minorities which have degenerated into dominant minorities, have become barriers in the way of man's continued development of self-direction. Moreover, they have at times misled man seriously. Childe suggested that religious ideas succeeded in making man "feel at home in his environment" and made his life "bearable." But he says they also often caused him to pursue "vain hopes and illusory short cuts suggested by religion and magic," thus deterring him from "the harder road to control of Nature by understanding." Yet Childe concedes that "magic and religion constituted the scaffolding needed to support the rising structure of social organization and science."[17] Yet man aspires to control nature and even to do more than that. He wishes to express his kinship with and his relation to nature or that which lies behind and animates nature. Indeed, in his mythic conceptions we see the mode and mood of early man's existential stance—his way of experiencing his world and himself. "The imagery of myth is then by no means allegory, it is nothing less than a carefully chosen cloak for abstract thought. The imagery is inseparable from the thought."[18] In these terms man tried to re-enact his relation with the deep essence of his world; in these terms he tried to formulate and wrestle with problems of his own humanity—its powers, its claims, and its place in the whole. Here, too, transcendence of self is to be seen. Man, as Toynbee observed, turned to problems internal to his society and worked out a new understanding of them. In this process, too, he made himself. Jacobsen comments about Mesopotamia:

> The idea that justice was something to which man had a right began slowly to take form, and in the second millennium—appropriately the millennium of the famous Code of Hammurabi—justice as right rather than justice as favor seems to have become the general conception. This idea, however, could not but conflict violently with the established view of the world. There emerged fundamental problems, such as the justification of death and the problem of the righteous sufferer.[19]

Structure versus Life

Out of their work and gesture, out of their efforts to relate themselves to their world and to impress themselves on their surroundings, men built internally differentiated societies which, despite the often great discrepancies between elites and people, assumed a stability of form and a marked continuity throughout a considerable period of time. One is reminded in this context of the suggestion of Herbert Spencer. Spencer felt that there were basically two kinds of societies. The first type was organized around the centrality of the military function, and in it the fighting classes became the dominant elite. Other functions became ancillary to defense and warfare—agriculture and industry becoming largely quartermaster and commissary. The second type came into existence with the decline in importance of the military role. There took place a rise in the independence of production, and the classes that organized and directed production rather than warfare became the ruling elite of the society. Spencer called this second type industrial society. He saw most of history as an alternation of these types. Joseph Schumpeter offers us some suggestive examples of military societies and thereby throws some light on the kinds of acting out in which men have found satisfaction. War has unquestionably been one of mankind's favorite dramas, a fact that prompted William James to suggest that in his own day what was needed was a moral equivalent of war to elicit and enlist in worthy directions man's potential idealism and energy.

Speaking of the "new" Egyptian Empire after the expulsion of the Hyksos, Schumpeter states that state policy became "more and more aggressive, and campaign followed campaign, without the slightest concrete cause." He then proceeds to diagnose the case.

> The war of liberation from the Hyksos, lasting a century and a half, had "militarized" Egypt. A class of professional soldiers had come into being, replacing the old peasant militia and technically far superior to it, owing to the employment of battle chariots, introduced, like the horse, by the Bedouin Hyksos. The support of that class enabled the victorious kings, as early as Aahmes I, to reorganize the empire centrally and to suppress the regional feudal lords

and the large, aristocratic landowners—or at least to reduce their importance. We hear little about them in the "New Empire." The crown thus carried out a social revolution; it became the ruling power, together with the new military and hierarchical aristocracy and, to an increasing degree, foreign mercenaries as well. This new social and political organization was essentially a war machine. It was motivated by warlike instincts and interests. Only in war could it find an outlet and maintain its domestic position. Without continual passages at arms it would necessarily have collapsed. Its external orientation was war, and war alone. Thus war became the normal condition, alone conducive to the well-being of the organs of the body social that now existed. To take to the field was a matter of course, the reasons for doing so were of subordinate importance. *Created by wars that required it, the machine now created wars it required.* A will for broad conquest without tangible limits, for the capture of positions that were manifestly untenable—this was typical imperialism.[20]

Schumpeter speaks of a similar example, the Assyrians, who, however, are a "warrior nation" from the outset and who conquer and cruelly pillage and oppress their neighbors. The author asks:

What answer would we get if we were to ask an Assyrian king: "Why do you conquer without end? Why do you destroy one people after another, one city after another? Why do you put out the eyes of the vanquished? Why do you burn their habitations?" We would be told the official—perhaps even the conscious—motive. Tuklati-palisharra I, for example, replied: "The God Assur, my Lord, commanded me to march. . . . I covered the lands of Saranit and Ammanit with ruins. . . . I chastized them, pursued their warriors like wild beasts, conquered their cities, took their gods with me. I made prisoners, seized their property, abandoned their cities to fire, laid them waste, destroyed them, made ruins and rubble of them, imposed on them the harshest yoke of my reign; and in their presence I made thank offerings to the God Assur, my Lord."

Schumpeter remarks that characteristically this account, obviously taken from a stone inscription, reads much like Assurnasirpal's report of a hunt:

"The gods Nindar and Nirgal, who cherish my priestly office, gave the beasts of the desert into my hands. Thirty mighty elephants I killed, 257 huge wild bulls I brought down with arrows from my open chariot, in the irresistible power of my glory."

Schumpeter's further remarks are illuminating for our inquiry.

Such an answer from the king does not help us much. It is scarcely permissible to assume that he was lying or pretending—nor would that matter one way or the other. But we can scarcely be disputed when we insist that the God Assur commanded and his prophet—in this case the king himself—proclaimed merely what was in keeping with acquired habits of thought and the emotional response of the people, their "spirit," formed by their environment in the dim past. It is also plain that conscious motives—no matter whether, in the concrete case, they are always religious in character—are seldom *true* motives in the sense of being free of deceptive ideologies; and that they are never the *sole* motives. Human motivation is always infinitely complex, and we are not aware of all its elements. The Assyrian policy of conquest, like any similar policy, must have had many auxiliary motives. Lust for blood and booty, avarice and the craving for power, sexual impulses, commercial interests (more prominent with the Assyrians than the Persians)—all these, blended to varying degrees, may have played their part in motivating individuals and groups; also operative was the unrestrained will to gratify instincts—precisely those instincts to which a warlike past had given predominance in the mentality. Such real motives are powerful allies of official motives (whether religious or otherwise), increase their striking power, or usurp their gaze. This aspect of imperialism emerges more sharply in the Assyrian case than in any other. But it is never altogether absent, not even today.

Here too, however, the actual foundation of the religious motive— and here is the crucial formulation—is the urge to action. The direction of this urge, determined by the nation's development, is, as it were, codified in religion. It is this, too, that makes the God Assur a war god and as such insatiable. For the fact of definite religious precepts can never be accepted as ultimate. It must always be explained. In the case of the Assyrians this is not at all difficult. That is why I placed the hunting account beside the war report. It is evident that the king and his associates regard war and the chase from the same aspect as *sport*—if that expression is permissible. In their lives, war occupied the same role as sports and games do in present-day life. It served to gratify activity urges springing from capacities and inclinations that had once been crucial to survival, though they had now outlived their usefulness. Foreign peoples were the favorite game and toward them the hunter's zeal assumed the forms of bitter national hatred and religious fanaticism. War and conquest were not means but ends.[21]

Schumpeter directs our attention to the sociological equivalent of what Gordon Allport calls the "functional autonomy" of motives which began as expressive of other needs and then became rewarding and self-reinforcing in themselves. It is an example of the conversion of what were originally means into ends to which John Dewey also attached considerable importance. The experience of a class or of a people gives specific form to their character, the social structure, and the values; and the type then tends to reproduce itself. The past rules the present; the situation conditions men.

Lewis Mumford has commented about the early civilizations that they "gave so much to so few and so little to so many"[22] and that they imposed a harsh regimentation and postponed, diminished, and denied life for great numbers. He states:

> The heroic efforts that enabled men to take the great step toward mechanical organization and sustained common effort far beyond the immediate needs for survival eventually gave way, in every civilization, to a dreary later stage, the unadventurous one of keeping the wheels turning. Then the will to order ceases to be self-sustaining and inherently purposeful: life becomes empty. Are not the sacrifices and burdens greater than the tangible rewards? At a certain stage of every civilization, accordingly, it reaches a point revealed in the early Egyptian Dialogue Between Man and His Shadow Self or Soul, when he asks himself why he should go on living: would he not be better dead? . . . Civilization begins by a magnificent materialization of human purpose: it ends in a purposeless materialism.[23]

In these early civilizations, Mumford suggests, religion kept interior life nourished.

> Both for good and bad, religion magnified the realm of creative possibility. In religion, civilization compensated for its own frustrations by creating aesthetic objects and ideal presences, deeply rooted in man's nature, and so imposing that man became more deeply attached to them than to life itself. For many it offered escape, but at the same time the human spirit was kept alive. It came forth, Mumford suggests, in what Jaspers called the axial period—in prophetic religion which at bottom concerned itself with "the recasting of the human personality.[24]

Self-control gave the person the ascendancy over the powers of his biological make-up; the emphasis on person gave the individual a greater significance than that of society or institution. From this period date many of our own deepest values, but this period, too, issued in a new traditionalization, and its values demanded a new kind of partial repression which could become mechanized and life-denying.

The Many Sources of Change
and the Upsurge of Vitality

Man makes himself in relation to a situation; he relates himself
to his situation and in the process "realizes" his own potential in
historically conditioned forms. He makes himself and creates
social institutions and a cultural tradition at the same time. The
society and culture become for succeeding generations the
learning situation. They become the setting for self-development,
replacing the environmentally conditioned original situation in
which the society and culture took form. Thus for many generations in many societies, the dead rule the living, as Schumpeter
put it. Such societies often fragmented men, making a large mass
of them in it human embodiments of their forms of toil and
allocating to a small elite the mental space for a more satisfying
realization. And even these established forms often imposed
themselves to suppress spontaneity and creativity. Yet in word, in
act, and in gesture, human creativity has always escaped its
containment. In religion especially it asserted its soaring
aspirations.

Human history exhibits considerable change—often far-reaching and fundamental change. It presents to our view rapid and
revolutionary change and slow gradual drift which over a long
period adds up to a great alteration in the conditions of life and
men's views of life's tasks and value. What introduces change
into the patterned culture and society, once they become established? Why are all mechanizations finally broken through or
overthrown?

A multitude of theorists have emphasized a variety of elements
as basic causes of such change. The biological flexibility of the
human endowment and the combinations and permutations of
genetics practically guarantee that the biological source of
potential response will be continually changing. Thus new
human potential is continually being brought into societies. The
manner of population distribution among the varied jobs of a
society, together with the unpredictability of the changing
biological substrate, reduces to zero the probability of matching
talent and temperament with role and function in society's
division of labor and reward. Hence misfits and malcontents are

to be expected in every generation in all societies. Under auspicious circumstances, they can become originators and supporters of change. Thus a basis for internal innovation, for conflict, and for protest seems to be built into human societies. Toynbee has emphasized the importance of environmental changes starting off a train of events leading to societal change.[25] Marx stressed the role of conflict of interests inherent in the division of labor as the source of protest, new aspirations, and struggle which in time lead to a major reorganization of the society or its destruction.[26] Weber showed that charismatic leadership brought new unroutinized impulses into a society and as a source of creativity for religious and political movements could lead to the reconstitution of important institutions or society as a whole.[27] Others have pointed out how new activities, arising out of a changed relation to the environment or new internal relations in the society itself, could provide the basis for the rise of new classes, with new values and aspirations. Some contemporary observers point to the significance of generational conflict—a usual social phenomenon in most societies—taking place under complex urban conditions and in the context of family social mobility as a source of disaffection and possibly of radical change.[28] Mannheim pointed out that the emergence of a number of points of view, all claiming legitimacy, contributes to an undermining of legitimacy, that in the clash of world views none appear beyond question and doubt.[29] The communications revolution, by bringing alien ideas in considerable variety to formerly provincial groups, hastens the passing of traditional societies.[30] Weber, following Kant, saw in man's continued activity in pursuit of any ends, and especially in his economic action, a tendency toward progressive rationalization of life and thought—a tendency which undermines the foundations of traditional and conservative cultures.[31] The notion of some kind of cognitive break-through—of disenchantment, of emancipation, of "demythologization," of a "withdrawal of projections," or of a loss of resonance with the sacral aspects of the human condition—appears to a number of observers to be characteristic of modern times and intimately related to the social and cultural changes of the age.[32] Others have seen the development of civilization—a process simultaneously creative and disintegrative—marked by increasing differentiation of human activities and thinking, accompanied by exhaustion of potential and a growing failure to maintain the products of differentiation in a unified and integrated whole. The relative and at times severely limited autonomy of systems of meaning and thought make religious and philosophical doctrines sources of change when they come into contact with groups of people predisposed with an affinity for them. Thus the sources of change are numerous, many-faceted, and complicatedly interrelated.

All forms of change "liberate" human potential from the established outlets into which energies were channeled under stable and traditional conditions. Many forms of change also bring stress and pressure on men and influence the direction of their responses and thereby the final product of their actions. What, indeed, of the mysterious human potential which is "realized" under all these diverse and different conditions? Our studies reveal certain general characteristics and needs and a staggering variety of concrete forms which these general characteristics and traits may take. It can perhaps be said that a society is the organized expression of the answer to the question, "What is man doing in his life on the earth?" It is the organized answer to that question taken in the sense of what should man be doing in terms of the kind of being he is. Men act in the world and at the same time act out their human potential under the press of circumstances. What we observe in the diverse variety of societies and cultures shown to us by history and anthropology is a multitude of variations of that realization brought into existence under many different sociological conditions. Human action directs energy and inhibits at the same time other modes of its expression. Thus in every society and culture men not only realize some aspects of themselves; they also repress or redirect the development of other aspects. Here a difficult and subtle problem arises. Man's malleability is not infinite, despite the flexibility of his potential mental structure and openness of his entelechy. Are we to say that the agriculturally based peaceful society of classical China and the warlike society of the Egyptian New Empire are equally valid or equally suitable self-realizations of man; or that the lower classes in these societies in their structured statuses and roles are given equally valid or suitable channels of expression and self-development? Can we begin to state in objective form criteria for examining such questions?

Cultural creativity always takes place under a definite set of circumstances and with the materials of thought available in those circumstances. It has been largely a further developing or embroidering of established patterns or the development of new patterns based on new activities which have come to be performed by groups in the society. When fundamental, it is a matter of changing the institutionalized answer to the question, "What is man doing here on earth?"—of changing it on the basis of newly evolved activities and newly emerged aspirations. For example, from the Renaissance on, the middle classes of the Italian cities and later in the north of Europe developed a way of life based on commercial activities. On the basis of this experience they asserted an increasingly this-worldly answer to that question against the marked otherworldly answer evolved by the church and its ecclesiastical intelligentsia in previous centuries.[33] Such creativity is usually moderate in scale and has taken place in the context of the established cultural and social system. There is an important, though at times difficult, distinction to be made between those historical instances in which men achieve a greater capacity for relative independence in the face of circumstances and those in which their scope for self-determination is curtailed. Yet never do men escape from what we might call the logic of the situation. Choices are generally structured by conditions, and transcendence of response is always relative. However, human history over the last several centuries testifies to the gradual, though irregularly, increasing capacity for human control over the circumstances of life. In Western civilization this has been accompanied by an increasingly critical tendency with respect to human thought and values and an increase in self-awareness. Social scientists who in our day attempt to predict the future find that they must predict a set of possible futures.[34] Some aspects of what is coming to be seem unavoidable, but others, together with the character of the total configuration of the future society and culture, are highly dependent on human choices. Moreover, those who ask what kind of future we should seek to bring about immediately discover that the vast increase of man's knowledge concerning what has made him in the past affects his present situation in two ways. It gives him an increased technical capacity for self-determination, but it also creates for him a severe value crisis, since value choice can no longer be made by the institutionalized canons of tradition and authority as they could in older situations. Today the past no longer rules the present, as in Schumpeter's examples. But this has not rendered modern man the unequivocal master of his fate and captain of his soul. Modern society and culture are open to innovation. Many seek for a new design for life which will provide a more meaningful identity and trajectory than the shreds and patches they have from the past.

The fact is that the two sides of the basic ecological relationship—men vis-à-vis situation—have been opened up. Man is no longer so highly conditioned by his circumstances since he has increased his control over circumstances tremendously and by his growing critical capacity and self-awareness has come to have some intellectual leverage over society, tradition, and the conditioning process. The forms of institutions and custom no longer enjoy the kind of self-evident validation and untouchable status that they had in earlier societies. Man is emancipated to some considerable degree from both environment and tradition. He is in a position to choose his activity, his values, his self-development. Man is being increasingly placed in the situation in which he must choose what he will do, how he will employ his immense technical potential, his vast capacity to make his world; he is simultaneously being put in the circumstances in which he must make major decisions about what is of true worth in the human venture. Here he discovers that his emancipation has had another side. The overcoming of tradition has too often been the emptying out of substance. No way has been developed satisfactorily to bring forward the insights of the tradition in universalizable and communicable form and at the same time profit from the development of self-consciousness and the critical faculty. In such circumstances men experience a most fundamental anomie and in confronting it often behave regressively and seek out old systems of belief and old postures which are unsuitable to the new conditions. What is more serious is that they often know at a deeper level, which they try to keep beneath the threshold of full awareness, that what they are doing is highly contrived. Emotional catharsis, an insecure identity, and stalemate result and substitute for more fruitful attempts to meet the issue. Man cannot avoid this situation which he has created. He must learn to face up to the challenge to make his world and to make himself, to realize himself according to a design which will do most justice to his potential. Man is emerging into the historical epoch in which the long implicit question, "What is man doing on this earth?" becomes a matter for conscious thought and genuine decision, a matter of practical policy—indeed, perhaps a prerequisite for survival.

America: The Contemporary Challenge

American history reveals two major historical "tasks" around which American society has developed and its values and social structure evolved. First we find the task of agriculture and westward movement on the basis of which the early United States was built. Next we find industrialization and the result of it, urbanization. In the century from the Civil War to our own day it was this second great task of building up the American industrial base which occupied the central attention and the greater energies of our countrymen. America was transformed from an agricultural to an industrial nation. Now in the two decades after World War II, service industry is replacing basic industry as a chief focus of occupational energies. We are evolving a service economy, with mixed public and private sectors, as the basic infrastructure of a welfare state.

An important social process is seen to be intimately and intricately bound up with these basic economic activities: the reception and assimilation of immigrants into the American society. Moreover, the republican and democratic forms which America evolved as an agrarian nation have been preserved and even strengthened. In setting out upon these tasks American society possessed two sources of strength which differentiated it from the older societies of Europe. It had the advantage of new ground, a vast continent endowed with rich resources and unencumbered by the time-honored precedents of countless generations. Yet even Frederick Jackson Turner, who emphasized the importance of the frontier in the making of American institutions and American character, was quite aware that the ideas and values which men brought to the settlement of the new areas were of great significance in affecting the social and cultural outcome of American settlement. But here, too, there were elements which strengthened the antitraditionalist effects of new ground. In the Calvinism of New England we find Christianity recast in a form suitable to find resonance in the mentalities of rising middle classes, a Christianity supportive of work in the world and of commercial activity—the strategic form of work in the world in that era—and shorn of its earlier sacramental and passive receptive characteristics. Puritanism is perhaps the most rational this-worldly formulation of Christian asceticism and the most antitraditional form of Christianity to be developed by the Reformation period. It represented an important ideological and psychological break with traditionalism. In a different but related way, those elements of Anglicanism in Virginia which led to Deism and the consequent acceptance of the developing English Liberal ideology must also be counted as important nontraditional influences in our history.

It was out of this kind of colonial background that America developed. The people of the new republic essayed their tasks supported by two general kinds of ideology: denominational Protestantism which was evolving out of the earlier situation of established colonial (and later, state, in some places) churches,[35] and the Lockean Liberalism with French touches of the Deists of Virginia and the evolving Congregationalists of Massachusetts. Protestantism was effective on the frontier (to a considerable extent because of the efforts of the Methodists), important in the rural areas of a country dominantly agricultural in its occupational structure, and was the religion of the old stock and the middle and the upper classes. Liberalism made its headway among the educated, and the second half of the nineteenth century saw Protestantism, which had gained much ground in the first half, slowly give way before a growing secularization of culture.[36] In church and university, the latter part of the nineteenth century saw conflict between conservative and liberal forces and between supporters of secularization and advocates of an earlier religious dominance. Catholicism, insignificant before the Irish and German immigrations of the 1840's, came in as the religion of immigrants, of ethnic groups (seen as foreigners), of lower and working classes which came increasingly to be made up of the newcomers and their children. W. W. Sweet has stated that Catholicism played a significant part in providing a meaningful orientation and a spiritual home for millions of immigrants and was a most important support of public order in an era of great change and hardship and potentially of great social disruption. Protestantism by and large split into a liberal and a fundamentalist sector, and secular liberalism to one extent or another made important headway among the sophisticated, though a vague Protestant connection or at least identity remained part of the self-definition of most old-stock Americans. Catholicism was highly affected by the openness and liberalism of its new surroundings. The nineteenth century was a time of

brisk and significant conflict in American Catholicism as a
vigorous immigrant community adapted itself to an entirely new
kind of society.[37] The general Modernist crisis in Catholicism and
the condemnation of the Americanist heresy, the defeat of
"Trusteeism" (a form of lay control fought and defeated by the
hierarchy), and the generally unpropitious atmosphere for Catholicism in the nineteenth century led eventually to a tamed but
highly Americanized version of conservative European Catholicism which remained typical of America to the eve of the Second
Vatican Council.

These two basic tasks on which American society was constructed gave rise to three great struggles. The first was the
continued westward settlement: a saga of heroism but also a tale
of brutal exploitation of land, resources, and fellow men and
racist violence against the aborigines. The second derived from
the two different kinds of societies and value systems which were
built in North and South on the basis of two vastly different-
forms of agriculture: one based on an independent yeomanry,
the other on the plantation and slavery. The unsolved problems
of the Civil War and its aftermath remain with us as America
tries after a century of callous neglect to do something about its
racial problems. Today this issue becomes related to and entan-
gled with that of the assertion of independence and the struggle
for viable nationhood by the nonwhite peoples of the globe, but
in the American setting it is a problem left over from the past. It
is an urgent problem, but it is hardly a new one. The second
task, industrialization, and its consequence, urbanization, was
also a relatively violent affair. It was closely related to the
assimilation of the immigrant. It gave rise to a considerable
number of important reactions as group after group felt their
interests and even their survival threatened. The farmers, victims
of the agricultural market and its fluctuations and disadvantaged
by the new large-scale capitalism, founded several movements:
the Grange, the farmers' alliances, the populists, and the progres-
sives. Workers developed a trade-union movement against great
repressive opposition: the National Labor Union, The Knights of
Labor, the American Federation of Labor, and the Congress of
Industrial Organizations. There also came into existence a radical
left—a socialist party—such an anarchosyndicalist movement as
the IWW. From the more public-spirited sections of the city's
middle classes came agitation and movements advocating governmental reform. Movements for Good Government attempted

to counter and curtail the rampant corruption which a vigorous, expansive, and unscrupulous capitalism had introduced into political life. In the administration of Grover Cleveland the federal government set up the Interstate Commerce Commission. It was weak in powers, but it symbolized much that was to come. Since then the establishment of numerous government regulatory agencies, the growing socioeconomic concern of congressional legislation, and the response of the federal government to social and resource problems slowly introduced a measure of social responsibility into the new economic structure that was emerging. Government regulation, a reformed tax structure of which a graduated income tax was a most significant innovation, strong labor and collective bargaining, together with what has often been called the "managerial revolution" in the structure of industry, have transformed the basic economic substructure of American society. The years following World War II saw a vastly increased prosperity with the development of a consumer-oriented service economy and saw this prosperity spread among an unprecedentedly large section of the total American population. Education tended to become democratized, and educational attainment became the chief route to social and economic mobility. Meanwhile America continued to play the role in international affairs which it reluctantly started to perform in 1917 when it entered the Great War on the side of the Allied Powers. This international role continues—and continues to be a main source of disagreement and internal conflict among Americans.

These two basic tasks and their many derivatives in city, town, and farm have provided the basic setting for American efforts for decades. American man has made himself in this work: his settlement of the continental expanse and his construction on it of an advanced technologically based society. In the process he has preserved his basic democratic institutions in altered form and his older ideologies, often much transformed. Today this American man faces two sets of problems. First are those derived from or left over from the two basic tasks which occupied him in history up to now: renovation of cities, justice to minorities, the structurally and spiritually dispossessed poor who cannot become part of the affluent society. This is the first set of problems; they represent a continuation of the tasks of the past. They are serious and urgent, but they are hardly *avant-garde*. Beneath these problems lurk the deeper, more radical, and more significant problems—the problems not left over from yesterday, but awaiting us on the morrow. What kind of society are we going to make with the great powers our learning and science, our past accomplishments and successes, have placed at our disposal? How now with our scientific leverage over our situation and ourselves are we to proceed toward self-realization and a society conducive to humane self-realization? A Christian and later a secular utopianism often inspired our ancestors; America was the "last best hope" of mankind, and Americans, in Lincoln's words, were God's "almost chosen people." Here on this continent we would realize the long-thwarted aspirations of men for a humane and significant life. How shall we give substance to that vision today? The question, "What is man doing on this earth?" in the sense of what ought he to be doing, now becomes a question which is to be found lurking beneath every problem and conflict in our current situation.

The identity crises of many of our youth,[38] the religious crisis of our time,[39] the tendency for many to seek a symbolic security in a radicalism of the right,[40] and much of the groping and seeking of our day are closely related to and, indeed, part of this deeper set of problems. Under these circumstances many seek what in effect are repressive modes of handling this basic crisis, of concealing from themselves the urgency of this problem. They seek modes in older causes and identities often stridently asserted and often quite symbolically and unrealistically perceived and formulated. Others manage to live not altogether comfortably in halfway houses, concerning themselves with the more immediate set of problems while avoiding the deeper questions which they cannot answer. Yet the deeper questions cannot be conjured away. The churches and the universities, the guardians of our religious and humane traditions, must begin to face up to what is involved here. The university becomes an ever more central institution in our total society, involved in many ways in the most diverse public and private enterprises. To be true to itself, it must take the lead in the human effort to understand man and to enable man to achieve genuine humanity. For the churches, their ability to render relevant support to this venture will test their meaning for the new world that must be built.

NOTES

1. V. Gordon Childe, *Man Makes Himself* (New York: 1951), p. 188.

2. Cf. Josef Pieper, "The Philosophical Act," Chapter 2 in *Leisure: The Basis of Culture* (New York: 1952), pp. 108 ff.

3. Theodora Kroeber, *Ishi in Two Worlds* (Berkeley: 1961), p. 180.

4. *Ibid.,* pp. 188–189.

5. Robert Redfield, *The Little Community and Peasant Society and Culture* (Chicago: 1960), p. 31.

6. *Ibid.,* p. 30.

7. Arnold J. Toynbee, *A Study of History* (Somervell Abridgement) (New York and London: 1947), I, 208 and *passim.*

8. *Ibid.,* p. 309.

9. *Ibid.,* p. 316.

10. *Ibid.,* p. 317.

11. G. W. F. Hegel, *The Phenomenology of Mind,* J. B. Baillie, tr. (London and New York: 1949), Chapter IV, A, pp. 228 ff. See also Louis Dupré, *The Philosophical Foundations of Marxism* (New York: 1966), p. 32.

12. *Ibid.,* p. 12.

13. The early manuscripts of Karl Marx quoted from *ibid.,* p. 149.

14. F. H. Heinemann, *Existentialism and the Modern Predicament* (New York: 1958), p. 192.

15. Susanne K. Langer, *Philosophy in a New Key* (New York: 1942), p. 41.

16. *Ibid.,* p. 39.

17. Childe, *op. cit.*

18. Henri Frankfort *et al., Before Philosophy* (Hammondsworth, Middlesex, England: 1949), p. 15.

19. Thorkild Jacobsen, "Mesopotamia," in *ibid.,* p. 223.

20. Joseph Schumpeter, *Social Classes and Imperialism* (New York: 1955), p. 25.

21. *Ibid.,* pp. 42–43.

22. Lewis Mumford, *The Transformations of Man* (New York: 1956), p. 67.

23. *Ibid.,* p. 69.

24. *Ibid.,* p. 74.

25. Toynbee, *op. cit.*

26. Karl Marx, *Communist Manifesto,* in Emile Burns, ed., *A Handbook of Marxism* (New York: 1935), pp. 21 ff.

27. Max Weber, *The Theory of Social and Economic Organization,* A. M. Henderson and Talcott Parsons, trs. (New York: 1947), Chapter III, pp. 324 ff.

28. Cf. Kenneth Kenniston, *The Uncommitted: Alienated Youth in American Society* (New York: 1960), and J. I. Simmons and Barry Winograd, *It's Happening* (Santa Barbara, Calif.: 1966).

29. Karl Mannheim, *Ideology and Utopia* (New York and London: 1949).

30. Cf. Daniel Lerner, *The Passing of Traditional Society* (Glencoe: 1958), and Lucian W. Pye, "Personal Identity and Political Ideology," in Bruce Mazlish, ed., *Psychoanalysis and History* (Englewood Cliffs, N.J.: 1963).

31. Weber, *op. cit.*

32. The word "disenchantment" is borrowed from Burkhardt; "demythologization," from Bultmann; "withdrawal of projections," from Jung; and the final reference to a loss of ontological resonance in experience refers to the work of Eliade.

33. Alfred von Martin, *The Sociology of the Renaissance* (New York: 1944).

34. See the Summer, 1967, issue of *Daedalus,* Journal of the American Academy of Arts and Sciences, "Toward the Year 2000: Work in Progress," and especially Herman Kahn and Anthony Wiener, "The Next Thirty-three Years: A Framework for Speculation," pp. 705 ff.

35. Franklin H. Littell, *From State Church to Pluralism* (Garden City, N.Y.: 1962), and Sidney E. Mead, *The Lively Experiment* (New York, Evanston, and London: 1963).

36. Merle Curti, *The Growth of American Thought* (New York and London: 1943).

37. Robert D. Cross, *The Emergence of Liberal Catholicism in America* (Cambridge: 1958), and E. E. Y. Hales, *The Catholic Church in the Modern World* (Garden City, N.Y.: 1960).

38. Kenniston, *op. cit.*

39. Thomas F. O'Dea, "The Crisis of the Contemporary Religious Consciousness," *Daedalus* (Winter, 1967), pp. 116 ff., published in Thomas F. O'Dea, *Atheism, Alienation, and the Religious Crisis* (New York: 1969).

40. Richard Hofstadter, *The Paranoid Style in American Politics* (New York: 1965).

INDEX

Aahmes I, 278
academic discipline, sociology as, 5
academic sociology of religion, 223–224, 230
Act of Supremacy (1534), 51
action frame of reference, 100
Action Theory, 226
activism, 73, 82
Adams, Henry, 54
Adams, John, 73
administrative order, dilemma of, 247–248
affluence, social mobility and, 8–9, 65
Agrippa I, 168
alienation: of Catholic Church from Western society, 59; from Christian spirit, 26; human, 275; objectification versus, 245–247; of symbolism, 247
Allport, Gordon, 280–281
American: Civil War, 289; colonial, religion in 45, 72–73, 287–288; contemporary challenge, 287–291; economic growth, 70–71, 287, 290; governmental reform, 289–290; international role, 290; managerial revolution, 290; migration to, 71–73 (*see also* immigrants); post-World War II, 290; Protestantism identified with, 92, 288; secularization of, 45, 73; as utopia, 143–144, 147–149; westward movement, 70–72, 144, 287, 289
American Catholic Sociological Review, 16
American Catholic Studies Program, 85, 87
"American Catholics and Intellectual Life," 86–87
American culture, 62, 73, 90, 91, 94, 103, 104, 160
American democracy, 79–80, 144
American Federation of Labor, 289
American isolationism, 53–55
American Jewish Committee, 7, 157
American nationalism, Protestantism and, 79, 250–251

American Protective Association, 42, 80
American Revolution, 72, 73, 160
American society, development of, 287–291
American solidarity, strengthening of, 164
American values, 163, 287
Americanism, Catholicism and, 89, 90, 94
Americanized Catholicism, 42–44, 47–48, 50; *see also* Catholicism
Amish, 42
Anglicanism, 288
Anglo-Saxon law, 41
anomie, 7, 36, 186, 187; sectarianism as response to, 187–189; test of hypothesis, 190–195
anti-Catholicism, 27, 41–42, 80, 81, 91–92, 160–161, 177
anti-Christian secularism, 76
anti-Communism, 27, 59–61, 63, 164
anti-intellectualism, 27
antiliberalism, 93
anti-Romanism, 93
antisecularism, 27
anti-Semitism, 6–9, 27, 37, 93; decline in, 155–156, 159, 177; in Europe, 159, 160, 165–167, 169–176; historical origins, 167–169; nationalist era and, 174–175; Nazi, 93, 164, 165, 176; political, 165–167, 175–176; present outlook, 176–178; Protestantism and, 161, 164, 177; revived, occasions for, 164; secularism and, 158–159, 161, 168, 174, 177; *see also* Jews
anti-Trinitarianism, 77
apostasy, 28, 83, 118
apperceptive mass, 57
applied psychology of religion, 17, 257, 269
Aquinas, St. Thomas, 32
Arendt, Hannah, 166
Aristotle, 16, 141
Arminianism, 72, 77
Aron, Raymond, 10